DARKNESS AND LIGHT:
Private Writing as Art

DARKNESS AND LIGHT:
Private Writing as Art

An Anthology of Contemporary
Journals, Diaries, and Notebooks

Edited by
Olivia Dresher and Victor Muñoz

toExcel
San Jose   New York   Lincoln   Shanghai

Darkness and Light: Private Writing as Art
An Anthology of Contemporary
Journals, Diaries, and Notebooks

This edition published by toExcel Press,
an imprint of iUniverse.com, Inc.

For information address:
iUniverse.com, Inc.
620 North 48th Street
Suite 201
Lincoln, NE 68504-3467
www.iuniverse.com

ISBN: 1-58348-560-0

Note

The purpose of this collection is to promote the notion of the journal/diary/notebook as a valid literary genre. The original manuscript was completed in 1991. In publishing the book eight years later, in 1999, we have refrained from updating the contents in order to preserve the original character of the book.

When searching for contributors, we wanted to discover "unknowns" as well as published writers who had never had the opportunity to release their journal and diary fragments. We also wanted to find writing that had not been published elsewhere. However, in the time since the anthology was first compiled, Mr. Haider's piece has appeared in a different form in the *Clothesline Review*.

—*The Editors, 1999*

Contents

Essays on Journal Writing

Introduction

The artistic possibilities of the journal have not been fully explored. Most published anthologies of journal or diary writing have attempted to offer a glimpse of an era or cultural milieu, or approached the journal as a vehicle for personal awareness and growth, or delved into the "intimate" lives of the famous. To these three ways of seeing private writing—historical, therapeutic, and voyeuristic—we would like to add a fourth: aesthetic.

This collection of journal writing is based on the premise that the journal can be art. It began as an idea for a literary magazine. We thought, initially, that a magazine's on-going nature would be the most effective way to promote this kind of writing as a genre. But since our idea was relatively untried, and considering a magazine's production costs and inherent impermanence compared to a book, we decided instead to advertise for submissions for an anthology.

At first we asked: How do we *find* these journal writers? Where are they hiding out? If the journal isn't yet valued as art, would anyone devoted to this form of writing look for or see such an ad? Ideally, we hoped to find those who valued journals as their life's work, as we do; realistically, we wanted to discover those who at least place independent worth on the journal, though it may not be their main work.

For lack of a more appropriate place to seek submissions, most of our ads were placed in national and local publications for writers. We suspected the drawback: writers would stumble across our ad as they searched for those requesting short stories, poems, etc.; we feared their journals would be sidelines to "serious" works, not respected as works in themselves.

Yes, we did get submissions like this. We also received conventional poetry and short stories that were only loosely tied to the idea of keeping a journal, as well as strictly autobiographical writing that did not contain the feeling of the journal's essence of immediacy and on-goingness. But we also found what we were looking for.

What *were* we looking for? Our guidelines read, "We are interested in literary, poetic, philosophical, and/or psychological writing which reflects a commitment to the journal (diary, notebook, etc.) as a distinct art form…writing which dispels the notion that journals are incidental to true artistic creation (i.e. short stories, poetry, novels), or merely a mundane, daily account. The journal writing which will be considered should also be much more than a tool for personal enrichment or self-help. We seek contributors whose inner life is already so rich that it spills out into their journals from a sense of urgency, not as a project or duty. Writings which are intense, probing, revealing, and insightfully critical of self and the world are encouraged…"

We were looking for journal writers who were unafraid of self-revelation, who told a convincing truth and told it well, who did not think conventionally, did not obviously borrow from the popular views of the day. We wanted to discover those who felt at home with the journal—those who were true journal writers, not just writers who dabbled in journals. We were looking for honesty, and (as one contributor put it) "the intimate feel of a sensibility that is hedging as little as possible."

We received more than 100 submissions—from 29 states, and two from outside this country (Spain and Saudi Arabia). The submissions from women outnumbered those from men, 3 to 1. Also, not many older adults—or very young adults—sent submissions, although the total range of ages was wide: 21–80. Most of the submissions came from the East and West Coasts; however, there was a curiously large number of exceptional manuscripts from the Puget Sound area, where we are based. Though it was not our intention to focus on this region, half of the accepted manuscripts were from this area, a phenomenon yet to be fully explained. The coincidence has inspired us to get to know some of these journal writers through long letters and also in person, which has heightened the experience of working on the anthology. A book of these letters would have been an interesting accompaniment to this anthology, especially since letters themselves are another neglected art form.

Ironically, a few writers expressed a prejudice against even their own journal writing in spite of its worth. For example, one contributor stated that she didn't feel the journal is a true art form, not as "true" as her stories, yet her journal reads like an engaging story itself, succeeding in the same way that a story does. These doubts are often a reflection of the prevailing view that denigrates journal writing as a literary art form, resulting in a lack of a forum or market.

As the submissions began to arrive, a variety of questions arose. We asked ourselves: What *is* a journal? At what point does it slip into a short story, memoir, or an essay? A few quality submissions were rejected because they did not quite "read" like selections from a journal. Some people, for example, sent us novel fragments or short stories which seemed to be composed with the intent of creating a self-contained piece, rather than being an on-going work that flowed out of the lived life. Even if the novel or short story idea originated in the journal, if the journal's essence was not retained in some authentic way, we felt it did not qualify for our anthology. Also, we did not accept fictional journals—fiction using the journal form as a device.

The majority of the submissions received, however, were authentic journal excerpts. Although many people keep journals, few succeed in maintaining the literary quality that we were looking for. We did not flatly reject writing that reflected the traditional and contemporary styles and attitudes towards journal writing (e.g., day-to-day and self-help writing), as long as something more was there, even if the writer seemed unaware of it. What made us interested enough in a submission to seriously consider it was both the care and urgency of the writing—voice, language, and the themes that evolved out of the writer's need to explore life on personal terms. Ultimately, we sought private writing which contained elements similar to what one looks for in fine literature, writing which is challenging and does not offer easy answers.

Though we wanted to present, in style and content, a range of journal writing, we leaned toward accepting serious, introspective writing. There are many sub-genres of journal writing we didn't include, such as strictly nature and travel journals, because their inclusion in the book would have forced us to expand beyond our specific focus. Instead of putting together yet another anthology consisting of a sampling of short pieces by many journal writers, we preferred to concentrate on a few selections, giving them enough space to have their effect. This accounts for some rather long pieces, and for a total of only 14 journal selections.

Many different types of journals exist because a journal can be anything the writer wants it to be. What is most unique about the journal form is its openness to the particular needs of the writer and the moment. Because there are no definitive rules, anything can be said, in any way the writer wants to say it. Journal writing can inspire one to take a leap in thinking and expressing, losing what is familiar and safe—even if just for an instant. The journal is at home in the darkness, the shadows, allowing its subjects and selves to be probed without the usual inhibitions.

We were looking for private writing which wasn't severely censored. Too many writers automatically censor their material, unaccustomed to the idea that the journal's value might very well be its function as a refuge for unordinary (and even taboo) thinking. Much of what we were sent seemed too timid. Even dedicated journal writers too easily abuse their consciences here, where the need is less than anywhere else. As a few of the selections in this anthology illustrate, the urge to censor the self seems to be battling with the urge not to. Somehow, we hope the publication of this anthology may give courage to those looking for the form to express publicly what can be so intensely private but no less the source of a great creative impulse.

There are those who dismiss the journal in general, because of the obsessive "I", not valuing the fact that everything that is written, not just journals, is an interpretation which comes through the self. The self is the primal filter; everything passes through it. We've been taught to distrust introspection and personalness. Commonly, we hear that journal writers are self-indulgent, self-pitying, "losers", loners, rather than persons who are a valuable source of knowledge and insight. (For a more rigorous discussion of this involved subject see the essays following the journal selections.)

What makes a journal art?—more than an historical record of the details of a life, more than a workbook for further writing projects or some other artistic endeavor, more than a place to keep secrets, confessions and problems in need of a solution, more than an excerpt from a "journaling" workshop, or a personal pep talk? These are important questions, especially for a cause such as ours, which is to encourage not so much the art of journal writing as the artistic journal. We answer the questions in two ways: by showing the journal in the act of being art (through the journal selections), and by arguing the case in the essays.

The 14 journal selections in this book are arranged subjectively so they will play off each other, darkness and light contrasting, and so the book will work itself into a whole. Perhaps the most dramatic instance of this is the placing of Ms. Gale's piece. Its surface lightness was varyingly interpreted by the editors as either deceptive, a parody of what we wished to avoid, the work of a rare comic spirit, or, alternatively, as the literal image of an almost mythical way of life. Whether it is anything but what it appears to be we leave for the reader to decide, but its placement before the unsettling vision of Mr. Luno was premeditated.

Both traditional and unconventional journal shapes are represented in this collection. As noted before, the lengths vary, often having more to do with how much was submitted than any desire on our part to cut an individual piece short. One selection reads like a story, which takes it a little outside the typical journal, but it is not a typical story since it is a journal entry (a story-of-the-day consisting mostly of dialogue); other selections are more fragmented and abstract. Some read like brief notes to the self, while others have much longer, detailed, descriptive entries. Specific dates are sometimes important for our writers, sometimes not: fragmentation alone is often the only connection with time. For some, their journals are their main work; others use them as a tool for something else, but still succeed in creating a piece of writing that has an aesthetic value of its own.

A span of subjects and moods can be found in our selections, reaching from poetic descriptions of nature to conversations overheard on buses, an exploration of a religious issue to a comic portrait of a contemporary life, aphoristic writing to the difficult details of a relationship falling apart, ironic philosophical writings to minute perceptions of the moment, literary essay fragments to an account of an afternoon spent in a graveyard with a child.

We began by asking how we could reach the keepers of fine private writing. Our goals have been to point out what the journal can be and to provide an outlet for serious journal writers where there hasn't been one before. In addition, this collection's purpose is to put writers, in general, on notice that a place exists for the artistic journal. We would like to present even more daring writing in the future, and we are hopeful this book will help us find it.

Olivia Dresher and Victor Muñoz
Seattle, Washington

Journal Selections

Sandi Sonnenfeld

Ways of Being: A Process Journal

In September of 1987, I enrolled in the MFA program in Creative Writing at the University of Washington. I had lived my whole life on the East Coast, first in New York and then, after college, in Boston. Seattle, not to mention attending a school of over 33,000 students, was a whole new world. I wrote my impressions down in a journal. I had been keeping one for close to six years, ever since my sophomore year at Mount Holyoke, but suddenly there was a pattern in my entries, my ideas were leading me to Ways of Being, 1988—a ballet piece performed not to music, but to spoken text. It was composed, choreographed, and danced by me. From March 1988 until June when the piece was performed, the work absorbed all my concentration and energies. When I wasn't in rehearsal trying to find the perfect link between dance and writing, it was constantly on my mind even as I continued on with my graduate studies. And I wrote down my thoughts. This is what I wrote.

&

27 October 87

I had an idea for a story tonight, as I was staring in the mirror that I stare into every night checking to see if during the day the body has turned perfect, if the lines on my forehead have disappeared, if the legs have grown long and the ankles strong.

I ask myself each night in that mirror, "Where am I? Am I hiding beneath all that? What is the evidence that I exist?"

I thought suddenly what it would be like to have a silent character, a woman completely silent, forever staring at the mirror, and how we would come to know her from the voice of others—her mother, her brother, her first lover, her doctor—for she would only be mute because the other voices have taken hold of her.

What could she say that they hadn't already said for her? Or created for her? Or turned her into?

I am not being at all clear about the idea of the story. In my mind I keep calling her "Beauty", but that would be far too allegorical and contrived.

But she *is* beautiful. That is all people see, they are blinded by it, fooled by it, in love with it. She is not beautiful like Grace Kelly, flawless, but if one were to take a look at each feature one could find it pleasing, and then when the features were all put together, it would be impossible to deny the fact of her beauty.

I don't know why this concept is so important, that it is so key, but perhaps it is merely my own obsession with it—with beauty as the idea of a mask.

Can a story like that be moving or seem shallow, or worse still, turn into a story about an "autistic" woman? I don't want to go for sentimentality, for pity, or if I do it is the pity that we should feel for each other, for this modern age that creates such vast isolation and loneliness, creates people without connections.

29 October 87

Had a talk with Hannah today about the idea of artifice in my dancing. She says I am much better than I was at Mount Holyoke. "Better." She doesn't say it is wonderful, delightful to watch you dance. She doesn't say a lot.

But underneath what she doesn't say is a woman who understands, a woman I respect tremendously because she has the integrity not to lie to me even though she knows it would be easier. She has been my teacher and my role model now for seven years. It is not so much that I want to *be* her, as I desire to be like her. To not only be as beautiful a dancer as she is, but to possess her qualities. Her electric charisma, her ability to laugh at herself. But most of all, to love life the way she does, to throw oneself into the idea of living.

Artifice. Imitation. The new questions of myself. Always before it was *why?* An external why, a query to the outside world, but now it is *what?* and *who?* The who is me and I am asking the most complex question about myself. Not just *who am I?* But *what am I?*

A fake? A phony? A cheat? How many layers of deception are there? And who am I really deceiving? Myself? Or the people who are trying to know me?

In writing class today I said that I was shy around people. Two of the students stared at me in disbelief.

"I never would have expected," Kevin said.

"It's hard to imagine you being speechless," Heidi said.

Am I really that good an actress, hiding behind the drama of myself? Can they not see my fear, the isolation in my work? And can they themselves truly be that two-dimensional that they are unaware of the other lives, the secret inner lives we lead?

No one is really who they appear to be on the surface. Perhaps that is what is so truly frightening to me about people—their unpredictability, that hidden surprise, the impossibility of anyone completely fitting the label "man" or "woman". No one can truly be "known".

22 November 87

Today is my half-birthday. In 6 months I will be 25 years old. It is time I stop writing about little girls, college kids struggling for understanding. I am supposedly, completely, adult now. I am supposed to know where I am going.

I had an idea today for mixing my writing with my dancing; a sort of multi-media project. Actually, it was receiving Kerry's letter that first brought the idea to mind and then, of course, being in dance class and hearing about the student dance concert and desperately missing performing.

I am no choreographer, but if I could write a good script, an interesting, slightly humorous, slightly sad script, overlay it with original music (I would need to get someone to write a score) and then put dancers on stage, not telling the script or acting it out, but dancing the images the words invoke...

Nothing at all technique-oriented. (What? This from Sandi Sonnenfeld, the worshipper of technique?) But the mood, the movement the words bring to the surface.

It is a challenging task, but one that intrigues me. If I could write it over Christmas, find a musician, I could rehearse it for the spring concert. I will never again have the resources that the university offers: dance studios, stage, dancers, and musicians all available for free.

My mind more and more turns towards performance-oriented work. A straight-forward play, this dance idea. It is not that conventional writing (i.e., short stories, novels) bores me, but stories are a personal private event, written alone and then read alone. Physical connection is what excites me, as does immediate response. I do not know if I have the patience to be a novelist. I don't lack the patience to write novels, but perhaps lack the patience necessary to wait a very long time for a reaction to my work.

1 December 87

My concentration has been totally destroyed. Words and images of Santa Cruz keep flooding through me, interrupting whatever I attempt. The magnificent copper-colored rock formations, granite covered with green moss and purple-flowered, the stone carved out by the eternal Pacific, the power of nature. Nature does not care about the people who inhabit its rocks, about their traumas and mini-traumas which go on day after day.

The power a man has over a woman simply because he is physically stronger. The anger of helplessness.

I see his dark face, his penis growing hard in his blue-jeans, his shiny Vaselined lips, his determined words: "Feel me. This is real. All else is bull-shit. Your work is nothing."

The force in those words, the conviction. How does one fight that?

How does one stop the face from coming at you again and again, those hands painfully running over your body, demanding, asking that you submit your will to his?

Danger, madness, anger; will the rage never leave me?

It is not that my heart has been broken. It has been cut out and replaced by hatred.

"Nothing," he said to me, "say you are nothing."

I am no longer my own person. I exist now only in terms of my anger and hatred towards him, the isolation I feel, how this man's fierce will, his own need to conquer, to overwhelm me, has taken control of my life.

Rape is far more than the violation of the body; it is the violation of the soul.

24 December 87 (New York)

Tonight on the way to the subway, three teenage boys called out to me, "Do you have a nice wide crack? Do you want us to look at your cunt?" They all laughed.

I clutched my coat tighter to me and walked on. Why did I remain silent? Why did I not say the words that were within me? What could I say? They wouldn't hear me anyway. They are fourteen and society has already taught them the power they have. The power of depreciation.

12 January 88 (Seattle)

There was an exhibit of photographs at the Henry Art Gallery. The pictures were all of people, mostly young people. They were beautiful. I looked at the photographs and was quite stirred. Something touched me, an immediate reaction, an apprehension, a definite recognition. Why is it that I respond so to the visual—photographs, films, paintings—and yet am so rarely moved by writing (the writing of others)? Is it merely that with reading there is more work involved? A picture is immediate, you can look at it for an indefinite amount of time, and the longer you look the more dimensions you will see, the more facets. But even the first glance evokes some reaction. A single frame is complete in itself. A single paragraph rarely is.

Perhaps it is just my feeling that writing isn't the purest of the art forms. Perhaps it is just that I know (as with dance) that if I could paint or sculpt or photograph, these are the mediums I would work in. There is some element missing in writing, a sense of the marvelousness, perhaps?

All I know is that looking at the photographs, just as when I view an extraordinary dancer, makes me feel ashamed, makes me long for that marvelousness, that mystery.

2 February 88

What is the social significance of my work and do I have a moral obligation to make it socially significant? Lately, I feel tremendous pressure from the professors to do so. Yet I am so against the mechanization that a cause turns us into, the dehumanizing element of an organized protest.

I know, whether good or bad, I am an American, have American values and American sensibilities. And yet I am so very critical of this country—of its hypocrisy, ugliness and blindness, of its inability to apprehend Art, the *necessity* of Art. Politicians and bureaucrats love to espouse freedom, and yet it is a specific, very closed sort of freedom they talk about.

I feel so caught up in a bind, torn between my inner artistic self and my complete submersion into American mass culture (including graduate school).

I feel sadness for this country because I see its possibilities, its potentials, and yet I see the waste, the poverty, the hatred and prejudice, the violence of rape and murder.

But perhaps this is what makes me so supremely like this country—the potentials in me, and the feeling of inevitable failure, despite the potentials.

11 March 88

Read Atwood's *Surfacing*. Nameless woman looking for herself, trying to reconcile her abortion, her married lover, her dead parents, the modern world. She goes to nature, turns into the animal she believes she was born as, an animal unable to hurt, or go to war, or lie, or turn into a machine.

She is a woman lost who goes to extremes to find herself again. Language holds no meaning.

And for me, and for me…why are words inadequate? I feel I live my entire life encased in this body of mine. My words echo off the soft innards of my flesh, dark red and soft and warm inside. The thoughts, ideas and feelings ricochet around, back and forth inside my body, but have no place to exit. The words, ideas and thoughts must not, dare not escape through my mouth.

For in the outside world ideas will grow cold, solid, and mechanical. The life will be gone—no breathing, sighs, half-whispered hopes. Daily I retreat from people more and more. My contact with them now seems only like a method of keeping time, a ritual I have to go through like sleep, so I can get back to the real world that is happening, growing inside me.

18 March 88

Reading *Volume II* of Nin's Diary. The Loyalists have begun rising up in Spain. War is imminent in this volume, threatening to overflow.

And in our own news, the U.S. has just sent troops into Central America. And Panama is on the verge of economic collapse. It is crazy, it moves from place to place like the wickedest of hurricanes, but it is always War and it always takes its victims.

I cannot see beyond its victims. I cannot see the question of who is right and who is wrong, the big picture. I cannot see the decision-makers in the Pentagon, the military bases. I only see the victimization, some of it self-imposed, but usually not. Mostly, I imagine faces. A few solitary faces walking tiredly, haphazardly through dust and merciless sun.

Like the Native Americans on University Avenue. Hands outstretched begging for money, but at the same time the dead emptiness of their eyes, not of resignation, but the look of people who no longer care, dazed by life, by pain, by the tired repetition of poverty, hunger, fear, and hopelessness.

I cannot picture a thousand victims, or a million, only one or two at a time, like they show you on the news. The dead I can picture, the corpses lying bloodied, still, not people at all, only rag dolls with their stuffing hanging out everywhere.

But it is the walking wounded, the near-dead that frighten me. Their ghost dance. They have no one to speak for them. I cannot speak for them. I am not them. At least, not yet.

For another voice is inside of me, thinking only of my own success, of my despair at the realization that the novel is not yet right, that it will fail to bring me what I want.

People tell me here that I am young. Over and over again, they tell me. Perhaps I *am* young, but somehow I must find a way to put the right words together. Totally apart from War. From America. From 1988.

28 March 88

First day of spring quarter. In Lois Hudson's Literary Genres class she kept talking about the "usefulness" of fiction, moral intent, of the power to change the world, etc.

But my work is personal. I write so that I may better understand myself and my relationship with the external world that frightens me so.

Fiction is the only way I can find the words to the silence that is myself. I cannot do it representing myself, for I, as myself, am coarse, like these journals. Words in my outside world are ugly, used wrongly; only in fiction can I trim the edges, break through the artifice of myself and find the true human being beneath.

I've never been one to change the world. It I tilt at windmills, they are personal windmills. My dragons are isolation, loneliness, ambition, fear, and a spirit that changes every hour, every second.

6 April 88

Lois agreed to letting me keep a journal about the experience of creating *Ways of Being, 1988*. (This is the title I have decided upon for my ballet piece, and the name of my silent character is Janie, not "Beauty".)

Just the fact that I am consciously recording this for someone to read—as opposed to my personal journal—makes me already question its authenticity. I fear that this journal itself will become constructed, almost as though my thoughts about the piece will become as "fictive" as the piece itself.

Still, as a technician the idea pleases me: the creation of a creation of a creation of an artist.

Tonight I wrote and recorded the text. After all these months thinking about this piece, after all the different ideas I want to explore, it seems almost ludicrous to reduce it to three paragraphs. Eight minutes long with the addition of the music at the end. Theatrical writing is different than straight fiction. I find myself being less specific, going after whole concepts rather than creating an individual. It is the dancing that will create Janie, it is the only way she can speak. I've used clichés for the script, in the attempt to capture the way people talk about other people, the way a gossip talks about a person he or she doesn't really know.

I envision something professional. I fear it will be amateur. My limited taping equipment makes the prose sound silly, not hollow. Ideally, I would like professional actors to read the various parts, not me. (Though W. did agree to read the role of the rapist—strange irony that, your lover playing the role of a rapist.)

I need the appropriate balance between violence and understatement for this rape sequence. It is the high point of the piece. Everything is so beautiful in ballet, and here I want to use this most beautiful medium to convey ugliness.

This is a piece about contrasts.

9 April 88

First day of rehearsal. You know how you picture and plan something over and over again in your mind? It becomes more perfect with every plan, every thought? And then reality comes and shows you the true nature of ideas. Conception is a beautiful thing. Execution, however, is often another situation.

I am torn between wanting to leave myself the freedom of improvisation and setting every move on stage. There are certain cues in the words (just as in music) that must always be the same, strictly choreographed. But the transitions keep changing on me.

I am glad that Hannah insisted that I have an advisor look over the project. She'll see the piece for the first time next Friday. I want it to be clean by then. At least up to the rape scene. I've decided to use the umbrella, not only as a fun prop for the opening sequence, but as a phallic symbol. I want it always to be on stage, half open, pointing outwards. This is very subtle. I do not know if the audience will register it or not, but unconsciously it might seep into their minds.

I am terrified of boring the audience (the monotony of my voice), therefore the choreography and, even more, the dancing must be impeccable, precise.

10 April 88

All my concentration is on WOB. I think about it all the time: walking to classes, at work, late at night, lying awake thinking. It seems to have taken on a giant proportion. It feels completely real—the process, the story, the idea—while the world of classes, schoolwork, and paying bills seems totally inconsequential.

I have become as obsessed with the process itself as I have with the piece. Perhaps it is because I know that I am recording it all for Lois or posterity or something like that. How does one go about creating a piece? In writing, straight writing, I worry about plot, continuity, always sure of my dialogue. But here I have no dialogue. Or I do, but it is the dialogue of the body and not the mind. I keep seeing the ideal over and over again in my head. And then reminding myself of my own personal limitations as a dancer and choreographer. I feel as though I am not expert enough to execute my own creation. As though my creativity is far more mature than I am.

I've decided on lights. I want it stark, a woman exposed. Bright whites and violets. The rape scene red and darker. The presentation of the rape scene torments me. I think about Santa Cruz and what I am trying to do, and I worry that the audience will fail to understand. I want the audience to feel assaulted, just as Janie is assaulted. Here they are in this nice theatre, going out for an evening of dance, and someone has changed the rules. I want them to be angry at me for putting them through such an experience, and then for that anger to turn into comprehension. I know I can do this. I just have to keep thinking through the channels, making the dance tighter and tighter, clean it up so there are no doubts as to what I mean.

Like Janie, I find myself growing more and more removed from the world of speech and hearing. I give stock answers to questions, and am annoyed when my thought processes are interrupted by the physical world. I keep up with schoolwork, but only because I know that when the piece is over I must return fully invested in the program. W. loves me, but he seems as unreal to me as the voices of my friends who call me every week on the phone from Boston. I feel like they are reading lines from a play, and I have walked in during the middle of it and have no idea what is going on. I am reading the lines of a different play.

11 April 88

I am in fragments. The pieces of my life are like pieces of a giant puzzle, each requiring my attention. W., and classes, trying to mail out stories for publication, and schoolwork, and my job, and dance classes, and Hannah, and my friends back East. And *Ways of Being*. The title takes on import beyond its eight minutes. Eight minutes and months of my life. This is not the first time a project has held me fixated. This happens whenever I am working on a story or a chapter. And each time I think to myself: "I am going crazy." And each time I think to myself: "What will it be like when it is finally done? Will I be any different? Will the emptiness inside me be filled at last?"

But this time I feel I'm spreading myself thinner than I ever have before. I am taking a bigger risk this time. I am taking the two things that matter most to me, writing and dance, and laying them and my feelings about them before the world. It is a vulnerable place to be. I am worrying too much. Worrying paralyzes me. It corrupts my work. I must be careful. To blow the fragile balance I have now would be fatal.

13 April 88 (2nd rehearsal)

The opening sequence is better, stronger. I think it is closer to what I want. Begun work on the rape section. I think perhaps the text is too long before the actual rape occurs. I find myself randomly wandering around the stage just waiting for the moment the man catches Janie. Which means the audience will just be waiting around too. I thought by taking it slowly I would build up more tension, but as I am already three minutes into the piece, perhaps the tension has already been created. Half-way through the piece, the audience is already expecting something to happen.

After rehearsal, I saw Hannah. She said that I danced very nicely in class yesterday. My heart soared. Such words make you feel humble and grateful, and secretly relieved. Then just before I was about to leave, Hannah touched me gently on the arm and her eyes went soft. When W. touches me, there is excitement, pleasure, but I know the single touch will lead to another and another. It is sexual. But with Hannah and me it is sensual, a different sort of desire, the desire for connection between two women. Will I ever be able to tell Hannah of my love for her, or will that, too, remain a silent emotion inside me?

How is it that we can deeply love someone and hate him or her at the same time? Because by loving them, we give them power over us? By giving them that power we are no longer their equal.

14 April 88

Lois talked about the experience of seeing a highway replace the open space where she had once taken her children to play.

But I was born into a world that already knew the bomb. It is my legacy just as Nazi Germany is, McCarthyism, Vietnam, and the homeless on the street. I have never known a world different from this.

Lois asks, "What, as artists, do we owe?"

I recall a conversation I had with my mother when I was fourteen years old.

"I don't want to help the world," I told my mother, "I want to dance." And my mother said, "Shame on you."

I was fourteen years old and my mother said shame. I had just told her the greatest secret of my life, my innermost hidden desire. I have never forgotten the exchange, nor my mother's anger. I have never forgiven her for not understanding.

But I was not born into the same world that Mother or Lois was. I have learned different lessons—that wars cannot be won, that everyone inevitably loses, that Watergate was only the beginning of decades of political corruption, that Jews die (and Native Americans, and blacks, and anyone else who is different), that Socialism fails to remain pure and that Democracy is not really about equality at all. I am not angry about these things anymore (well, sometimes I am); I merely accept them.

I read somewhere that the best artists of an age come when an age is about to end. We haven't had too many good artists lately, so maybe we should take that as a positive sign. I weep inside almost every day at the cruelty of this world. At its injustice. Its unfairness. But that is the way it is. It has always been that way. Perhaps it is only that we are no longer afraid to recognize life for what it is. Contradictions. Half-truths. Bittersweet.

And so I stop reading the news and listening to the statistics. I tune out the debates. Instead, I use my eyes and look at the world as it is now. I walk the streets of the cities—New York, Boston, Seattle—but more importantly, I walk the streets of myself and write about what I find there.

15 April 88 (3rd Rehearsal)

Hannah didn't show up for rehearsal, so I worked on alone. The rape scene is definitely too long. So I have changed it. Right now, however, I am more worried about the transitions. They are not smooth enough. They do not register. A dance composition must be like a story. A dance phrase is like a sentence. And phrases must form into paragraphs. And paragraphs must be linked one to another. *Ways of Being* is a story, just like any other kind of story, but as I am working against the literalness of words—seeking out the real truth, the physical truth as opposed to the subjective truth of words—it is crucial that each transition be precise. I think I need to slow down the movement a bit. I am pacing it too evenly. I've got to use the text like music, with a rhythm and a time signature.

Three bloody toes today. The *pointe* shoes rip into my flesh, a painful reminder of how much farther I have to go.

19 April 88

Janie is everywhere. She pervades all aspects of my life, my alienation from my parents, my separateness from the external world, in W's grief for his dead father and Hannah's grief for hers, and in the abused child in my new story, "Telling Lies". She is everywhere but where she is supposed to be—on stage.

I feel her living inside me, yet she does not come to life in the ballet. I am too much aware that it is me dancing on the stage and not Janie. I have to let her fill my body, take over from Sandi, who is busy worrying about her ego, about what her body looks like, if her feet are pointed enough, if Hannah will be moved by *me*, not Janie.

How would Janie dance? She would not be dramatic. She would be grounded, suppressed by all the voices that possess her, yet have that one element of strength from which the new Janie, a free Janie, will be born.

I am trying very hard to work from the inside out, but so far I seem unable to reach inside and turn it into external movement.

How does Janie move?

22 April 88 (6th Rehearsal)

The piece is going better. It is starting to become a part of my body, the movement doesn't seem quite as awkward. Ironically, I now believe the rape scene is the strongest section. Which is good, since it is the climax. I still worry about the correlation between the text and the choreography. Sometimes I worry that the movement is too abstract for some of the words, and in other sections I worry that it is too literal.

I have to rework the end, the solo with piano music. This is crucial because the text ends there, and we finally hear Janie speak through her movement. I am using the theme of a circle, the definition of a face, and then expanding it to encompass the whole body. I've decided to speak in the last four counts of the music, the first live words heard. Janie is dancing her circle dance and she re-encounters the umbrella/phallus. She wavers, unable to decide if she is strong enough to live within her own voice and not the voice of others. She reaches out to the umbrella as if to pick it up, but at the last moment she covers her face and draws the circle one last time. And she says…I AM.

A bit melodramatic on paper, but story ballets are bigger than life. It is part of their charm, their ability to captivate. Actually, I am just trying to stack the deck in my favor. If I were a better choreographer/dancer I wouldn't need those words to help me, the audience would be able to tell simply by the movement. I believe everything can be expressed through movement; only my limitations as an artist create the need to rely on both words and dance.

Writing this journal makes me aware of how I create fiction and how I write this prose. When I write fiction, I hear the voices inside me, the dialogue of the different characters, the voice of the setting. When I write in here, I speak out loud as though having a conversation with myself. Of the two, I think journal writing is far more self-conscious and therefore not a true art form. Fiction, whether it be a story or a play or a dance, is the best part of me, the selfless me, the moment when I come out of myself and let the world come into me. It is like the difference between masturbation and intercourse. In intercourse there is much more humor. But here, I take myself too seriously. I suppose I am compensating for being five foot three and weighing a hundred and four pounds. People tend not to take you seriously when you look like that. People stare at the body but rarely look at the soul. I am 14. I am 96. I have died and lived and died again.

Janie is the product of one of my deaths.

2 May 88

Things have changed with *WOB*. Hannah has given me the name of a costume designer at Pacific Northwest Ballet. (I want a unitard—jade to match the umbrella. The only colors on stage.) I am still unhappy with the end of the piece. Do I tell the story effectively? Will the audience see, understand the transformation? Most of all, is it boring, or still worse, melodramatic and, therefore, a farce?

In writing class today, the instructor said that there was no doubt I wrote well but there was a problem with the interaction of my characters, keeping them separate, establishing relationship, feeling. Perhaps too much distancing from my work. I love the irony of all that. I, who feel so much, I who worry constantly that my characters feel too much, that they border on melodrama, cannot elicit sympathy or pathos from my readers.

One student said of my work that he would feel more sorry for my characters if they weren't so intelligent, so obviously materially well-off. As though the pain of the intellectual, the "over-privileged", is invalid simply because they seem (to the outside world) to have everything.

Perhaps I really am that spoiled, self-indulgent child. Perhaps my attempted suicides, my vast sadness, my mammoth fears come not from my supposed suffering, but simply because I hate not getting my own way.

I see myself as Janie, and yet the rest of the world, the outside world, only sees me as over-privileged.

I have no money now. I owe the government $15,000 in student loans. I work 20 hours a week, besides going to school. In Boston I held 3 jobs just so I could dance and try to write. And yet, though I could not even afford oil to heat my apartment, I too have never seen myself as poor.

Yesterday W. and I had a conversation about how to market art. He is looking for a way to make it accessible to everyone, to the masses, and thus guarantee financial success. I simply wish to be read and understood, knowing that I am only writing for a select few. Of course I would like to be successful, of course I would like to have enough money so I can get to Italy, so that I do not have to deliberate over every dollar I spend. But everything in this world, or at least in America, has a cost, and the cost, one of the costs of being an artist, is an uncertain future.

Therefore I must live, as hard as I can, in the present.

4 May 88

Gave my report on Shahn's *The Shape of Content*. Actually, it was more like "Art According to Sandi Sonnenfeld." Lois asked me if there wasn't something dangerous about my way of thinking. She meant for the world. I replied, "Of course."

But danger is what makes me keep trying, that *frisson* of excitement, that moment when you hover on the brink, unsure if that day is the day you fall over the edge.

Life is red. Death is black. I am in love with both of these colors. And I am never quite sure which I will choose. But somehow, despite myself, red continues to win out. Perhaps that is why I do not worry about the danger Lois is talking about. Danger lies in the red zone. Danger lies with life.

Every time I write something, it is new—either an emotion or an idea I have never explored before, or a different way to approach the same emotion or idea.

5 May 88

Hannah has finally seen the piece. She was very quiet afterwards.

I said, "Is it boring?"

She said, "Not at all. I just didn't expect it. Right up to the time she was raped, I didn't expect it."

She said perhaps she wasn't the best one to be my advisor because she knew and loved my writing so much, that she couldn't be completely objective. But she knew exactly what I wanted. What I was talking about. And so she can help me without changing its intent.

First thing she suggested was to cut all music entirely. The last section (2 minutes) didn't add anything. The "I AM" was already in the movement, she said, it was there. There is no need for me to talk.

She also said that to make the rape scene even more powerful, I should have it occur in complete silence. She objected to my use of the word "thing". I suggested "penis". She said they were both bad. I said, but rape is ugly. She said, but it will knock them dead, the silence. She is right. Besides, this *is* a piece about silence.

I am so grateful she liked it. She said that she was very negative coming into it. She didn't like the idea of spoken text. She was afraid it would be corny. She said, *Somehow it is not.* In the midst of all this, another dance instructor came in. He said, *How is it going?* Hannah said, *We are talking about rape.* He looked uncomfortable, and left the room.

After talking about the piece, Hannah and I started talking about my other work. How frustrated I am that few people seem to understand what my writing is about. She said that it isn't so much that the artists out here are shallow as much as they rarely explore the dark side of life. (She excluded Seattle theatre in this.)

"You and I—we explore it in our work. The dark part of our souls and the dark side of humanity."

I asked, "Are they afraid?"

She didn't know. She didn't answer.

6 May 88

They must be afraid. Because tonight we had preliminary showings of everyone's pieces. I could not believe how nervous I was, just for a showing in the studio. I haven't been nervous the whole time I have been rehearsing. But suddenly, in front of twenty-five dancers, I balked. I realized the emotional impact of the piece. How personal it is. And I was scared. My legs shook on *pointe* the entire time.

Afterwards, there was polite applause. Nothing else. But Hannah touched my leg and said, "Yes. Yes. I like the changes you've made." (I had quickly re-choreographed this morning before showings, using her suggestions as a guideline.)

She said, "It is very powerful."

"But they didn't say anything," I said.

"They can't talk about it. It got to them. But I'll ask around later. See what the other faculty thought."

The six other pieces were all abstract. Some were quite beautiful. Some quite funny. Some dull. But they all avoided anything sad.

But later, after everyone had presented their work, Hannah's assistant, an older woman, came up to me.

She said, "Are you okay? It is a beautiful piece. It is very strong." And she hugged me.

I was still shaking. Somewhere between dance class and the showings I had become Janie. I felt exposed like she did, vulnerable like she is. People have so much influence over us, about how we think—not only about the world, but about ourselves. I felt the audience's silence within me.

8 May 88

W. teases me because I insist my work is not political. He says, I read your journal, don't tell me that's not political.

I said everything is political, but mine is personal politics, not world.

I do worry about that though. I want Lois to come see *Ways of Being*, but I do not want her to misunderstand. I am not trying to tell people rape is wrong. Everyone knows rape is wrong. To me the piece is not about rape. Or if it is, it isn't so much about physical rape as emotional.

I can't dictate what I want the audience to see or understand, that is up to them and their own experiences, but I don't want anyone to believe I am preaching. When you have confronted that ultimate weakness in yourself, suicide, you feel you have no right to pass judgment on others. All I can do is try to make them understand me through my work and, somehow, for me to come to understand them.

Who is *them*?

13 May 88

There are only four rehearsals left before dress rehearsal. Hannah talked some
more about *Ways of Being* today. She wants me to make it not more dancy, but
more dramatically expressive. Right now, she says, it is a very well-executed
dance piece, but you want it to be more than that. She thinks I should make the
beginning sections funnier, more playful, to counterbalance the ominous tone
of the text. (Yes, and yes, she picked up on all the contradictions I intended.)

She says that I understand the correlation between person and artist completely in
my writing, but I have never quite understood it in my dancing, my performing.

"Don't worry about technique," she says, "You have more than enough technique to last you. I don't want to see a ballerina, I want to see Janie, and
through Janie, see you."

So I was right earlier when I questioned this. At least I am accurate in guess-
ing what is wrong. This lack of "humanness" in my dancing is what has kept
Hannah from casting me in her own pieces these long seven years. Some people struggle to be artists; I have to struggle to be human, to be real, and not
just some falsely created image of the unreachable, always beautiful, always
unhaveable ballerina.

Artifice. Imitation. This journal has gone in a circle. It is back to where it
started. But I do not think that I am. Because I am going to try this time. I
mean really try and not pretend to try. Even when conceiving this piece, I had
no idea that *WOB* was going to be the work in which I finally must confront
myself, challenge myself. So far, it has been too easy—not living, but writing, writing has been too easy. But now I cannot hide from myself any longer.
As Janie I must at last confront the world outside. God, what happens if they
really do see inside me? The ugliness?

A sad, slightly mad Pandora's box.

20 May 88

Awoke early. Before the alarm, which is unusual for me. Thinking about Janie and writing and Hannah.

In rehearsal yesterday it took me three runthroughs before I rediscovered Janie in my body. The first runthroughs were Sandi, remembering the piece, the changes I made. It was too studied.

I find this realization remarkable. My immediate reaction in dance is to cling to technique, to keep the humanness out. It is only by running the piece again and again that I slowly transform steps into Janie's opening walk.

On Hannah's suggestion I have created a story within the story so that everything Janie does on stage has a particular purpose or narrative. This is an internal narrative, one that will only read to the audience in the context of the external story on the tape. Hannah said that most of the changes I had made dramatically were greatly improved, though I could go still farther with it. (It is funny. I try to hold back in writing, not to reveal too much…no, that is not true, I just decide exactly what it is that I want to reveal, yes, and this is what I must do for *WOB*.)

Hannah said the arabesques still look too much like ballerina arabesques.

"What is Janie thinking about there?" she asks.

"Being sixteen and being a ballerina."

"Has she studied?" Hannah asks me.

"No," I say.

"Then perhaps she can emulate one arabesque correctly, you know, from having watched dancers. But then on the second one, perhaps she looks around to see if anyone is watching her, and on the third one, it feels so good she goes too far and ruins the line."

"Yes," I say, "that is the point of the overdone Balanchine arabesque."

"Let us see her more self-conscious, let her want someone to notice her."

"You're asking me to bring back all my old bad habits," I say, "all the ones I've worked so hard to get rid of these past ten years."

Hannah laughs, "So after June 4, you'll never do the piece again."

I laughed too, but the word "never" ran through me. I am going to be terribly sorry when Janie leaves me.

Live performance is not like a story you can read over and over again. After closing night, Janie will no longer exist. (On videotape, yes, but that is only the ghost of Janie.) I am going to miss Janie and the work I am learning from her and in her.

After rehearsal I sat in the hallway by Hannah's office to take off my *pointe* shoes. Her office door was open. I watched her. Very often I feel like a thief, stealing people's lives, observing them without their knowledge. She is the most feeling person I know, and so I can watch her for hours. I know I watch her with longing, like looking in the jewelry window at Tiffany's. There are things I cannot have.

31 May 88 (Dress Rehearsal of WOB)

Sunday, W. finally saw *WOB*. We ran the piece twice because there were still problems with lights. As for myself, the hardest part is being able to become Janie from the very beginning of the piece.

I'm not going to get two chances on opening night.

Hannah didn't say much—she just yelled at me because my *pointe* shoe ribbons were hanging out, looking sloppy. I must be sure to sew the ribbons down tomorrow. Aside from that she said it went "okay." I am not even going to bother tormenting myself over the obscure meaning of such a word.

W. wanted to stay and see the piece following mine, but sitting in the darkened, chilly theatre, the sweat still wetting my leotard, I knew I couldn't stay. I had to get out of there. I felt a desperate need to run.

Maybe it simply was the exhaustion of running a difficult solo twice in a row, maybe it was because when my piece came on nobody in the audience clapped, maybe it was Hannah's reticence, maybe it was the fact that W. was there—I don't know what it was, but I began to shake uncontrollably.

W. took me out of the theatre. And I began to cry. I was filled with an incredible emptiness, beyond sadness; I was reliving the void of Santa Cruz.

In these past few months, I've not talked about Santa Cruz to anyone, or about that man whose name I refuse to utter, or the betrayal of my friend who married him knowing what he had done to me.

I've talked about Rape, but in distant terms, the way most people talk about it—as one more problem in a long list of problems in society.

But I know Santa Cruz has never left me. *WOB* came about because of it. W. says I can't let that man have such control over my life. W. would like to destroy him.

I said, "But that will make you as bad as he is."

He said, "Sandi, you've got to get over this."

I don't think he understands. *WOB* was the way I was going to get over it. It was my way of confronting both the anger and the fear inside me. It was my way of dealing with the silence that I have been living in these past 6 months.

So close to performance, yet I am aware that the piece fails. It *just* fails, but it fails nonetheless. I do not know whether it fails as art (I am totally unaware of it as "art" while I am doing it. I'll have to wait for the videotape to decide about that) as much as it fails me personally, in that I do not believe it will succeed in bringing people into my silence. And worse still, that it will fail to bring me out from that silence.

And if the audience fails to understand, I will know it is my failure, not theirs, for I am supposedly, as a dancer and as a writer, a communicator of life. Until I can be that, I will never be able to write about anything other than myself. I will never be free of that self-absorbing I.

After all, this is a journal about myself, a song of myself, as *Ways of Being* is a dance of myself. But this is the end of the dance, the end of the song. For tomorrow when I go on stage, Janie belongs to the world.

I hope the world treats her kindly.

Kathleen Hunt Dolan

Journal Essay-Fragments from The Alchemical Heart

The following excerpts evolved from reflections on journal entries made during the period between 1977–1989. As I re-read these journals, making notes for what would eventually become a book, I became aware of the recurrence of certain themes: passion, time, solitude, landscape, wandering, the archetypes of light and dark, illusion and disillusion; and above all the persistent search for points of vibrancy and illumination in the midst of the bewilderment, attrition, and just dumbstruck groping of daily life. As I abstracted the subtext of my recorded days, the reflexive art of journal writing doubled back on itself; a collection of essays emerged, which I call The Alchemical Heart. *(The book is composed of six essays, three of which are represented here. The remaining three are: "Yo Amo Madrid," "Clouds and Alchemy," and "The Philosopher.")*

At times I have been conscious of journal writing as something done in a state of near-helplessness; more rarely the obsessive, ritual chronicling I have performed now for eighteen years has approached the repose of controlled reflection and analysis. In any case, there is a sense in which all autobiographical writing attempts to break the trance of the quotidian even as it documents it, wrenching an authentic subject from its thralldom to a half-conscious life. Journal writing deals the first blow, so to speak. It instigates a liberation which may advance itself through a subsequent process of artistic filtration. And, as the subject is liberated, so too is time, transformed from a corrosive duration to a recollection of flexed, reverberant moments.

I have come to think of my original journal entries as "engendering moments," sparks or seeds that yield a thought which does not wholly detach itself from these moments, but affirms their particularity while clarifying and fulfilling them. Am I saying, then, that each such moment is a question asking to be resolved—and the self the awakening, expectant sum of these moments? Perhaps. Each moment in a life is both ash and spark, loss and discovery, darkness and light; and the cumulative, heightened awareness of such moments divulges a unifying theme: the journal itself is a wandering which reveals the (alchemical) hope of the wanderer to be nothing less than the ultimate lucidity of the transfigured self.

℘

In the kitchen

(1)

I'm sitting at a small green metal table—all that will fit in this tiny room. Soup simmers, the lid lifting a little, steam on the windows. Afternoon light seeps between the narrow red metal slats. One of three dogs lies under the table. My feet can't avoid him. He doesn't care.

Last night I awoke hearing voices, and saw what seemed to be a kind of signaling light in the room. Later, when I woke again, under the skylight, I felt that the light-message had to do with you. Your approach. I could hear the water gurgling softly in the fountain beneath my bedroom window. I could see the clouds moving across the patch of sky above me. I was afraid to stay there, got up in the dark, and went down to the kitchen.

(2)

The green metal slats of the chair prompt one of those funny associations: I think: green—ladder—Don Quixote's latticed stockings. He's in his room, in the Duchess' palace. He's alone, dejected—this is Part II of his story, and his defeats and humiliations are beginning to accumulate. He's having some serious doubts about his whole romantic enterprise, his life plan. He's bruised, battered, manic-depressive, and about to take the final plunge.

30

He's getting ready for bed now, having firmly closed and bolted the door against possible feminine intruders, and he sees that his green stockings are badly frayed.

"The worthy gentleman was distressed beyond measure, and at that moment he would have given an ounce of silver to have had a bit of green silk thread there; I say green silk, because the stockings were green" writes the translator, John Ormsby.

The intermittent shimmer of green—the only color in this long, long, impossible novel. He rises to open the window—just a little, he's on guard, cautious—with reason, as it turns out. In the moonlit garden women are murmuring about him, their voices sonorous and plaintive. Siren-like, they sing, and play soft harp music. The almost unbearable allure of this cruelly contrived scenario spreads its silver light throughout his solitary room. And for a few moments he is able to forget his miserable condition. Roused from his melancholy by the threat of this mood of languor and sensuality, he re-dedicates himself to the pure and unattainable Dulcinea, and slams the window.

(3)

February, an icy day, bright sunlight in the kitchen; I'm cleaning up after a lunch of garlic soup, toasted gruyère on french bread floating in it. I feel a surge of joy, even after a dreary morning spent at the dentist. Music, good hot food, my bright little kitchen with the red blinds! And freedom—freedom from you! That's how I felt, in that instant, loving you but rejoicing in my freedom, my ability to walk away. Did I walk away? Yes, I did.

And then the phone rang and it was you. I set the teakettle to the side of the burner, and listened. Your voice, with Irish music loud in the background. You're in your kitchen too. And the joy that had been expanding like steam in the room seemed to funnel into a small closed space for a few moments. I felt it quiver in the wires, it went from steam to electromagnetic waves, humming back and forth it went—weren't we happy? As we talked I pulled up one blind, to let in more light, and rinsed my bowl, and made the tea.

The blue coiled cord of the phone, that stretches the width of the room. The blue walls. The sunlight. The stainless steel sink. The white bowl with the broken blue line around the rim. Damp paprika coating the bottom of the soup kettle. The steam. Winter outside, laced and streaked with the currents of heat between your frozen neighborhood and mine.

(4)

The green stockings. Green, a secondary color. Nonetheless, primary, pure, archetypal green. Neither dry nor humid, but something like the green of earth viewed from a remote, yearning distance.

And the green of unraveled hope. Threadbare green. The green of hope darkening to the ash-green of disillusion.

When does the conviction of perpetual renewal, so crucial to emotional and spiritual life, become illusion, enchantment? Green becoming silvery green, *verde plateado*, a baroque, alchemical green. Silver, the lustrous feet of the messenger who promises the gold of revelation, the resolving chord and alchemical terminus, Dulcinea. It is this silver-green, the silver-green of hopeless hoping, of lunatic expectation, that Cervantes is intent on lashing out of his character throughout 800 pages. That is to say, he subjects him to *a life*.

(The most illusory of greens is perhaps the iridescent, metallic green of the Quetzal, which is no more than a brilliant greenish light cast by microscopic granules in the feathers which fracture white light into shimmering blues, golds and greens. A green not there at all. Iridescence. But enduring—unlike the pigmented red of the bird's breast—for having the nature of an *aura* rather than a substance.)

(5)

How dark that kitchen was, in Tacoma—even darker than the view beyond the window, which was of Orchard Street, partially obscured by a dripping camellia bush positioned artfully under a downspout. Antique, cracked linoleum frequently flooded by a leaky refrigerator—the kind of refrigerator whose door banged shut. The house sat on a peat bog, and of course was slow-

ly sinking. A raving woman, mustached, haggard, haunted, roamed the unpaved streets, peering in windows, dressed in the same thin cotton dress, whatever the season. I could see her a few yards beyond the lugubrious shrub, pausing in her ramblings to gaze dementedly towards my kitchen window. Neighbors said she was looking for children.

A Middle-European fairy tale atmosphere to that part of town, not far from the copper smelter. Fine yellow dust on the front porch. Sulfur dioxide fumes. Illness caused by the fouled air no one would talk about. Weird religious cults, cases of severe depression, a pack of wild dogs. A Yugoslavian neighbor and her German husband shared their plot of garlic and lettuce with me, and cut my grass with an ancient scythe. Maria and Karl.

(6)

Your mother is finally dying, you say. Five times she tried and failed and now the end comes, as love or inspiration may come, when you finally stop chasing it. I reach for the phone and drop the receiver. Its long cord uncoils and it clunks against the side of the stove, bounces against the floor. I say "sorry whoever this is" and I hear your voice laugh, though the name you give (why *this* joke, *now*?) is another's, belonging to that man we both know is better not spoken of.

Your mother, after a long lifetime of practice, finally falls from her purgatory into a heaven of no breath, no pulse, no voice; her practice has been to perfect just this expiration, this fall which is her ascension.

Sometimes you make me silent and wary, like my father, who stopped speaking to a friend for twenty years after a quarrel about a gun—we left the coast for good, Nick's Cove, the cabin, the path along the cliff.

From this later cliff I'm speaking to you now. I know it's you, splendid in distance, and freighted with the dense havoc of your life. I hear you say "she's going," and "I'll be back later in the week."

(7)

Before me on the table is a letter from my daughter, and a photograph of a row of white pigeons on a perch, in a market near the Seine. Their spread tail feathers like white peony blossoms. I'm imagining the sound they make, like the sound of a spring or a fountain, water gathering somewhere, circulating, burbling and filling. A cistern of water. In rain. In a hidden garden, one of those patio gardens glimpsed from the narrow Moorish streets of Córdoba. With lemon trees in pots, and pelargoniums, jasmine, myrtle. I contemplate their soft whiteness and imagine the river flowing past them.

Colombier, that was the word I was trying to think of, dovecotes in Provence. Houses and towers, or a pyramid on top of the barn. Holes in shapes of hearts or clover, just big enough for the birds; the interior full of perches, the droppings used to fertilize the fields.

To look, to be absorbed in seeing. In front of the doves, whose heads and orange bills are turned towards my daughter's camera, are the black vertical bars of the cage that holds them. The birds are lit from behind, so that their fan-like tail feathers are translucent, and brighter than the curved form of their breasts, their necks and small heads. The black beads of their eyes.

My daughter's face—is it also illumined by this wide diagonal path of light that reaches for the bars of the cage? But no, the light seems to stop a few inches from the bars, where the pale yellow straw—so fine and delicate-looking under the pigeons' feet—is cast in light shade.

To see is not enough. I want to touch, and to hear. I want the world of the white *colombes*, to be present *beyond* the retinal event.

To be more than an image. (Candlelight on the table now, the red wax dripping onto the wood.) For the bars to be dissolved between myself and the doves, for the space between us to become supple, continuous, to flow like water.

The only color in the photo is the faint yellow of the straw. And perhaps it is the near-monochrome of the scene that prompts this leap from optical to auditory appetite? Immersed in this textured whiteness, visual perception isn't held by the spell of color, and seeks music of a different order.

But it's the whiteness I crave too, the whiteness of the perennial, of the new moon, the whiteness of beginning-again.

Despair of buses

(1)
On my way downtown to board the university bus. (Why do we have to go south, then north? Why do we always have to go downtown, when that's not where we want to go? Recently a woman on the radio claimed this question was being asked forty years ago.) The frail old cop climbing on at the Counterbalance bus stop on upper Queen Anne. Exchanging a few words. "Camelot" rain, we agree, would be best—let it rain at night, say, between 1:00 and 4:00 A.M. He smiles, waves me on first, making a little joke.

On the bus he sits sideways, in the front. Across from him, an El Greco figure in a leather jacket, elongated, sallow, a little dazed, no one you will ever know. His attenuated form suggests an interrogatory mode, unconfirmed by the expression on his face.

On Eastlake now, gazing numbly back across Lake Union to my hill, its radioactive radio towers. As a woman wearing a blue plastic harp in her hair gets off, an old hunchbacked man tries to rise from his seat, then falls back down and dozes under his tweed hat, lower lip pushed out like Churchill's. Students begin to board as we draw nearer the University. The space around the bus contracts as grayness thickens. A telephone pole near East Lynn Street has so many scraps of ripped-off announcements still stapled to it it looks leprous. Suddenly, inexplicably, I'm seized by the desire for this old man to wake, to not go any further north on this bus. Now! I say silently to his clenched, slumbering form. Wake up! Get off here! We pass over the ship canal.

Back downtown now: Third and Virginia. A small crowd waits, silent, separate, atoms in a void. No one talks. A dwarf appears, running—a woman, upper front teeth missing, dressed in skirt, denim jacket, large pearl-like beads that bounce against her chest, as she pants and pounds the pavement, determined, a small whirlwind—to catch her bus. The #4 pulls up and I climb on,

35

as the dwarf pushes in front of me and seats herself across from a man in a dirty red jacket who rotates his head methodically while holding up his left thumb. Head rolls right as thumb bends right, but no system here—it's random, though the two gestures, more or less coordinated, are clearly favorites in his repertoire. Variant: caresses the back of his neck with right forefinger. Grimaces. Raises right fist, eyes shut tight. Reaches down to tug on soiled white nylon sock on left foot.

The bus moves east across the intersection at Fourth and Cedar, and bends north past the Five Point Café, where the bronze statue of Sealth, visionary Chief of the Suqamish, stands above an extinct fountain. His right arm is raised; his eyes have the gaze of all statues—distant, monumental. Around him in the mild October air the Sycamores (or are they London Planes) are beginning to turn. Wake up! I say silently; get off here, now!

Approaching the east side of the Hill. Head-revolver exits, ambles west on Mercer, gesturing to motorists with upraised forefinger. Now up the Hill. Groan and whine and wheeze of buses. Despair of buses. Slowness of buses, especially up hills. Three passengers left by the time we reach Queen Anne Avenue and Boston. Then only me.

The human voice, its cries, its songs and its prophecies: a fountain. And statues, human figures without breath or movement, grave simulacra exalted by a mineral poise. In statues the dead have returned to the silence of the mineral kingdom, yet magically they stand, aloof, upright, almost defiant. Here I am, still! Destitute, and still faintly musical, in rain and snow and poisoned city fog and the slow slow rot of condescension and abandonment. Mute fountain.

(2)

Climbing up, we find ourselves in the condition of having stepped down; purified of all ambition, we let ourselves be carried by a kind of listlessness, temporarily released from the pressure of achievement, even the achievement of walking or driving from one point to another. We aren't ambitious—we ride the bus. But here's an anomaly: the sprightliness of this woman who just climbed on the #13; yes, this is a notable event on the route between the Hill and the Market, especially at this time of day. Her neat little black boots, their thick soles and cotton laces. Slender legs in faded blue-green cords. I can't take my eyes off her. But it's her jacket mostly that entrances me: tri-color, the torso blue-gray, the sleeves blue-green, and the hood plum, or maybe mauve. It blouses out above the waist. Silver pendant earrings that end in a point—that's sprightly too. Light brown hair, cropped, billowing at the crown.

(3)

And now the sun cracks the shell of the afternoon, right as we're sitting here, six or seven passengers content enough with our portion of light—it's almost November, after all, and the dim, occluded light lets us be what we are, affirms our condition: we ride the bus, we are without aspiration, or even any hope of some improvement. So here's brightness, an unhoped for visitation, plucking at the black fisherman's cap of an old, white-goateed passenger holding a QFC bag. Then the yellow trees in Regrade Park at the corner of Third and Bell flare up, and sunlight warms the bodies huddled or sprawled on benches. The blue trim on brick buildings brightens. A sprightly bus ride now. *Sprezzatura nel autobus, sprezzatura nella città.* Two men get on the back of the bus and stagger to their seats. One asks the other, in a hoarse, tremulous voice, Free? Is this a free bus? Free says a passenger, Free echoes the driver, Free Free Free. The sprite-woman has large gray eyes. She bites her lower lip. The bus turns west on Stewart, and there's the Market, and the bay behind it, the sharp, delirious blueness of it, and West Seattle advancing towards us waving its banner of orange trees.

(4)

First and Cherry. Cold strong wind. Climb on the #7. Young man in jeans and plaid flannel shirt pulls on a sweater, complaining of the cold to the older man next to him. Just out of jail—six weeks. Old man in camouflage cap reminisces—it's been a long time since I've been in jail. At least it's warm. They go on like that, companionably. Younger man says he's thirty—time to turn over a new leaf. Now a plump blond man in tight, bleached denims climbs on. Will it snow, he asks the dark-haired woman next to him. Will it snow, what's your nationality? Persian. Will it snow? She doesn't know. Turns away. Asian women on the left side of the bus look into themselves.

What else can you do. Drive it, pass out, get lost, read a book, fall off, be born again. The English boy on his way to Nordstrom to buy "LA Gear" shoes to take back to London. "Everything's right there in the Bible," he assures me. (He's not very aggressive about this—he's just saying he's got some things resolved, he's o.k. now, and I don't feel put off.) I ask, politely, Were you raised in a particular religion? He looks down, there's still some conflict here, maybe some guilt. Yeah, I was raised Catholic, then I went to Australia and became a born-again. His face looks stubborn, a little tense, but also vulnerable, as he describes the anger of the priest.

I show him—we're turning east off First Avenue—where the store is, further up and just north of Union. His new religion is simpler, he feels. Everything's spelled out, right there, all the rules you need. Bright and well-defined with firm outlines around it. I like him, but when he wants to talk some more, following me north along Third to my transfer point, I stop, as he's about to cross Stewart, and shake his hand. "I don't want you to get lost."

Later I'm on the #3. As it curves around onto Boston Street near the top of the hill, I look out over Lake Union, and I see the curve of the hill in all directions, and feel at home. I like the tilted places, the dropping-off places, the curves. And I think about the Fool on the Tarot card, stepping off a cliff, right into space.

The shadow side of the saved English boy is the Fool, who finds his bliss in a perennial condition of setting forth, of being born again, but always into *errancy*.

With an utter faith in her wandering footsteps she strides forward, stroking, absent-mindedly, the obscure thresholds of her fate.

(5)

The driver announces that there's a power outage on the hill ("but we're operating on d.c."), on Boston Street and all along Queen Anne Avenue. A fine rain combs through the trees now and the air is a silvery green glow. Not quite a storm. But clouds are moving and the streetlights are down, and shops are dark and closed, or empty. One person sits in the window of the Standard Bakery, still reading by the late afternoon light. I like it, this disruption. The mood of randomness. I am closer to where I want to be now, though I can't say where that is exactly.

To be saved or lost.

To be lost in the Way of being lost, in a storm of color. Everything is uncertain for us here, on the path of amazement. Information is ambiguous, unclear, subjective, and may drive us to seek the white light at the end of errancy, of all wandering.

(6)

About a block from the Bon Marché, the driver announces it's 7:30 and we'll stop here for about five minutes. I guess no one's in a hurry. He gets off. Some of the drunks get off too, and there's an argument, some want to stay on. One man reels off and slams into the back wall of the bus shelter. Two men are left. They pass a bottle back and forth, laugh, curse, splutter.

Another man on the bus mumbles about not giving a shit. We're all gonna blow up together anyway. Then something about "niggers". A bottle rolls across the aisle, under the seats. What are you lookin' at punk he says to the black driver who's just getting back on. Watch who you're callin' a punk. The man goes silent, broods. Gets off, looking murderous.

Then, as we're about to pull away, two young women get on—another world. Aerobics. "But the weight just goes back on…I'm trying to cut out dinner and just do lunch…"

In front of the Bon Marché, a dark figure of a man with outstretched arms, surrounded by no one, haranguing the empty streets and sidewalks.

Further on, near Blanchard, a man careens into the street, nearly colliding with the bus—the driver honks—the man spins back, vanishes.

Cedar Street now, the bright lights of the Five Point Café, the fountain. I look out and into the dark window and see the lines of my own tired face superimposed on the statue of Chief Sealth.

(7)

First and Cherry, waiting for something, anything to come along, to carry me north towards the area of the Public Market. It will have to displace this huge "Maverick" tour bus occupying the entire bus stop. (Who's on this tour, I wonder; who would pay for a tour of the Pacific Northwest on a bus, in early February—like those people my mother tells me about, tourists visiting "Old Sacramento" in July.) I'm standing under the roof of the kiosk, which I share with some women and a little boy who's with them. Rain pooling between the cobblestones. One woman mutters to another: Whatever you do don't take a drink now there's a cop over there.

In the center of First Avenue the Sycamores, or are they London Planes, with last year's spiky seed pods hanging from bare branches. Daffodils rising from ivy—dark green, where the eye seeks its rest. A wonderful poem by Thomas Centolella begins "Every day is Easter or ought to be." I want to rise, and to see everyone around me rise, from this spot, from this darkness; I want the darkness in their hearts, in our hearts, to be lifted, and to find another motion to existence, the essential gesture, efflorescence.

(8)

The kiosk billboard announces, drably: Myra Stahl: Masks and Myths. Concerts: The Posies, The Beltanes. A Tea Ceremony. A #7 pulls up, a long one, pleated at the center, an accordion-bus. A boy wearing spotless white running shoes stands eating a slice of pizza from a paper plate, rain falling on it. He gets on the bus, saunters towards the back, still forking his damp meal. On board now, in front of me, a young woman with a powder-white face wears a message attached to the back of her jacket, black letters on a white plastic square: THE END IS NEAR. The sky a uniform dull gray, with faint tufts of darker gray here and there, above the northern end of the waterfront.

It's as though a fallen body, still alive, had been uncovered. You find its breath, its pulse. But the muscles don't move yet. Torpid, not quite convalescent.

The greenness of life without the animation. A body fallen, succumbed to a spell, not yet risen.

To yield to this dulled, muffled world is to float, cloudlike, in that anesthetized zone in which euphoria and the outer limits of pain are equally implausible. Beyond the reach of that ecstatic light that casts such deep, annihilating shadows. All that is rhapsodic is compressed and hidden, like a gold seed sleeping underground.

(9)
Grayness: inflected, or uninflected, it has the tender, yielding quality of a sleeping human figure, of human existence at rest, passive, stilled. Relaxed nerves, defenses momentarily down. Not abstract, like black and white, but not quite a color, either. Unawakened.

Tashihiko Izutso writes of the "killing of colors" as a principle of "Wabi", the spiritual and aesthetic attitude which turns away from the chromatic splendor, in retreat from the painful illusions of the phenomenal world. ("The Elimination of Colour in Far Eastern Art and Philosophy.")

It's not difficult to grasp the refined pleasure of this ascetic reduction. It's more or less the visual equivalence of silence. (At the other end of the spectrum of visual sound: the color red, the lucid pure red of a great major chord in a Beethoven symphony or piano concerto; the bright phosphorescent red of a scream, the dark cavernous red of a howl, the sweet rose-red of a love song, a love song in which the singer is hopeful that love is returned.)

(10)
First and Cherry, mid-afternoon, January. Soft rain begins to fall, straight down, and my daughter and I move back from the sidewalk to the scant shelter of the kiosk. Three women stand near the curb, talking together, their zippered jackets stuffed with cats. The cats' heads peek out. A drunk with one leg in a cast approaches, bellows into space, cursing everything and everyone, staggers past the group, unseeing.

A very small girl stands with the women, dressed in a fuzzy yellow jacket, wearing glasses with thick lenses. Her tiny doll's head tilts upwards. She strays a little from the group. An arm shoots out, and with a single ferocious grip the child is plucked up by a shoulder and put back in place.

The rain grows heavier. The child is weeping, quietly. The cats are warm against the breasts of the women. I say to my daughter, whatever bus this is, get on. We board a #1, ride as far as Kinnear Park, and walk the rest of the way.

(11)

Spiritual loneliness. To embrace winter, when "the world's whole sap is sunke." There may be a danger in embracing this wisdom, this spiritual art, prematurely. Before one has had time to fully experience one's life and to acquire a true understanding of the hidden richness of winter. The danger of appropriating the wisdom of old age too soon. First the child has to be recovered and given its home in us, and that may take a long time.

First we are the child, and then we abandon the child. The child steps forward again.

Near Third and Blanchard, a man lies sprawled in a doorway, covered with leaves.

The "killing of colors". Colors like the presences of native tribes said to linger all around us, and beneath us, arising from beneath the pavement, haunting the molded and erected surfaces of this city.

The pathos of colors. The child that reaches towards the world, running and stumbling and picking itself up to run and seize and explore. The ache of color; a child fallen, scraped and cut but undeterred. How much of that child do we want to give up? How do you know when it's time?

Soyez mystérieuse, soyez amoureuse, Gaugin inscribed in the redwood portal of his house in Tahiti.

To live in color is to live ensnared, in a state of perpetual amorousness.

(12)

The subject is the woman's friend—she's fed up with this girl. She had a good job, "not too hard, a receptionist." Her boyfriend beats her, and also made her lose her job.

—I was there. I started hittin' him with my umbrella. And police started to arrest *me*! I said I'm protectin' my friend! Now she's pregnant and he's doin' the same thing. They're gettin' married. Her parents gave her a silver Mercedes. He drove it two blocks and wrecked it. And you know what? They won't give her a dime until she moves back home.

—She had insurance on it didn't she?

—No. And she didn't have no license.

A grayhaired lady wearing a long, flowered skirt, silky white blouse and a fixed smile gets on, sits next to the first woman and turns to her, "Nice day isn't it?" No response. She turns away, smile unchanged, except for a slight twitch.

—When the police came she said (high falsetto) he didn't do it—*I* did it!

Driver shakes his head.

—Then they took him down to King County—she about had a nervous breakdown! She's out of a job, but (in a confidential tone) she's still got another job. Uh-huh.

—No.

—Oh yes. Mm-hm.

—Oh no.

—Uh-huh. I don't let her sit on my couch 'cause my couch is white, that's what I tell her. That's my excuse. I got kids. I got to protect my interests. And she gets on my nerves!

—She just turned 21—got her whole life ahead of her!

—At the rate she's goin' she's got her whole life behind her. That the guy you call "Red"?

—I call him *low*-life now!

—Pretty soon it's gonna be *no*-life!

My mother listens, face turned towards the window. I can see the reflection of her teeth, her squinting eyes, the blue-gray of her hair. She's making a series of those grimacing, coy expressions I can't and don't want to interpret, that make me sigh and stop talking. She has her new purse in a bag. The talking woman gets off near Seattle Center. We continue up First, west on Roy and up the hill. The revolving sign in front of Tower Books declares, stri-

43

dently and boringly, WHEN YOU GET THERE YOU'RE NOT THERE. I hope my mother won't ask me what it means, won't try to read the sign out loud. Please don't ask me about it. My brain, no my spirit is so tired from trying to unravel your remarks and questions.

The huge, hideous white blob on Roy Street (wasn't it once a Mexican Restaurant? In the Seventies?) is showing signs of life—a big dirty ghost about to stir. Unkempt but saved, maybe tenanted. I'm looking for something attractive or interesting to fasten my eyes on, and I'm keeping quiet about everything, because my mother thinks I'm too critical. When I'm around her I feel monstrous, and lugubrious. *Para mí, siempre es de noche.* A cyclops stuck in a cave. Yes, that's what I am. But look, there's a blade of water, shining in the west. I am silent with this gift, my secret, the white nymph whose moving, musical light I carry always in the back of my terrible eye.

Darkness and light

(1)

What's missing here is that polarity from whose tension, according to Goethe, sprang the entire spectrum of colors. Chiaroscuro: monster and nymph, their marriage, their varied offspring. The jeweled valley of color towards which the god of the platonists, starved recluse, yearns, stretching down his gold roots.

Union of opposites: beauty and beast. But polarity is usually subdued here, if not buried, and those of us who have chosen to live under these skies may be predisposed towards ambiguity. Connoisseurs of mood and tone and atmosphere, we are at home in this landscape of blurred boundaries, with its air of being removed by a veil from the hallucination of vivid color and vehement outline. We embrace the postponement of definition, though we live near earth's boundary, *finisterre*, the edge, the place where you have to stop.

(Three days of rain and atmospheric gloom. I'm seated in the dining room, nibbling at a bowl of pistachios. Three lamps on at 11:00 A.M. In the instant

44

that I read the words "immoderate, a red to shatter crystal," a pattern of dark diagonal lines appears on the white page in front of me, making a grid over the words. I'm aware of the shadow cast by light striking the blinds behind me before I feel the sudden sunlight at my back, and see the sudden red of the maple across the street, the sudden oblivion of the lamps.)

(2)
Where is the home for the soul? Between absolute darkness and absolute light, the boundaries of the human psyche. In Nietzsche's words: entangled, ensnared, enamored. (Though he didn't say he was actually speaking of the soul—he was cagey in these matters, and about his deep preoccupation with his own feminine self.)

A city abandoned to its clouds.

It's like a prolonged twilight, it has the shape and mood of postponement of form, of self. Realize yourself—just keep doing it, it doesn't end, the journey just keeps going, the journey of self-realization, the Aquarian dream. Mist, twilight, a soft current carrying you. Not visible not invisible. You're *almost there.*

Nietzsche, as his mask Zarathustra, achieves full identity in the extremity of a mythic noon hour, moment of plenitude, of consummation, of complete, jubilant disclosure and affirmation of the will. And yet Nietzsche's favorite painter is Claude Lorrain (nicknamed "Orrizonte" by his Flemish friends in Rome), autumnal painter of idyllic landscapes and twilit harbor scenes, horizons of mist mingled with a tentative, lyric light.

(3)
Shadow: light hurtling up against—and finding its limit in—shapely, articulate, opaque bodies. Interrupted, not filtered light. A collision of luminosity and density. An avalanche of light is needed to produce the drama of a shadow. Spanish, or Italian. Caravaggio: his painting of the Conversion of Paul, in which the twilit Greco-Roman world yields to a drama of absolutes, a violent embrace of light and darkness. The saint falls from his horse, struck blind by the light of heaven.

The unyielding metaphysics of foreground, of absolute light, has cast the saint's historical existence into an absolute darkness. Do you trust this bolt of light?

(4)

I saw him for the first time, several years ago, at a poetry reading. "Poetry Theater", before it moved to its current, less democratic locale (a tavern), convened in a room on the lower level of the Public Market. You could hear the street musicians, the voices of the produce vendors, the butcher upstairs pounding his "special cuts". You could hear a beat-up transient read a rambling monologue about 40 guys on a beach north of San Francisco playing poker for fucks.

We spoke, had beer and cider in an alley café nearby; only when I registered his tense insistence on taking the seat that faced the door did I begin to suspect his condition. Erudite, visionary, persecuted, lost. A Vietnam war vet, formerly a surgeon, he claimed. Leaning against the wall of the alley, an old bicycle with a few archaic-looking gardening tools strapped to it.

A few days later I visited the Dawn Horse bookstore (at that time around the corner from the Sunlight Café on Roosevelt) to see a film about William Blake. It's evening, late November. Rain is about to turn to snow. When I step through the door into the small, softly lit shop, I see his face look up, as though he's been waiting for me. He's holding an open book: Blake, of course. As he fixes me in his gaze he points to the lines, "Tiger, tiger burning bright…"

He follows me into the chapel-like screening room, and seats himself directly behind me.

The audience is quiet and reverent, and I'm the only one who laughs at the image of Blake racing a plough crazily across a field. It traces a zig-zag pattern, and makes me think of the furrows in the visionary fields of Van Gogh. Green sparks fly. Then we see the poet knocking down a soldier in his own sunlit garden, as his wife looks on and coughs. The lights go on, and I turn to take my sweater from the back of the chair, a white Irish fisherman's sweater, still damp with rain, smelling faintly of lanolin. But it had fallen to the floor, and he's already retrieved it, and waits to drape it gently over my shoulders.

Much later, I imagine a flame in a blue cell. The rain surrounding the heat of your exhausted gaze. Good-night, good-night—I never even said those words in my rush to escape you, and the passion of your codes, systems of meaning sparked from the brooding forge at the heart of so many solitary rainy evenings. Darkness, blueness, watery sparks of light reflected in flooded streets, the blueness of speculation, its fiery heart... Goodnight to your broken and still-turning life, that no one of my frail and uncertain powers could ever mend.

(5)
Alternation, duality, the children of darkness, the children of daylight. Who can see furthest? Do not whistle out of doors at night; sweep the hearth and leave a well-made fire. Wait for the crowing of the cock before you go out of doors. If you must go out at night, in this season, do not look behind you if you hear footsteps on the path.

(6)
>"It was rocking and rolling and heaving and caving in"
>>—resident of Santa Cruz recalling the 1989 earthquake.
>"Everything was moving and lights were flashing"
>>—Seattle woman stranded in San Francisco during same.

October 17, 1989. The Marina blazing, and phone booths scattered throughout the city's streets—small islands of faint light, where a man might stand for hours sobbing as the phone rings and rings in his house on the other side of a shattered bridge.

That city of my origin, distant to me now, in time, is always the lyric city, as well as the original city. Its poetry is composed of peninsular distinctness, ghostly summers, steep hills, a sense of precariousness and unfading lustre. A city whose scents and sounds alone, without the sight of its hills and fog and water, would be sufficient to identify it for me. Fragrant, lyric, mist-wrapped precinct. I like to think of it now, as it shudders and falls and struggles to stand up again: gallant, fragile, possessed of numinosity which depends on no monument or single scene or vista, or historical cycle of splendor and decay, but on mood, atmosphere, a mysterious definition of space: set apart, not only from the inland territory of Northern California, but from an entire continent. For like an island, a peninsula can be a magical precinct. Earth, and the westwardness we impose on it, finds its limit here, and ending, rises up to affirm itself, to become its own monument, these eloquent cliffs of my earliest memories.

(7)

I am a small girl, barely more than an infant, wearing a red, hand-knit sweater. I can walk, I can run. I run from my mother. In the vestibule of my first home, a second floor apartment in San Francisco, stands a marble bench. It marks the threshold, the passageway between the street and the upstairs rooms where we lived during the war.

My infantile world was divided by this radiant and, as I came to see it later, pearl-like object. I clung to that stronghold, running around and around it in order to escape my mother, who wanted to bring me upstairs. The stairway was dark and narrow, and led to confinement; the bench reflected the fog-filtered light of the street. Children do not want darkness, sleep; they cling to the daylight. The light of my world was condensed to the mineral light of this passionately possessed and remembered object, the first instrument of my resistance.

Upstairs, my mother would pace behind the bay window, waiting for my father to return from the Presidio, or from the city's taverns. Food was rationed; I was "finicky", turning away from what was offered. My father grew bored with his uniform, refused his promotion. When the war ended, we moved inland.

Space is universal, general, vast, anonymous. Place is particular, personal, intimate, creaturely. Space is no-place; place of origin places us; it attaches us, it is a heart.

(8)

The enamored, the impassioned embraces a dream, a spell, a malaise, a darkness. And sexual availability may not heal the affliction of romantic passion, in fact may only drive suffering to a higher pitch of intensity: Psyche with burnt wings and still yearning. Immersion in a night, a night without solace, lacking even the assurance of the punctual arrival of daylight.

Every such love is a chaos—chaos not only as in a microcosmic confusion of elements, but a primal substance, a condition that precedes and seems to call into question all the fragile constructs of our historical being, our evolution towards conscious, responsible existence.

In Hesiod's *Theogony* chaos is primary. Something stirs, inexplicably. Upheavals follow, and unions, incestuous progeny at war with each other, or their begetters. Great clashings, then stillness: the hierarchy of Olympus, order, of a provisional sort. The forces of darkness pushed out of sight, far down into the earth, into invisibility. The monstrous, the deformed fall through a space not yet infinite. The upper world prevails, the world of the sublime.

But look how darkness can come again! A fissure in the earth, Hades heaves up his dark, ravenous heart.

Earthquake, temblor, rupture. Winter, winter, barrenness, the weeping mother, the lost and buried soul of the world.

The chaos strips away the qualitative time of evolving identity. We do not know who we are, we are *as winter* to ourselves, without substance or skin, a speech that chokes on itself, a cold vapor, a shivering bird. We are a verb in the passive voice; we suffer love, Eros has uncovered the darkest place of our souls and made a home there, and says: this is who you are. This is *all* you are, forever, forever, only this.

(9)

It is winter, and see how we are crying again! The old light falls in the gutter, teasing the ice. A bird walks over it. The drift of leaves, the tentative flare of dreams in which you rise, or fall. Winter—the grimacing face stationed beneath the surface of the pond. Let him lie there; glide over him. In his eyes there is a question. If you try to answer him the water will freeze and crack open and you won't want to see his face. There is not enough sky, not enough day or night to contain the tremor of his question.

As you wake in the early hours, listen to this tunnel of pacific wind that inspires the trite geography of the alley, scattering trash and dry madrona leaves. Reader, is it winter where you are? Think how you are as light as a leaf or a dragonfly, skimming the surface of the mysterium, as Hirsute Hades grimaces from the abyss.

(10)

I was in my small garden, it was night. I had gone out to plant a white dog-wood, an azalea, red tulips, anemones, crocuses, a couple of lilies...my shoes were caked with mud, I couldn't stop working, and the radio broad-cast a live performance of Beethoven's Ninth symphony; as the chorus sang the "Ode to Joy" I happened to glance at the basement window, and all at once, for a fraction of a second, I thought the house was on fire. Late October: it had been very cold, and now the night air was soft, mild, and enveloping. It had stopped raining, and I could see, when my brief hallucination waned, a bare light bulb suspended from the basement ceiling, not far from the window. I dug, first with a shovel, then with a trowel. I imagined the redness of the tulips, the white of the dogwood blossoms and of the lilies whose bulbs I hoped wouldn't rot in the muddy, heavy topsoil I'd shoveled and spread the week before. And now I thought of the mystery of so many hidden things, of the heavy darkness of soil, and of the flame-like presences all around us.

We say that white contains all colors, and darkness negates them, absorbing them. Yet colors lie hidden in darkness, becoming concentrated in recoil, like voices preparing to sing.

(11)

"Just now my world became perfect; midnight too is noon," Nietzsche exults in *Zarathustra*. The philosopher's climactic, fearful "abyss of noon"—this moment is akin to Caravaggio's painting in which Paul's noonday epiphany on the road to Damascus is rendered as an invasion of darkness by noon's sovereign "abyss". An ecstatic image, the specialty of the baroque age: Paul, the saint, suddenly fallen outside of his own history, which the groom behind him (and facing us) still tends, the history of animal-breath-muscle-bending neck-hooves—furrowed brow. Worry and tending, the road.

The "abyss of noon" is the inverse, according to Nietzsche's hard-earned euphoria, of the "soleil noir" of melancholy. Midnight, the darkest hour, absorbed to the shadowless world of noon. In this rapt proclamation, this supreme spasm of denial, the philosopher overcomes himself, becoming ecstatically one with his beloved alpine landscape, above the clouds, above the disturbingly veiled and humid undertow of his own soul's life.

(12)
The power of these boundaries: absolute darkness and absolute light, the places where the soul goes with trepidation, doubt, passion, reaching for—oblivion? Knowledge? Absolute beauty? Desire, Eros, I know, is bound up with it. And there is darkness and light woven into music too, into tonality itself, and in all visionary experience. The last movement of the Saint Matthew Passion—that mystery, soul-shaking, terrible. How is it that the human voice can sound so unearthly? What is happening when we sing? The *tenebrismo* of massed voices, a nocturnal procession moving slowly over the quiet countryside, thousands of candles covering the hills, their bearers invisible, moving like waves. The quavering flame-tips, the higher voices, the invisible hands, the lower voices; the moving, gathered lights of voices.

(13)
Fragments of darkness: the inescapable, irrepressible crows that haunt the alleys and streets, *corvus brachyryhnchos*, the short-billed crow. Darkness that probes, pries, hunts and tears, peels, plucks, scolds, a fretting, vexing, scattering, agile, swooping, mobbing darkness. Power outages: the fledglings perch on transformers, rub their heads on the high-voltage porcelain bushings, immolate themselves and a whole block of windows goes dark.

(14)

An old Spanish play, a brilliant jewel of theatrical allegory, depicts the Redemption of the fallen human race (Eve) by Christ as Orpheus, archetypal poet. But first we see Satan, black-cloaked, cruising the newly-born world. He's got a partner: Envidia, or Envy, identically garbed. Two crows, surveying the groves and meadows of paradise. They wait, watch, plot. Later we see them lurking behind the dancing figures of the seven days of the Creation. Stealthily interposing themselves in the circular dance, shadowing one figure and then another, they instigate a rhythm.

In the last scene there's a white ship with gold lanterns and masts, and an operatic Eve climbs onto it, surrounded by the lovely original Days of Creation, released from the surveillance of their dark night-twins. They sail away: Eve, her Redeemer, the Days and their creatures—the flora and fauna of the radiant, primal world. The human soul, nature, and history plucked and plunged into a vat of liquid gold. Now a timeless ornament for the white sea-paths of eternity.

The human voice submerged therein. Music ends. Desire ends. The engendering power of moments ends. Satan and Envy sink back to their underworld, and dream of the next cycle, and of the voluptuous cadences of time.

A day, an interval of light. But see—they're all dancing onto the ship, serene, in perfect unity. A luminous wreath of days. Unhinged from their molesting shadows, they rise into a purer music, a music without rhythm or melody, without the figured anguish of separation and absence. What are moments? Is there anything more beautiful, or more terrible? What is the source of their radiance? What is their enchantment, cut free now from precariousness and possibility? Is there anything left to watch?

(15)

I saw him again, only once more, but we never spoke. It was at my father's funeral several years ago, in early May. A pacific storm darkened the valley that morning, lashing the dusty old walnuts and oaks with torrents of rain. Wild roses bloomed in the little pioneer cemetery behind the plain country chapel, a small, shaded precinct fenced off from the flat

52

expanse of surrounding wheat and tomato fields. I remember lichen on the old, tilted stones, an angel with its head broken off, and inside, a nest of birds wedged between a window and a shutter, their loud, persistent cheeping during the service.

At weddings and funerals only would I see him. And the dreams continue. In the most recent one, we're seated at a table, quiet, watching each other with wonder, and perfect happiness. He's only a boy, as he was when I last knew him, and I am as I am, but when he looks at me I can see that he thinks that I'm beautiful. Like the other dreams, visitations through the years, the decades, this one too is utterly clear—it radiates certainty, light, perfect love; clear and calm as a pool of water in which you can see the grains of sand, or pebbles, the small choreographed movements of fish, the light falling all the way to the bottom.

(16)
November, afternoon, upstairs: never more lost than in this house, dreaming of your hands, your face. Nimbus, the waving branch and little stars, wait for me, I'm on my way. The dog on the rug nosing the spider, the voice on the radio, the sun moving behind the huge madrona in the alley. Blinded by it all, then not, then wishing I were. Cascades of voices.

That nocturne, the "Flight into Egypt": the family crossing the blue desert; just ahead on their path the shepherd's camp, its beckoning orange glow. That's the way I hold your image, hidden, almost, in so much night; and I always moving and watching.

(17)
In Caravaggio's painting, there really is no visible beam of light as such, though it's easy to imagine that this photic event occurs in such a form, because of the violence of impact. We see only the effects of the spiritual missile—the bruises, so to speak. The moment of impact, seizure, convulsion.

We do not know if Paul's arms are flung out in a gesture of supplication, embrace, or mere helplessness and surprise. The light invades a prior darkness; thick, muddy, claustrophobic darkness. Not the enamelled, lyric dark of Caravaggio's contemporary Adam Elseheimer, whose starry night in the "Flight into Egypt" is vast, intimate and maternal, lit by galaxies and moon and reflected moon and torch and campfire and the pervasive illuminating lyrical love of the painter.

This dark is a prison, closely woven, dense, oppressive, and the light projected into it suggests a dubious release.

A world without foliage, without water, without foliage reflected in water.

(18)

A spasm of light. Suggesting perhaps the interior, meaningless light of migraine. Rapt involution without meaning, a cruel caricature of ecstasy. The incommunicable. I remember: gyrations, explosions of light inside cerebral dark. Clenched dark, clenched light. The head—its tension, its agony. How we are alone in it. No one looks at us.

(19)

Fallen, stricken into an essence. The saint's face is turned away from us, facing—nothing, or an unspeakable plenitude. The groom looks down at his master, brow furrowed, in an attitude of consternation. But he already belongs, like the horse, and the horse's warm breathing, to a prior world, an abandoned world, the world of footsteps and hoofprints and falling and waking and falling again...of going forward on the path, from one earthly point to another. The light-beam has eclipsed that history which bound these figures together: Paul, the groom, and the horse, still caught together in the moment of the painted scene, but severed, as the light has forced a wedge between the time of the road and the place of everlasting arrival.

(20)

Against the almost impenetrable dark, the glowing crimson robe of the saint, the pallor of the groom's forehead. The gleaming flanks, belly, mane of the horse.

Not a beam but a flash of light, something that bursts, detonates, sears, scars.

The soul on the road, invisible, still restless, wandering in the flickering light of foliage. Not having arrived.

A alma é um sopro. A alma é um vento.

(21)
Now all of my dreams are of that lost one, the lost brother. A bird circles a white cliff, flashing its red wings. Above, and below, is darkness.

Noëlle Sickels

From Journals: 1970–1989

I am not a faithful journal-keeper. I don't write every day, though for stretches of time I have done so. And, in recent years, I've gone for long stretches without making any journal entries at all. I turn to my journal most often when I have been emotionally struck by an experience or a person and when I am traveling. I have also used journal writing, especially when first awakening in the morning, as an exercise to "warm up" my subconscious for other word-work, most notably fiction.

Anytime we are about to use words, whether on paper or in speech, all sorts of internal censors leap to action. In some instances, they are of practical use; in others, they are foes to be wrestled down. The journal form catches the censors napping. What may have begun as a straightforward diary-like entry on some small event of daily life flows subtly and strongly, with a seeming will of its own, into a delineation of beliefs or an insight into the many intricacies of even the simplest situation.

My journal writing reveals me to myself and helps me make sense of the world. It does so not because that's what I set out to do, but because the journal structure—private, process-oriented, cumulative—sets free a mechanism that finds words for the wordless in me and then lets those words rise up into the spaces between the planned sentences to claim my attention.

৪১

June 13, 1970 / Age 24 (Oxford, PA)

Keeping a personal journal has always seemed sort of pompous to me. I begin this one out of a great need to formulate my feelings in some communicative manner; this need has been sharpened by my loss of Leo, in two ways. Firstly, the suddenness and definiteness of our recent break-up and the constantly recurring evidence of the depth of his involvement with Ann has plunged me into a whirlpool of some frighteningly strong emotions; these are rendered less ominous to my mental equilibrium when I translate them on paper. Secondly, Leo's absence from my life has shut off the most receptive and significant outlet for my feelings and thoughts, so I must turn within and manage as best I can alone.

Alone—the word is so evocative. There can result from being solitary such a wealth of insight and exciting perceptual experiences that the prospect of aloneness holds promise and a unique value. Yet there can be such a desperate desolation in it too. Perhaps the difference lies in intent, the touchstone of most human activity.

If being alone is one of several vehicles of growth and experience, if it is a state entered by choice and used with respect for its powerful potentials, then it holds only strength and beauty. But if being alone is in any way imposed or serves to separate or exile, then it brings agonizing pain and fear. Since Leo, I have still known the former aloneness, but the latter edges closer and waxes stronger every day.

I saw an underground movie last night, and one scene touched me deeply—the rawness of it almost embarrassed me because I knew so well the feelings expressed. It was a close-up of a young woman's tear-stained face; she was doing a monologue of some very personal emotions and fighting for control and dignity. She was saying things like: "You say that this will make me a better, stronger person. I want to believe that, but I don't know. I think I will be stronger. I know there's supposed to be something noble in human suffering; if it's my lot to suffer, I want that nobility. It always ends in tears, everything always ends in tears, and I'm so tired of tears." That says so much what I feel, I can't even comment on it without becoming superfluous or repetitive. Even as I write now I am crying...

I think I should write about Ann a while. Whenever I think of her, I experience actual physical dismay: trembling, nausea. I don't talk about her when discussing my troubles with friends; it's strange, but somehow that seems more private and unshareable than things which have passed between Leo and me only. I barely know her, really; I always felt a vague sense of threat from her, probably because she had been Leo's mistress once before. I am ashamed of my jealousy, or at least at the vehemence of it.

It is almost incomprehensible to me that Leo could love anyone else. Cathi says she believes he is really serious about Ann; Dave says it appears to be only a passing thing, a "vacation". I know for my sanity that if I accept either opinion it must be the former. I have endeavored to hold no opinion. I refuse with equal firmness to relinquish my love or to expect any development from it.

Leo once said that each of us was the best possible counterpart for the other. He admitted the arrogance of such a belief, but encouraged me to hold it, which I did and do. Obviously, Ann is making him happy, but how? Is it mainly because right now she is safe to love, easier than I? Is it possible that Leo could have found an equivalent to the intensities he and I knew? Does he even want or value the kind of relationship we had, anymore?

I know if I asked him these things point-blank, his answers would be evasive. He would not agree to thinking in comparisons, but would only speak of differences in experiences. I think he might admit to some copping-out in his involvement with Ann and exclusion of me, but would not act on that admission and would posit sincerely other more worthy elements in his feelings for her.

I am at a complete loss to even guess at his evaluation of our past and our potential. There is concern there, I know, but is it just a paternal worrying about my individual future or does he ever consider a reunion of some kind for us? He has said no door is ever shut as far as he's concerned. I suppose I would be wise to bolt this one from the inside, but I long ago replaced that bolt with hinges that swing.

February 22, 1981 / Age 35 (Rosemont, PA)

On Tuesday it will be a year since Mom's death. That she is really alive somewhere in secret, escaped the family she made and was a part of and apart from, is still an idea I cannot totally discount. I recall the dream some months after her death where she appeared to me in the kitchen as I was frantic to prepare dinner and get everyone to eat together. She warned me not to even try, and said that she had had to die to get away from the demands and frustrations of that household.

Maybe that's one reason I don't like her ashes being in that house in my father's narrow, tidy closet. I want to free her from there and even from him, as I have been freed from them—more than I have. But would she want that? Did she? I am afraid of either a yes answer or a no answer.

I haven't begun the project of finishing her novel and appending a biography to it, except for sifting through her papers and some tentative form-seeking. I blame it on my job, the time pressures of a family. It would be a staggering undertaking even if I were single, unemployed, and free of fears of hurting my father, exposing my mother to unseeing hearts, failing her.

I am much like her. This I have long known. It is amazing that I am still discovering parallels as I age as a woman, as I learn as a mother, and lately as I compromise, postpone, and submerge. For didn't she, too, shelve dreams and longings to divert energy to her job and her ever-present husband and six children?

When she was young, sex, intellect, a passionate observation of life, and a full savoring of what was attainable and attained satisfied, even as it pained her. But what did she have as she aged? When the writing stopped? When the love affairs were sparser? Her inner labyrinth must have continued. She allowed me glimpses of it. Is it only wishful, wistful self-torture to think I could have known it more as she and I shared my son's growing up?

There are surface answers to my questions, but I want more, hope for more for my own sake. I almost feel pre-destined in the old Protestant sense, and she is my blueprint. Her writings are my codices, but they end so soon. I try to fill the gaps with her letters and my memories of talks, expressions on her face, what dismayed her and what made her laugh. Why must we always die alone?

I've digressed from my "discovery" today: that I am taking second-best, making do, as she did; that I have richness and love but that I see more and am too timid to reach for it. Will she help me be more content or be more bold? My son has her chin, I have her soul, but I don't want her fate.

August 27, 1986 / Age 40 (Big Sur)

Amazingly, I have found an uninhabited driftwood niche on the beach to shield me from the constant wind. My hand makes a shadow on the page. A slight lift of my head and the spectacle of a sparkling, rampant sea, huge rocks, sloping hills, and birds soaring across a blue and white sky is before me. The noise of the waves is steady and surprisingly varied.

I am compelled to write of my encounter this morning with Emil White at the Henry Miller Memorial Library. Brief and simple though it was, it moved me deeply. I was so entombed in the feelings it set off that I felt distant from the beautiful cliff scenery we visited right after and from Victor and Jude. I wanted only to sit down and set it down, and now at last, an hour or more later, I get the chance.

I knew it was he as soon as we drove up, though I had never seen a photo of him and supposed him possibly dead. He stood beside a mailbox on which EMIL was lettered in large, bright characters. He had the look of a startled fawn, his eyes wide and watery, his pose momentarily frozen. His face was soft and sweet. Thick white hair stood up from his forehead in waves.

He waited for us to get out of the car. Very slowly we entered a gate and walked together down a gravel driveway. He asked if I had read any Henry Miller, and when I said I was reading *Big Sur and the Oranges of Hieronymus Bosch*, he grinned and tapped his chest, saying, "The man in the dedication, that's me." He seemed proud and shy at the same time.

Inside, he showed Victor the dedication: "To Emil White of Anderson Creek, One of the few friends who has never failed me." A fine thing to have someone say of one, especially someone as perceptive as Miller.

The Miller Memorial Library is really an intimate, L-shaped room in White's small, lovely house. In it are photos, White's naive paintings, and books owned by him and by Miller. It wasn't much, really, but there was a feeling of grace and spirituality there. It was, in its way, a shrine to a great man and, with White's presence, to a deep friendship, but it had avoided being too reverent or overly sentimental.

As usual, I was pretty tongue-tied. I couldn't think of a thing to ask about Miller. At any rate, I felt I should be satisfied just to be there. It seemed rude or vulgar to treat White as a living storage bank of Miller memories. So the few comments we exchanged were about his house and his former gallery, his problems with Parkinson's disease, even the beautiful weather.

I bought a poster reproduction of a painting by White of the Bixby Creek Bridge. He offered to sign it. He had to lean on my arm to walk to a table in the kitchen. Once we paused a minute while he stood rooted to the spot, unable to move forward. The signing was a great task for him, as his hand was shaking and his grip on the pen was slight.

I sat opposite him. Through a wide window beside the table I saw a plot of red and pink hollyhocks swaying in the breeze. I recalled Miller's description of the hollyhocks in his own yard as "starved sentinels with big, bright buttons." One of White's hollyhocks pressed against the window. I touched the pane.

"The hollyhock wants to get in," I said.

"They're racing each other, trying to reach heaven," he said.

When we left, I shook his hand. He held on, saying, "You have beautiful hands." Then he kissed my hand. An habitual gesture with him perhaps, but lovely nonetheless.

Why did this little visit affect me so profoundly? The answer lies in several places. The influence of Big Sur on my spirit, namely a swelling of it. The thoughtfulness provoked by reading Miller, the inspiration of it for my living and my writing. The frailty of the old man White juxtaposed against photos of the younger, exuberant White. His paintings. His modest and beautiful home. My own silent absorption of the place and of him.

And still I feel the explanations insufficient. I felt while we were there that I held some rare, delicate thing in my hand. I was lent a piece of time and the pulsating existences within it to peer at and touch. I was in a room built as much by love as by wood and nails, filled not only with memorabilia but with a vibrant body of thought. Beliefs and ideas and even actions faced me in titles, photos, paintings. And it seemed so right, as we left, that he asked us to drop his mail at the post office for him.

August 28, 1986 / Age 40 (Big Sur)

Some morning thoughts after one cup of coffee and still with the torpor of sleep upon me. I feel soft, newly born. Ideas arrive unbidden, uncluttered, modestly. It came to me that I misheard or (more likely) misrecalled White's words about the hollyhocks.

"They're trying to reach heaven. It's a race."

I'd thought he meant the straight, straining stalks of varying heights were vying with one another to be the tallest, the first in heaven. But now it comes to me he could have meant the race was between them and him.

The hollyhocks, in bright array, full of vigor and life, confident, longing. And the old man, trembling, clad not in brash new blooms but draped with the pressed flowers of memory—patient, tenacious yet accepting, longing.

September 3, 1986 / Age 40 (Los Angeles)

Am feeling a little claustrophobic. Was more so a while ago when Joe, drunk enough to be very sentimental, and his helper, drunk enough to be loud and obnoxious, were here working on tiling the hearth. I considered throwing them out. If Victor had been here, *he* probably would have, but I wanted this project to go on, so I tolerated them.

At Big Sur I had thought to hold on to the full, happy feeling it gave me. At Big Sur I thought I could. By Salinas it was slipping away. I felt the shadow of a headache. I wearied of driving. The tourists in Monterey had pressed in upon my serenity.

Simplify, said Miller. Let go. The world will come to you. What you genuinely need will come. But he was a genius. People and things were drawn to him.

I do agree with much of his philosophy and have reached some of the same conclusions. But sometimes moving from understanding to living is very difficult—more difficult than moving from living to understanding, and *that* is far from easy.

I lack what Miller had to fire his philosophy, to blend so ferociously living and understanding: far-ranging knowledge and intelligence, guts, egotism, bravado. Not that I feel stupid or weak. I know some of the strong feelings he speaks of. But in me their expression is more private, more controlled.

Still, I can simplify. Act with more conviction. And push my writing further. Even in L.A. Even in my crazy-quilt existence. I have a piece of Big Sur yet in me, like a smooth pocket stone to caress secretly whilst in the midst of clamor and movement and the swarm of others' dramas.

Action springs from ideas and feelings, sometimes from long ago. In turn, ideas and feelings germinate in actions, a variation of the phoenix. The mystical body of Christ; the great mandala; the Ganges; the ecological web; the global village; the Tarot. Unities. Syntheses.

The impossibility of being alone co-exists with the impossibility of thorough connection. And reality sees no contradiction there. Only we, trying to grasp instead of allowing ourselves to be grasped, have trouble with it, gnash our teeth over it. Except at certain holy moments before the sea or a page or a rock. Or in our own dreams or epiphanies, when an unspeakable clarity is ours and a glowing harmony, and we feel made of pure energy, of light, an amalgam of everything ever. And we can only say yes, yes, yes, and so be it, and don't move too quickly now or the meniscus of this vision will slide off me and down and I will wonder if I really felt and saw what I did. But such moments are never really doubted in our deepest hearts. And we are never the same again.

January 8, 1988 / Age 42 (Los Angeles)

Jude turned nine yesterday. A shock. I had thought what a good companion he is just the night before as we walked out of the theater after seeing two Beatles movies, which he declared wonderful. We had to dig out and play "Help" the next day.

In a true step out of childhood only this week he discovered that there is no Santa Claus. He cried. For days after he made sidelong, almost bitter remarks about it. Perhaps his first taste that growing older is not all fun. And though my intellect shakes its head, my heart wishes to save him from every pain, every disillusionment.

When I tried to recall my own Santa discovery, I conjured up two scenes. Rustling, whispers, maybe even giggles in the bathroom on Terhune Street, and my parents, surprised by me, bent over stocking stuffers wrapped in aluminum foil and piled on the closed toilet lid. The other scene I may have confused with a facts-of-life talk, or it may be that the two blend a little because the setting was the same. Again the Terhune Street bathroom, my mother in the tub, me on the closed toilet seat. She asked me what I asked Jude: "You sort of knew, didn't you?"

Jude said no, he had no idea. As a child, I had prevaricated. I knew somewhere in me I knew, but I didn't want to admit it. I wanted to be completely innocent of my own disillusionment.

Somehow I was aware I was relinquishing more than Santa Claus. It was a first step, albeit a small one, outside a protected world, outside the beneficent arms of generous, reliable elves and complicit, shielding parents. How could I want to take even partial responsibility for such an awesome step?

The step away from Santa was the step toward life on my own, the step toward sex, death, truth. It was the first step away from guarantees.

Am I giving my nine- or ten-year-old self too much credit? Yes and no. All these ideas were not there, certainly. But I felt trepidation. I sensed significance. I sat on that toilet seat cover and denied any suspicions, denied curiosity, denied my own rational powers. I felt an inevitable separation beginning. I was, in this bit of knowledge at least, separated at once from my younger siblings. And I felt a shift in my relationship to my parents, too. In essence, I was inching towards them, towards the adult world, but I felt parted from them. A magical link was broken. And, in fact, the adulthood I was embarking on was not theirs, would never be theirs, so I wasn't really joining them, but setting off on my own to some as yet unformed community.

I wonder if any such uneasy feelings were behind Jude's tears and remarks. I certainly feel he is moving on. Not just because of this. He is maturing slowly. He is still the little boy, affectionate, playful, free with his tears. But I have been seeing him pull in more, too, take painful or difficult situations on his own. And though he still comes to me for comfort, sometimes I must go to him and press it upon him. He takes it. It even calms him some, but there is in his acceptance a politeness, a keeping to ritual which makes me feel he is letting me comfort him for my sake.

He is beginning to see, I think, that his solutions and sorting-outs are on his own shoulders ultimately. What a lesson to have so young. Yet memory tells me it does begin where he is now, and experience suggests it is begun young because it takes so long to learn.

June 15, 1988 / Age 42 (Los Angeles)

Through a series of phone calls I learned at noontime that Eduardo's neighbor, Patricia, had blown her brains out. She left behind two very young children.

I barely knew her. She and her first baby, a beautiful dark-eyed girl, came with us to the river on one of our Mexican trips. Last August, on my solo trip there, she and the little girl came with us to the river again. She was pregnant then. She had considered abortion, but friends talked her out of it.

I recall Eduardo saying there was tension in the marriage because her husband stayed all week in Mexico City, and on weekends (at home in Tepotzlán) spent a lot of time visiting, playing soccer, and sleeping.

I think of her alone day after day and night after night with first one baby and then two. I remember her as slender and pale with dark hair and eyes, an intelligent face, a reserved air about her.

Marilyn says she remembers her as overly attentive to the baby. She didn't strike me so. I can remember that stage of motherhood—the direct, physical demand and connection of it, the steady, fierce, inexorableness of it, "the seamless days and brittle nights," as I once wrote. It's a wonder, in a way, more women don't break under it. Perhaps the difference is in how we break and how much, not in whether.

I met Patricia's husband once, though "met" is overstating it. We were introduced in the little cafe, La Luna, where he was holding forth on some political topic. He was there on a Sunday morning without his pregnant wife and baby. I swear it is not hindsight to say he disturbed me. He was almost ugly, but saved from ugliness by intensity. To me it was an unnerving intensity; there was something dangerous about it, something blind. But to others, it seems, it was attractive. He was the village intellectual and politico. His opinions were deferred to. It's said, too, he was a womanizer.

And Patricia. Seemingly bright and strong. Seemingly in love with her first baby. Patricia alone in that village despite the friends, despite her husband's admirers, despite other mothers and babies. What was it like, that dark place she finally entered just before she took the gun in her hand? Or was it simply the back wall of the dark place she had entered when her second baby was born? That baby came out into the light and its mother retreated from it.

I pity the children, yes. And I see the selfishness in what she did. But it is Patricia my heart cries for and rages about and sympathizes with. I cannot fully comprehend her desperation and despair, but because I am a woman and a mother, I can taste it. I can say, even ignorant of details and personalities, that this was a death that did not have to be, that shouldn't have been, and at the same time that this was a death that was "planned", that was a known and accepted (though not by the women, not willingly) expense of bearing a child in a patriarchy.

I resist getting dictionary-feminist, but it is unavoidable. I am struck by this event so hard, I think, because it reminds me of sisterhood, and the neglect of fathers, and the burdens of mothers. Will anyone there in that village mourn properly for Patricia? Will all the balm go to her survivors and none to her memory? Will anyone say she died of a system of maternity that asks too much? Will anyone see what she gave and how much she gave in before she finally gave up?

Her death is appalling on many levels, but it is only the ultimate and crudest expression of what many, many women lose daily. And I say these things and feel them even though I love my own child and his father, and find parenting rich and nourishing and am not alone in managing it. Perhaps it is because of my state I can feel this, for if I were even remotely as unhappy as Patricia in my role, would I dare to feel it? Could I risk contemplating such a descent if I myself lived on that cliff?

September 16, 1989 / Age 43 (Los Angeles)

Went with seven other women to the Korean baths last night, then to a very expensive restaurant. It was a mixed evening.

The baths were relaxing and invigorating and purging in a way I had never experienced them before, perhaps because I used the cold pool so often. I felt so good, so pleasured, that near the end, alone in the sauna, I was singing.

Dinner was less enjoyable, though the food was excellent, the place posh, and laughs frequent. Mainly, I think, I was uneasy with the superficiality of the women. That word, really, is too harsh. But there was a quality to the conversation, and by extension, in some people's cases more than in others, to the lives that disappointed me.

To be fair, it was a light social evening and too large a group for easy intimacy or seriousness. Even so, some serious veins were probed, but always, always through humor, and often at the expense of ourselves, our mothers, or some other women.

I was particularly disconcerted by Susan, Valerie, and Martha, who seem to live such short-sighted lives. Only financial inferiority keeps Valerie from being as dedicated a consumer of luxury clothes and experiences as the other two.

Susan has always mystified me by the way she glides along, pampered by her husband, ensconced in good taste, intelligent and yet never seeming to think—certainly not to agonize. She has certain fears about physical safety that perhaps belie her serene exterior.

Martha is grittier and is so extroverted and generous-hearted she is impossible to dislike. I know she struggles with some emotional conundrums. But her responses to them, ultimately, are facile. And her constant pursuit of good times and her gushing sentimentality wear on me.

I like all these women and would like to get closer to some of them. But I don't feel a part of them. Ages, lifestyles differ. And there is my perpetual loner-observer stance and what I am afraid is my judgmental appearance. I feel there's something else, too—some structure in which we are all caught and which, despite the camaraderie, sadly separates us. I don't know how to breach either the structure or the sadness. Maybe it was this sort of feeling that spawned consciousness-raising groups years ago.

I get the impression (or perhaps it is just a hope on my part) that the core four women, who are often together, have broken through some to realities beyond clothes, weight, and kids. But I fear it could be just as true that they have achieved only a partial or token breakthrough, that they are not really connecting on deep, basic levels but merely exchanging more thorough and personal gossip and questioning their status in the world, especially as related to being female, only enough to let off steam and not really to challenge anything.

It's hard, what I expect of them, what I wish for them. They all have children they love and men they need—in most instances, caring, "good" men. They have comfortable, interesting daily lives. They have the potential for work and creativity and even exercise it irregularly and safely. Safety. Yes, that is what I am asking them to relinquish, or at least endanger.

But am I so different? To an outsider, my life must look much like theirs, with some unconventional twists, like not being married and home-schooling my son, that are actually only variations on themes. I have my broiling thoughts and the odd searching talk with a friend, but mightn't they as well? I am making a stab at being a writer, but only I know how weakly.

So the agenda I set them, I must set myself. I must think of some way of shuffling off the cloak around myself and encouraging them to do the same— or, in reverse of the fairytale emperor, to admit we are clothed and not naked.

Audrey Borenstein

Gleanings
(From the Journals, 1964–1989)

For this manuscript I chose passages from my Journal writings during the first twenty-five years of its life in celebration of the range and versatility of this form. Some years ago I began to prepare volumes of my Journal writings for preservation and also perhaps for publication, and I am arriving at the halfway point of this undertaking. I have made many discoveries along the way. In my foreword to one completed volume, I wrote that the retrospective of the Journal-keeper teaches how variable the past proves itself to be—"every retracing of the journey changes the look of the landscape and its figures,...every contemplation of the canvas invites a pentimento." I found that words for my Journal are protean—"cobblestones, lodestones, grains, keys, leafboats, worry beads...pigments, musical notes, tracings and sketches, diagrams for the memory palace I never built, much else besides." And I found that they "follow labyrinthine ways," and in so doing they hint of "an apprehension of the circularities of life.... For me, the movement of Journal writing...describes arcs, spirals ascending in a dream of the template of the double helix."

In another volume I am just now completing, I explore possibilities of arrangements of Journal fragments into compositions. Among those I made for this volume are compositions of journal art as readymades, life-studies, self-studies, collages, montages, still-lifes, cartoons for tapestries to be woven in late life, samplers of dreams. My revisitation of its tens of thousands of pages have disclosed the Journal's gift for shape-shifting. One who braves the full encounter this return journey becomes will recognize the shape-shifting of the Journal itself—into that other form of private writing, a letter, continuously writing itself to one's later self.

Much of the examined life, the life deeply and intensely lived, is lived in moments, heart-thoughts, stirrings of the soul. The Journal writer gives words to these; the Journal gives them keep. Manuscripts of Journal writings are offerings to Journal lovers and to students of 20th-century American life and literature. In preparing my own for preservation and publication, I have wrestled time and again with the gift of capaciousness that is unique to this form of writing. I recognize it for the Trojan horse it so swiftly and easily becomes. My artist's soul knows it is made of wood and what cargo it carries, yet sees with its God's eye flutes within spears, hears with its God's ear music's counterpoint to battle cries, dances as the whirlwind around the divine voice calling through the horns of its hooves for its keeper to release its holy sparks.

⇛

It is 1964. And the violence of the Four Days in November still hovers over everything. I still am stunned, grief-stricken; the memory of it burns as an incense. It is just as the rabbi said, every time someone dies in violence the image of God is diminished.

* * *

This morning, Will Herberg gave a lecture contrasting Hebrew and Greek society. He spoke of the Greeks' sense of the continuity of the human and the divine in contrast to the Hebraic notion of God's imposition of law upon humanity (immanence in contrast to transcendence), the Greek anthropology (man's mortal body and immortal soul) as opposed to the Hebraic emphasis upon will and conditional freedom (engagement), God's involvement with humanity, and the covenant between God and the world, humanity and the animals; and the Greek *polis* wherein the totality of humanity is the social order, in contrast to the Hebraic concept of God's primacy over society. He quoted a philosopher whom he greatly admires to the effect that this struggle between the Greeks' concepts of reason and nature and the Hebraic concepts of involvement, will and freedom—this struggle is the source of the energetic creativity of the Western world. As I was walking the children to V's to stay there for the hour, L honked his horn and offered to drive me to the lecture after he picked up Herberg at the motel. As I walked home after the lecture contemplating the trees, their branches almost bare under the late October sky, it came to me that I would not exchange the understandings I now have even for the most exquisite hour of my youth. Herberg has the long, sad face and the beard of the Prophets.

***

The day before yesterday, the first snow. It came down in a flurry, but turned into a real blizzard today. My poor children, my poor little ones, born in Louisiana and seeing their first snow, could only look and look from the upstairs window while I played in it for them, making snowballs and tossing them away. They've had colds for six days now, so could not go outside. The house is comfortable, but has become somewhat of a prison for us. I walked to Mrs. P's tonight and saw, as if for the first time myself—deeply, deeply moved—the banks of snow bordering the walks, and on the street the hardened grey ribbons of it made by tread marks…sights so intimately familiar, so cherished after living for ten years in a region that has no winter.

***

The news about D's death arrived today. How fresh the paper is on which she wrote her last letter to me, how bright the ink. There was an ice storm yesterday. The trees are threaded with ice, the ground is glazed, the earth like glass. The colors: thin lemon yellow, and grey and pearl-white and black.

***

All of us are in the dark, carrying lanterns that shed a little light on the cobblestones.

***

W observed yesterday, again after I just had been thinking the same thing, that people who live together for a long time begin to have the same handwriting.

***

I am close, more and more often, to the infinite.

* * *

I have just finished Freund's book, and I see the stars rushing away from one another; I see their fiery flight, and the incandescent spools of cosmic dust. It may be that the least suspected part of ourselves is the part that has eternal life. And that the most authentic, most glorious aspect of ourselves is longing, cosmic longing.

Rapaport (sp?) gave his lecture in King Chapel. Evolution, he said, is a vast lottery (the gene pool). Excellent point: in attempting to control human behavior, the social engineer unwittingly fosters revolution, sabotage.... In recapitulating the history of science, he emphasized the importance of written records and said he finds it no accident that the world religions, with their emphasis on human brotherhood, arose with the invention of writing—he suggested that people who live by the oral rather than the written tradition have a sense of community only at the tribal level. I question this, because of what I learned from Durkheim's *Elementary Forms of Religious Life* and Lévi-Strauss's *Totemism*. Rapaport (sp?) has a wide, generous mouth, a warm smile.

* * *

At night, beyond the two windows of the hotel room, Chicago sparkled in the darkness, close to me as it always has been, and expansive and blustery and friendly. In the morning, with a child's hand in each of mine, I walked on Michigan Avenue for the first time in many—*too* many—years.

* * *

Yesterday afternoon, at the Ink Pond, we saw a hooked silver fish leap and thrash and struggle for life, and later saw the boy who had caught it carrying his pail with that gleaming creature suspended from the bait line.

* * *

Was indescribably happy in last night's dream of playing in the surf with F. The waves rose higher and higher; they looked like grey glass. Joy in being alive. Afterwards, F's car passed mine; I saw his lips form the word, "Tomorrow?" I nodded, happily. I was driving, breaking every traffic regulation, and laughing. Laughing.

***

Last night, dreamed of *L'autre*—the deep-set eyes, the beloved face. He said, "What drew me to you was that you were so…feminine." I was close again, to ecstasy, to eternity.

***

What if the world you're building within yourself counts the most? What you leave on this earth matters, yes. But it may be that the inner palace and its walled gardens are another Reality we haven't even dreamed of as our keep hereafter.

***

It seems the more one understands, the more silent one becomes. I want to fling myself before God and say, Take everything, everything from me, only watch over them, protect them. This is, of course, the price the older parent must pay: the awareness of all that lives inside people and of all that might befall one and one's most beloved children.

***

The moon that night: smoky-glowing, and full: a pearl in mist. A werewolf moon.

***

Perhaps life is theatre, I suggested to V. The dead and the unborn, all spirits are in the wings…and take possession of us now and again, flying in and flying out. Life is so long, Journal. The radiance is sometimes so intense. And then it leaves as it came—in an instant.

***

Was very happy today thinking about, and talking with W about, writing a book, a whole (little) book on Compassion. Let that be my New Year's Resolution this evening: I enter the new year quietly, aware more keenly than ever before of how fragile time is, and even more, we who imagine we enter it.

* * *

One can be possessed. As I have been, by Montesquieu, by Rousseau, others...the trick is to be aware of this, and to learn how to sustain the spirits inhabiting us and yet remain on earth until we also learn what it is we are to leave here. And, even more importantly, what it is we are to take with us. Remembering the magnificence of what we came from, we imagined we were here on earth to re-create this. Yet we persisted long enough that we now know we are meant to take something away with us. Some offering, to give us passage to continue this journey.

* * *

Dream: Someone told me that if I put a nickel in a machine and stood on a certain platform, I would see scenes from my childhood. We were in a hotel at a convention. My childhood was projected on a screen. First I thought this was done by projecting the photographs in my wallet on the screen. But soon I realized this was not possible: there were too many scenes I did not have photographs of, and what I was watching were not scenes, but movies. I was afraid of what might be shown, and could not believe the show was running on and on for only five cents! There were my sisters and brothers and me...and there I was, going down a ladder into a pool at the YWCA, and I ducked my head two or three times under the water and came up laughing. *There,* I thought, I *did* try to swim when I was a child. I was almost afraid to look my earlier self full in the face. I felt apprehension: I might learn things about my former self that I had forgotten.

* * *

Rain today. Worked all day on the story about Joel. He's got hold of me in some strange, unanticipated way. All day I puzzled over this character who is trying to speak through me.

* * *

Journal, I was thinking yesterday that a writer who couldn't get his works published might translate his work into, say, Spanish. And then translate it back into English, and submit it for publication as a translation. He'd have to invent an author, but that is all right; the main thing is to have it published. W said this morning that getting published was not a problem for the Spanish writers: it was inexpensive, and one could publish in newspapers, too. The main thing wasn't getting published, but to have one's work *discussed*.

* * *

Dream: a snow leopard: blue spots on white. An *imitation* of a snow leopard, fierce and little and beautiful. I understood that it was not "real", but a facsimile—a replica of an individuation of the Platonic Ideal of the snow leopard.

* * *

Far within, I long to let go of life. Solitude, however brief, restores me to myself, and with the sorrow there comes a beautiful peace. And the awareness of the vanity of all things, and that I am meant both to leave something on this earth and to take something with me when I leave.

* * *

Dream after dream...I can't recall any of them but one, rather unpleasant because it had a morbid atmosphere. I was in a semicircle of women, hooded and shrouded in grey, who one by one stepped off a stage, and in that moment was cremated—either that, or the coffin was pushed away. It seemed it all was theatre, and I knew this as I stepped off the stage; even so, I hesitated before doing so. This was a reincarnation dream, I think, or at least a dream that suggested the body and the spirit are separable. That the life of the one doesn't depend upon the life of the other. I remember that the woman who was directing us in the dream remarked that we would be better off if what we were doing was true and real and we *didn't* have our bodies anymore.

* * *

The writer is not a person anyone could love. Hawthorne was right when he had Coverdale say these things in *Blithedale Romance.* I am afraid to go too deeply into analysis of my work; I'm not that tough and relentless. Therefore, I withhold certain truths, and they keep changing all the while.

* * *

The other evening as we drove to the M's, seeing double because we were so tired, and not wanting to go, I saw the failing light on the marsh at the foot of the mountain—pale yellow, earthlight, so soft and lovely—and felt how much of this I turned away from these past years because of obligations. I can't bear to live another day of this self-denial.

* * *

Meant to write in here this morning of the pungent ecmnesia (Beauvoir's word in *The Coming of Age*—I can't find it in my Webster's New Collegiate Dictionary—for the sudden return of a scene or moment from the past, acute, compelling) I've been experiencing these past few days. Some are stirred as I read Mary Austin's *Earth Horizon.* Others come unbidden. Just now: I am riding the Michigan Avenue bus, coming home from my voice lesson. Scenes, moments suddenly coming alive. And not at all connected to one another.

* * *

The snow is falling in *huge* flakes. A snowfall of doves. W and I talked of how precious time is as one grows older—one doesn't want even to give up three hours for socializing, even though one wouldn't have accomplished much in solitude during that brief period of time.

* * *

I felt I was dying last night. And I *was*—the being in me who is losing ascendancy to the Other, the writer.

* * *

Told J last night when we were talking about writing that I am sad to think of all the fictions I might have written over the years and that I *could* write in the years to come. He said that's in "The Snows of Kilimanjaro." I feel my silence as betrayal, but what can one do if one can't break through with one's fiction? As we talked, the past—things I hadn't thought about for years—came alive again. Places, people I knew—all that I've yet to give utterance to, given time, given the chance.

* * *

J told me about the disclosure through the Freedom of Information Act that unexplained UFOs were sighted near nuclear silos. While others leap to the conclusion we are being visited by beings from other planets, he says there is another possibility, that we are unwittingly producing things that may prove to be beyond our control—we are tinkering with forms of energy that are powerful beyond our imagining. Nuclear physics is awesome, it can be frightening. He asked me if it frightens me to think about these forces. No. I am not frightened, but *intrigued*.

* * *

The only moment I felt truly alive in a long time was when I gave an impassioned reading of my "Rites of Separation" at the Festival of the Arts in West Hurley. The young men who read earlier on the program were so talented and filled with energy—original and gifted and strong-voiced—they *ignited* me, they restored for a time the old faiths. I *reveled* in their words. Noticed a young man in the audience watching me very closely as I read.

* * *

I see D more clearly each time we meet, as I see myself emerging from the mists of my life, with that huge dark flower of my heart of darkness. I have never liked myself less than during this long and brutal year of revelations.

* * *

Coming back from the Recycling Center yesterday: the leaves a deep, deep yellow. The storm yesterday was violent. W said, One day it is all over; we will not see it anymore. Yes, and for a moment perspective is regained. If only one could hold on to it! Then there would be no more war on this earth.

* * *

When we came back from Poughkeepsie today, the wind was blowing through the willow, the sun glinting on the bare withes: chimes from an Elsewhere.

* * *

Last night, talked with S about her paper on Nemerov's poem, then read some of Millay's later letters. As I was reading, I became aware of the soft sounds of falling rain, and grieved for the lost poet in me. I felt I had betrayed my destiny, that I wandered very far from the course set for me. That I am a traitor—or a lostling.

* * *

Sartre said everyone feels he or she *must* write his or her story. I am impressed that one could have this powerful faith in writing, that one believes so utterly in literature. That is my aspiration, to believe in it this fervently, and to live for it as the highest vocation. I admire Sartre for this; had he accomplished nothing else in his life, that would have been more than enough.

* * *

I see—*vividly*—the marvelous chink of light under the door in Sargent's painting of women in the interior of the courtyard; and the dark tones of "The

Pavement," 1898—the stones wet, gleaming. S wants to shake people, to wake them up, make them *look* at the buildings, at the white light in that area in Manhattan in the summer. "You want to change people," I mused, "and I want only to observe them, to read their characters." It's true—and odd, because I've been a teacher for many years. I really don't want to change people; I want to console them.

* * *

I think that everyone can find some spirit in the other realm to whom to pray for intercession. Anyone who has faith can do this, and *any* spirit can answer. All the dead are potential saints for the living, then. It's vital that one make—and keep—the connection.

Yesterday (and I've experienced this many times before, although not so persistently, so overwhelmingly) voices, faces, trailings of words from conversations rose up in my thoughts with a lucidity that was forceful. And I despaired of writing—the whole raging sea of Life, its fierce vitality beat against my hope of making art, *ever*: I felt despair, hearing B's voice, remembering countless little phrases, all disconnected and yet so dazzlingly alive, pulling me this way and that. You can't contain it, I thought. You can't catch it and make anything coherent of it. But this morning, I'll get up from the table here where I'm writing to you, and go "once more into the fray." *Jusqu'à*, Journal.

* * *

H and I talked about our mothers' deaths, and I told her Anaïs Nin wrote that when our parents die, we give birth to them inside ourselves.

* * *

It seems to me you have to make a choice between being good (virtuous) or being the Artist—that you can't have both (at least not all the time). W said I sound like many editors today who are prejudiced against a tale having a moral. He's pointed out to me before that he doesn't see any clear dividing lines between genres in the literature of this century, and when I told him a criticism some readers have made of some of my work—that it's not fiction but an essay—he said there's no formula, there are no rules about what fiction is and isn't. At these times, he reminds me I'm taking a position that makes me critical of some of my own work. (Well, it's *true*! I *am*, Journal!) Last night, he asked, What about Picasso's *Guernica*? THAT was an idea! (I'd just said Art isn't ideas, it isn't arguments.) "And Picasso was *obsessed* by it!" Then B asked, What about midrash? Midrash is the use of tales, of fiction, to teach. I replied that as I see it, in midrash (and literature began as a kind of midrash, I suppose) you know where you're going, and the problem before you is how best to *get* there. But your aim, your objective is clear from the beginning. In literary art, you don't know where it's going to lead you. That's why art is thought to be risky, even dangerous. Because you can fall into the hands of the Devil.

* * *

The past did have shadows, I said to J, and we tend to "forget" them in moments of nostalgia. But I find them, I said, in my Journals. My Journals remind me that the times I long to return to at certain moments *did* have shadows.

I said I believe there is Judgment, and that what I most fear is the unlived life—of having God tell me I did not live the life I was given.

* * *

N said she had been amazed at S as a child: S didn't just draw deer, she drew deer running, a deer looking over its shoulder...all her deer were moving, were alive. Yes, I said, how true this is. I reminded S how every animal she drew was doing something or supremely *not* doing something (as sleeping)—that the animals she drew *lived* on the drawing paper.

* * *

The question the young woman asked had to do with recognizing a "turning point"—the recurrence of something a third or fourth time, indicating that it is a turning point. She asked what difference it makes whether one recognizes it as such or not. ("Why worry about missing it?") B answered that if one misses it, one's life doesn't move in the direction that it's meant to move in. I felt we were really *on* to something here. We also talked about a book (beginning with the Bible) being read as one incredibly long sentence. (W had mentioned the long phrases in some literary works, and had given examples in Latin.) B suggested that this way of writing, speaking, thinking may be the closest approximation to Life, to Reality. (García Márquez writes in this tradition. And so do I at times in here, Journal.)

* * *

When the talk came around to telling lies—and the example given was the parents of an unattractive baby asking, Isn't he beautiful?—someone said people are dishonest if they say Yes. B explained (marvelously!) that the question here has to do with a much more profound truth, the depth of the parents' feeling for their baby—and the beauty was about the beauty of the bond each of them felt, not about physical appearances, surfaces.

N was being philosophical—and *she* thanked *me* for calling the feeling of being overwhelmed by the great suffering of all humanity and the expression of impotence as "ethics-on-the-cheap," and for suggesting that the moment of truth is the concrete instance, the encounter of someone reaching out to you in need: it's *then* you describe your moral code.

In another exchange, I said I thought that no one knows beforehand what he or she will do or say in an encounter, and that what one does on Tuesday may be different from what one would have done on Monday, or *will* do one day in the future. (I am suspicious of the feeling of self-confidence; the Trickster always waits in the wings.)

* * *

Have just seen Tavernier's *A Sunday in the Country*. An exquisite, very moving film. W said they'd never make this film in the U.S. It moves, arrests itself as a composition of color and light, and dissolves. And again the movement to another composition, and again it dissolves. The music: Fauré. The old man was dreaming of Moses at the moment he knows he is about to die (fully aware he will not see The Promised Land). Rapture. The realization of having Love, Art—of having "seen" The Promised Land in this way—and that it was enough.

This morning I felt the presence of the Shechinah. Not an embrace; rather, a kind of shawl of light fallen upon me. My mind was a crystal.

***

When W and I came in, I told B that in my novels I'm working on relating Quantum Mechanics to the Kabbalist idea of exchanging souls. "That was going to be my doctoral dissertation!" he cried in happy recognition.

***

I want to record this while it's floating up to my memory, Journal. B showed us some *Life* magazines from the late Fifties and early Sixties they'd picked up—at an *antiques* sale! Among them was the JFK Inauguration issue, dated, as I recall, January 29, 1960. The cover photo shows JFK and Jacqueline Kennedy smiling and waving; in the jumpseat in front of them is a man who looks like Connolly. Jacqueline Kennedy is even wearing a pill-box hat. The cover photo is a foreshadowing of the cover photo of the couple in the limousine moments before the fatal shots were fired in Dallas. R noticed it just as I did. "It's scary!" he exclaimed. It is eerie. As though it were all written. As though we had been shown in January of 1960 the sign and portent of what was to come.

***

This morning, I told W the idea that had come to me in the early morning hours: I would like to found a repository for unpublished manuscripts of *quality* literature. W suggested that I try to get a grant. He also suggested that I found a repository here in New Paltz, and that I limit the eligible mss. to prose. This is because poetry is a vast world unto itself, and poets can publish chapbooks of their work. I like all his suggestions. I am thinking of writers over the age of, say, 55, who want their works to live. Writers who have sought valiantly but in vain to find a publisher for their work. Writers of quality literature. And what about younger writers who have a terminal illness? I would include their work also. What I want is to do away with the sociological categories that the M.B.A.s in the publishing industry translate into "markets". Good Writing is All. And length wouldn't be a problem; long stories and novellas would be as welcome as novels. W gave me excellent advice: think of it from the *public's* viewpoint, of making these good works accessible to readers for whom Good Writing is All.

* * *

Dream: I was in Mount Vernon, Iowa again. I had the sense there was an airport on the outskirts-of-the-town/boundary-of-the-dream and that I'd packed up to leave. I was walking on Fifth Avenue and came to the corner where the bookstore was, where we first lived when we moved there in '64. I went up the steps and onto the porch. There was a little table there with papers on it. I stopped to pick up some of the papers; one was a child's poster. A woman in a housedress appeared, carrying a basket of laundry—a woman in her fifties or sixties. I understood in the dream that now *she* lived in the house. Her face was so like my mother's. She looked at me as if to ask what I was doing there. I felt I was an intruder. I mumbled, "I *used* to live here," and went down the steps and began walking away—toward the airport, out of the dream.

I felt the same meaning that W found in this dream when I related it to him this morning: he and I both have recurrent dreams of going back to Mount Vernon because that's where we lived when we were happiest—when the children were little. I told him that I used to wake up in the morning aware of the presences of the children in their rooms near ours and feel pure delight, looking forward to the day with them. Looking forward to beginning again with the adventure of being with them once more...the whole day before me opening its radiant path.

Journal, the dream says that enchanted time is over. That I don't belong there anymore. "I *used* to live" there. The Mother Image looks at me as though I'm a trespasser. I took away a little paper from their childhood, a souvenir. I was "packed up," and my flight was waiting to take me away.

* * *

What's changed is that no one will be nostalgic for these times. Nostalgia may end with backward looks at the Seventies; there may be no longing to return to the Eighties.

* * *

The characters in my story "The Cameo" are still so close and real to me, I have to wait in patience for them to depart. It's a kind of rite of separation the writer has to undergo, perhaps. A burial, a funeral has to take place in the soul. I feel this story is my "breakthrough". Mailed it yesterday, and told W that whatever the editor decides, the story will be forceful as a fist—it will affect her deeply. I am one of Unamuno's "disturbers of souls", it's my mission, I said. And *this* would make a good story, too—the story of the writer who disturbs the souls of readers and editors who reject the manuscript, but whose consciousness is changed forever by having read the work.

Guy Gauthier

Water & Earth
a journal

In my journal, I've been trying to capture the moment, writing down what's happening while it's happening. I tend to work with a loosely structured sentence which allows me to take off in any direction, at any time. It's the only way to keep up with what's happening around me, and sometimes several things are happening at once. I like to write impulsively, spontaneously, without any preconceived plan, without knowing what I'm going to say. I seem to do better with this unplanned, unrehearsed type of writing. When I'm doing something long, something carefully planned and structured, I tend to bog down, I get stuck, and writing becomes more of an effort than a joy. The journal is one of the loosest structures you can work with, which is another way of saying it's one of the least structured types of writing. In a journal, you can say anything you want. No one has ever been able to lay down the law as to what a journal should be. This could be because there's no market for journals. No market pressures operate on the journal, dictating its content and style. Editors and critics don't have any set notions of what a journal should be. It's the least defined, least theorized about genre of writing.

Lately, I've been thinking about writing an autobiography. Not because I think the events of my life are particularly important, but as a companion piece to my journal. I think of the two as opposite, yet complementary. The journal records the present moment. But as a result, it shows no hindsight. Usually, when you write something down in your journal, it's something that just happened, and the impression is still fresh in your mind. But the memory, working over a period of years, sifts through events, sorting them out, giving more prominence to some, while it reduces others to insignificance. So when you write an autobiography, you're writing things that have

85

already gone through the sifting process of the memory. But in a journal, you have the undigested, raw materials of reality, before the memory has had time to re-evaluate them. Both the journal and autobiography answer my need to write the truth, i.e., to write down what happened exactly as it happened. I don't like to invent anything. I have a kind of aversion to writing fiction. With me, memory is much stronger than imagination.

ℰↄ

1972

On the train to New York / Sunday, April 30, 11 P.M.

Looking out of the black window, I can see my face brightly reflected, but when I move closer to the window, when I stick my nose right up against the glass and block out the light with my hands, I can vaguely see black shapes moving behind my face, unrecognizable shapes moving through blackness. My reassuringly familiar face has faded away, the thin and insubstantial image of me is gone, and I can see the disquieting and frightening shapes behind the glass. My life is like that, black shapes moving mysteriously through darkness, but I see the surface only, like my face in the window. Take this train. It has all the familiar markings of a train to New York, and I know I bought a ticket for New York at the station in Red Bank, and I know the last stop was Perth Amboy. But what is this…this raw mystery hurtling through the night, this light advancing feebly through blackness, a blackness I conveniently reduce to the night of April 30, and what are these lights, and the hats, and the hands, what is this *strangeness* transparently disguised as a train to New York? Things are only recognizable because of a convenient algebra of feeble notions like ticket and train, and words like Red Bank and New York, which neatly package the raw incomprehensibility, the mystery behind the glass.

FOOTNOTE (Days later)

Things are more real, more total, than we think, but their reality escapes us. Things escape us. Here in front of me is a pipe specifically designed for smoking. But the purpose of man-made objects is the most superficial part of them. We identify them only by their purpose, and we see only the surface, things escape us, we think of them only as a pipe, a cup, a chair. But they are much more than that. Finally, things are independent of us, the pipe is independent of me, and it is only the merest part of the pipe that I use for smoking. We think we recognize things, but what we recognize is only their man-made purpose. Take the phone. The phone has a total reality which goes far beyond making phone calls. Things are very elusive. They are more total, more absolute, than we imagine, and there is a part of them we never use, which is their own true reality.

Sometimes, when I am very drunk or stoned, I can no longer recognize the objects in my room, and the pipe seems no longer something made for smoking, but something strange and unrecognizable, and my convenient notions of a pipe are shattered, and I am faced with something strange...with God?

Things that are man-made, they are only partly man-made, only in a superficial way, but in themselves, they remain unchanged, alien to our purposes and our will, waiting patiently to return to their natural state. Those of us who live in cities live surrounded by man-made objects, and we are the ones who are most completely fooled, we see only the surface of reality, its man-made purpose, and we are missing the elusive reality, the totality of things. We live in a world where everything is easily and conveniently identified by its purpose: tables, doors. They are not tables, they are not doors! This is only the use we make of them. Only when things become absolutely and utterly unrecognizable can we begin to see reality.

4 A.M., June 11

I was lying on my mattress reading Kierkegaard, and the water was steaming on my hot plate. Now I'm sitting in front of my tin foil, having a cup of Lipton tea. What is there, besides now? Kierkegaard, tea, now. And now is just now, now is nothing, splendid, glorious nothing, perfectly empty, the final reality of this cup of Lipton tea, now, on West 80th St., at 4:20 in the morning. There are no birds singing outside. Not yet. It's hard to keep writing, because it forces me to narrow my attention down to the business of typing, it makes me lose my awareness of the moment, and this moment is everything, and as I go on writing, I'm missing it, it's passing by unlived, unknown. But often, when I hit a comma or period, I pause and then I can feel it, now, it's there, raw, thick, dense, a perfect mystery, it opens like a window on...on nothing, the purity, the pure present, NOW, purified of all value or significance, because to attach any value or significance to this moment would be to force this moment to march to the tune of some abstract concept or principle, to make this moment step in line with some philosophy, and this moment is really only this moment, free, independent, absolute when you realize that it will not fit into any...any what? I can't find the word. Abstract is the word I like best. That's the enemy, the Abstract. And this is abstract, much too abstract, because in writing this, I'm missing the wonderfully concrete moment, the...what? I can't find the words, and it's no use, in such cases, pretending I can find the words, pretending that I know precisely what I'm saying.

8:30 P.M., June 12

What am I doing here? *What am I doing?* I'm drinking a can of Munich beer. Sitting on a plain brown chair, with my jacket slung over the back. But mostly, I'm indulging an old habit, the habit of sitting here doing what I'm doing. You move your fingers over the keys, you marvel at the way they hit exactly the right keys, as if they knew what they wanted to say, but meanwhile, your mind is drifting, and thinking, what am I doing? I'm opening another can of Munich. On the 20th, I'll be moving to Bailey's on East 2nd St. So I won't be looking at this wall any more. Over the past year, I've seen the world on my wall. But maybe Bailey's wall will be interesting too. That's what I *really* do, I spend my life facing the wall. So I hope Bailey's wall is...psychedelic!! But it's not the wall, it's you. You just project your own mind on the wall like a film, and if you're bored just looking at the wall, that's because your mind is dull. My cat Willy can't stand my typing. The moment I sit down and start pounding, he leaves the room in protest. He *knows*. He can see what I'm really doing: *making noise*. And you know, sometimes, I can hear it too, the noise, sometimes I lose the sense, the purpose of what I'm doing, and I can only hear the noise, I can see what I'm *really* doing: making noise.

90 Park Ave. / Thursday, Nov. 16, 4 P.M.?

I have to get some sleep. Today's sunset is more yellow than yesterday's, and not as spectacular. Too many clouds on the horizon. They're moving to another office, moving files, typewriters, everything, and there are tons of paper piled on the floor. The white smoke from the chimneys reminds me of St. Boniface, the winter days when I walked home from school at noon, following a path through the snow in the College yard, looking at the smoke rising from the chimneys, not rising but swept away horizontally by a strong wind. The horizon is a milky blue. There's more haze, and the lights of Brooklyn are very dim. I'm tired. Now that it's getting dark, I can see the whole office, my desk, and myself, clearly reflected in the window. I see my face on a building, the short hair, the neat shirt and tie, enormous on the shrunken skyline of downtown Manhattan. I'm transparent, like a TV ghost. Through my face and body, I can see the skyscrapers of Wall St., and lights are shining through me! Rochelle, the girl from Kennedy, just came up to me and said, What's your name? Sounds like we're going to be on talking terms. Oh, wow, the smoke from the chimneys is blue!

90 Park Ave. / Nov. 28, late afternoon

On this IBM is a sticker, and the sticker says: MORGAN MANHATTAN. And on my phone is a sticker that says: 983-5021, Ext. 5021. That's me. The phones keep ringing, and I'm drinking this awful Nestea, and on my cup of Nestea is a cow smiling, I kid you not, there is a cow with a big smile, and under the cow, it says, ELSIE! And here, beside me, is a brown box of Kleenex, with one tissue sticking out. And a white paper cup. And two washers. Now, what are those washers doing there? They've been there for days! It's the most perfect mystery to me, two washers, one with little teeth on the inside, black and with teeth, and the other a faded silver. What are they doing there?!! They just sit there, they exist, like a universe of unknown origin. Oh, wow, there it is, right there, across the room, two smiling faces, a mother and her little girl, it looks like, clean, healthy: it's *McCall's*! And a novel, a paperback open on the desk, *Angle of Repose*. I hope it's good, but I'm glad I don't have to read it. And a clock, and the time on this clock, the time, ladies and gentlemen, is now 3:45! Fantastic. Another hour and I'll be out of here!! But there's a problem, and it'll take considerable ingenuity to solve it: what do I do until 5 o'clock!! Ahh, a package of Kent's, and a little booklet of matches with the word FREE in big red letters. Actually, all I can see is the first three letters: FRE... And there's a plaque on the wall that says, Donald J. Slattery,

Jr. As G.K. Chesterton once said, nothing is insignificant, and this, surely, is of monumental importance, I'm serious, what could be more important than this, there is a plaque on the wall, and this plaque says Donald J. Slattery, Jr.!! Oh, and this is something really special: CHARMS. Candy Sour Balls! A can of charms, a dark blue can with lovely painted candies, orange charms, yellow charms, green charms, and man, I feel good, I feel drunk. Just the effect of…what? Killing time. I love killing time. But in the end, time will kill me. I couldn't resist adding that. I'm getting a bit giddy. Hey, this lady in black, no kidding, *black*, appeared out of nowhere, and opened the can of CHARMS, and with a guilty smile, took out a charm and put it into her mouth, and then, still smiling, left the room. Am I dreaming? Now somebody's hanging his coat on a hanger, I caught a glimpse of a hand, on the other side of an open door, putting a coat on a hanger, and then it all disappeared, it was gone, hand, coat, hanger, all gone, poof, presto, and now there's just an open door. Ribbon Clear Set IBM Gardner Adv. Co. 634 Mar Set Back Space Shift Lock Return, and up at the top 1234567890-= that was the top row of my typewriter, and with the Shift Lock !@#$%¢&* Wow. Isn't that something? Just feast your eyes on that! !@#$%¢&* That has got to be… Wow. It's a symbol of something, something so profound, it's hard to say just what it stands for. A portent, an augury! Here is my prediction: !@#$%¢&* You want to know what I think of life: !@#$%¢&* I'll send postcards to all my friends, full of glittering Manhattan skyscrapers, with the awesome message: !@#$%¢&* It's a hieroglyph assembled by IBM mechanics who had no idea it would become a magic formula, the great ABRACADABRA!

90 Park Ave. / Nov. 29, 4 P.M.

I was staring at the rug, a grey rug, actually, it's got 3 colors, black, grey and brown, but the total effect is grey. Anyway, I was staring at this rug, and my eyes slowly got lost in a maze of interwoven threads of color. The patterns on bathroom tiles and table tops are incredible. Take the door to Walter's office: it's a wooden door, and the streaks in the wood, the dark fibres are…indescribable. Like a great abstract painting. Something tells me there's going to be a gorgeous sunset tonight… Excuse me, while I walk to Walter's window… It was a bright orange sunset, the sun flaming coolly between the Empire State and some other building. It's somewhere around the 30th floor now, and it's going down, down to the 29th, like an elevator going down, floor by floor. People keep walking into our office to sample one of Elaine's charms, her charms are very popular... What do I write next? I'm trying to think. I'm looking around desperately, let's see, door hinges, I see door hinges, and of course, doors. I see the grey keys of my IBM typewriter, they're an awful shade of grey, but the letters are white, so white they look like cracks in a grey wall, openings, almost as if light was shining through them. I feel like a prisoner looking outside his prison, looking out through the white cracks in the wall, and let's see, what else, oh, I wish I had a window!! H... Wow, that was really something, I just typed out the letter H and then my mind went blank. Well, there you have it, the contents of my immortal mind at 4:20 in the afternoon, on Nov. 29, 1972: H... That's all, just H... There's a sign on a black door, and the sign says, EXIT. Actually, from where I'm sitting, it says...XIT. In big red letters. Doesn't that sound ominous? EXIT through the Black Door. The End.

90 Park Ave. / Dec. 1, 4 P.M.

Hey, there's a sunset. Walter's gone for the weekend, and I'm sitting at his desk, with a splendid view of the city, a yellow sunset, yellow and orange, and Christmas lights on 5th Avenue, and white clouds moving very slowly toward the top of my window. What a way to end the week. I've sure missed my view, and Walter...ahh, I can't tell you, the sunset, there was a cloud over the sun, and suddenly, its light flashed many times brighter, the sun, it's blinding, a blinding orange sunset sun, I was sitting here looking a bit like Rodin's thinker, when suddenly, the full sun broke out from behind the cloud, and caught the corner of my eye... The phone rang and I was talking business, missing the sunset, but it's still there, now more red, it's red, I may not see a sunset like this for months, and all the clouds are pink, pink on the sunset side, and a strange gray blue, or maybe a very light purple, on the other side. Ah, no, no, the sun is slipping slowly behind the Empire State building, it's going so fast, I can actually see it move, now it's half gone, somewhere around the 20th floor of the Empire State, sliding behind the building, it's going, this moment is slipping away, and now it's almost gone, the sun, there's only a tiny...only the edge, just a spark, and it's gone, it's gone. But there's a red glow from behind the building. Wow. I can see the sun through one of the windows of the Empire State building! Isn't that incredible? Wow. Two windows, actually. I can see through a window which shows another window (on the other side of the building) full of red sunset. Just a tiny square of glowing red, and in the other windows…only a dull white light. But it's gone, now this window is like all the others.

Back at my desk

Some guy on the radio just said, it is 14 minutes to 5 o'clock. My last few minutes at Gardner's. I just left a note for Gretchen, wishing her a very Merry Monday. The sky must be getting dark, but I can't see a thing from Gretchen's desk, only that water color of the Manhattan skyline, seen from Brooklyn. I think I'll switch back to Walter's typewriter, and spend my last few moments here looking at the city.

Walter's

Ahh, this is the life! I think a view is essential for mental health. Hey, now that it's dark, I can see myself in the window, and I see I'm smiling, I didn't know I was smiling, and I'm enjoying these last moments so much, I feel like I could stay here all night, knowing it's my last day… But Rochelle wants me to help her staple some commercials.

1973

April 3, 4:30 P.M.

I spent the weekend in Cookie's friendly apartment in Flatbush. Lawns, bare trees, rain soaked streets, and Mircea Eliade. I was reading Eliade's *Images and Symbols* and *Myths, Dreams and Mysteries*. More than anyone else, he has helped me understand the origins of religion, even more than Freud and Jung. It was raining, and I opened the little plastic storm windows, and I stuck my head out into the rain, but the opening was so small, it was like sticking my head out through a porthole. The sound of rain, just the sound is enough! It was 3 A.M. and

I had stuck my head out of my porthole, my head, me, I was out in the heavy rain, and in the light beaming from the roof of our neighbor's garage, I could see the raindrops clearly, I could see them hitting a huge puddle of water on his driveway, and it was such a perfect moment for me, it was so…perfect, I just stayed there with my head sticking out of the wall, I stayed there thinking, this is a moment in eternity, and this moment is passing, passing, and staying here longer, getting my hair wet is not going to make time stop, or make this moment any more memorable. Only a brief flash, an instant of rain, the fresh smell of the lawns and the bark of winter trees, only a flash and I would never forget, and now it's gone, the rain… Now it's April 3, and I'm sitting at Bailey's typewriter, and I can still see the rain, the light over the garage, the raindrops hitting the little lake by the garage door, and I can still *enjoy* that moment, even now, but do I really see the rain, do I, here, now, really hear the rain, really feel the rain wetting my hair? Proust says yes, Sartre says no. Rain, Inglenook wine, and Mircea Eliade. Does Eliade know, will he ever know that for me, the experience of reading his books was mingled inextricably with the taste of Inglenook wine, and the sound of rain in Flatbush? What is the origin of religion? I would like to answer that question within my lifetime. This great question has never been asked until now. The first men to ask themselves this question, Freud, Tylor, Eliade, are…it's not that my thought ended there, my mind did not really go blank, I think I just started the sentence the wrong way. There's a crystal ball in my head, and when I look for an answer to that question, what is the origin of religion, I'll look in this little crystal ball. I don't deny that I've done some research on the subject. But finally, when the time comes to answer the question, I'll find the answer in the crystal ball in my head, this is my method, my new scientific method of finding the answers to such questions. And I insist that my method is just as *reliable* as Mircea Eliade's method of studying and evaluating all the available data. I'm really hungry, and my mind keeps wandering to a bowl of New England Clam Chowder, Campbell's 35¢ Clam Chowder. And I wouldn't be surprised to hear that anthropologists actually *do* use my method, you know, just a bit, every now and then, on the sly, without telling us.

April 15, 6:30 P.M.

We have gone beyond decadence. Now we live in a state of chaos. We are entering the twilight, the darkness that comes at the end of an Indian Yuga. But every man has his picture of the world today. Arthur C. Clarke, for instance, has a picture of the world very different from mine. But that's what's wrong, that instead of one great picture which all men could recognize and accept, we have...chaos. I'm a *reactionary*. A revolution is a cruel thing, a revolution always sacrifices something to its ideal, like human lives, etc. In the face of the great technological revolution, which asks us to sacrifice *nature* to its ideal, I'm a reactionary. But there is something futile about being a reactionary, or at least, the word implies futility. To be a reactionary is to make one's exit from history. I'm a medievalist, think of me as the Grand Inquisitor, and think how Torquemada would feel if he could see Europe today! Being a *gothic* Catholic, I tend to see the world today as chaos. With my gothic glasses, I see the world as a disintegrated Middle Ages. We live in the decomposing corpse of the Middle Ages. God is dead, and *there is no substitute*. The King is dead, and chaos reigns. But this is not a pessimistic view. On the contrary. I find the myth of Chaos very appropriate to the present situation, because Chaos, in the ancient myth, is what precedes Creation. Out of this chaos will come a new and ordered universe. When the time comes, men will say, let there be light, and there will be light. But for the time being, we must grope in darkness, in *Chaos*.

2 East End Ave. / Thurs., May 17, 7:00

I had to work overtime, and at 6 o'clock, I went out to dinner, I had a spaghetti and sauce at John's pizza, and...the floor is still wet, the janitors have just finished washing the floor, my play *Tonto* will be opening at the Cubiculo at 9 o'clock, and... OK, why did I feel so intensely the nihilism of modern literature? (Isn't this exactly what you would expect from a Catholic?!) Why did I experience the Youth Movement of the Sixties as decadence? My view was an outsider's view. (Your own ideas are never nihilistic, only those of others.) The word decadence has fallen out of use. So has the word atheism. And why are these words and concepts, which still seem to me the basis, the foundation of our experience of the world, disappearing from our vocabulary? Are these things taken for granted? because they constitute our past heritage? And why is there at last, thank God, a note of hopefulness...*what is this*, the EUPHORIA of the drug culture, or what?! The Hare Krishnas think they are exempt from the moral death of Middle America (a man in the throes of orgasm does not experience his orgasm as decadence) but as Nietzsche said, there is no escape from decadence. Nobody is exempt!! We will all pay our dues!! But this is an outsider's view. And here you see how the medieval mind is able to shed light on the present situation. With my 13th century point of view I can clearly see...the confusion and chaos of the 20th, yes, I can read the weather, and the forecast is...more rain, a deluge, followed by sunshine. I was born in the Middle Ages, though for many years I harbored the mistaken notion that I was born in 1939. But one day they lowered the drawbridge and I caught a glimpse of the Brave New World outside, the world that Arnold saw on Dover Beach. I made a belated attempt to leap over the centuries, in 1959 I absorbed the Renaissance (and that was a bitter pill to swallow) and then there was the Reformation, an even more bitter pill, then I was shocked by the Enlightenment, the rise of science, the French Revolution, my progress through time was a kind of electric shock treatment, it was like being Thomas Aquinas and being given a sudden horrifying glimpse of the future. But I greeted each new jolt with enthusiasm, I made an effort to absorb, to digest, to...but my attempt to leap over the centuries was a failure. I almost succeeded in my prolonged and determined effort to identify with the 20th century, but finally my mind slipped back, regressed, if you like, to the simplicity, the Light, the great *All under One* of the Middle Ages. I was born with all the answers. It was only later that the questions came. And even now the ideal solution seems to be: entering a monastery and sinking into the bliss, the purity, the warm womb of the Middle Ages. Infantilism. My nihilism has been replaced with a new philosophy: *infantilism*!

1974

Saturday morning, March 23

It's nine in the morning, and I've been working on *A Moon in Cancer Memory* all night. Karen's sleeping. And Willy's asleep on the couch. Now I'm going to sit in my canvas chair and relax, reading *Ariel*. Sylvia Plath's use of metaphor is teaching me things I didn't know about metaphors. It's 1974, and Jupiter is in Pisces, but the way I feel, it could be Virgo. Tonight I'm going to the Bronx to meet a friend of Karen's. I'm always me. It's always the same. I mean, Stanley's in Brooklyn, and he's always Stanley Nelson, nobody else. And I'm always just me. Stanley doesn't see the wall in front of me, the cracks in the white wall, he doesn't hear the song I hear, he must be asleep, in Brooklyn, Stanley Nelson. Sometimes, he's looking at me, and I'm look-ing at him, and his lips move, and my lips move, and we see the same walls, the same table, but now, he's asleep, he doesn't see the calendar on my wall, he doesn't feel my shirt on his back. I'm not Stanley Nelson. He's not Guy Gauthier. What does that mean? I'm always me. And then I won't be. Bailey's in Oklahoma, in OKC, asleep. He doesn't see the cracks in the wall either. He doesn't hear the song, now it's another song, and the DJ, he's babbling some-thing about UCLA, basketball, the DJ doesn't see the wall in front of me, he's maybe looking at another wall, another calendar, and I don't see his wall, John Denver, sunshine on his shoulders makes him happy. I'm stuck with myself. I have to live inside myself for the rest of my life. I can't be John Denver, with sunshine on my shoulders. I have to be me, like yesterday, and the day before. I have to be Guy Gauthier, I have to be the animal I am while I am that animal. Wow. The Space Age, the Atomic Age, the Age of Television, the Age of the Heart Transplant, the Age of Bell Bottoms, no, that was last year, the Age of Aquarius, the Lost Generation, the Beat Generation, and the Pepsi Generation. The Nixon Era. The...

June 13

It's almost Friday the 13th, but not quite, it's Thursday the 13th actually, which is not so bad. I wonder about the origins of this idea, that Friday the 13th is bad luck, I mean, I wonder who discovered this...law of nature. My approach to reality is the "Total Suspension of Disbelief," I'm only skeptical about science. But I'm getting interested in philosophy, questions about the nature of reality, like What is real, etc. I find philosophy restful, it's pleas-ingly removed from my own problems, it's like reading fiction, and I've been reading the Introduction to a book called *Phenomenology and Existentialism*, but once I got into the actual body of the book itself, I felt that old weariness, that empty feeling I get when something gets too heavy. I'm always doing that, reading introductions, like I get a book, an anthology, I look at all the Bios and pictures of the writers, I read the Intro, the foot-notes, and that's it, after that, BOREDOM. Why do I like to get everything second hand, I seem to be afraid of the source, as if I wanted the source to be...a mystery, sacred and unknowable. I love books, I like to carry them under my arm, but somehow, I can't read them. It's the bright covers that get my salivary glands going, I read the rave reviews on the back cover, I look at the author's picture, I carry the book home, I can hardly wait, I'm flipping from page to page, reading a sentence here, a sentence there, but then, when I get home and sit in my canvas chair, BOREDOM, I'm suffocating, I need air, I want to take a walk. The best moment, when I come home tired from the office, is when I see the bright cover, the colors, it seems to me that I can experience the book that way, in a more essential way, like the book designer has given me the essence, the gist of the book, I put the book in my lap and sit relaxing, looking at the bright colors. But then, unfortunately, I start reading. Like my book, *Existentialism*, I can't get past the Introduction. Husserl, I say to myself, Edmund Husserl, those words…speak to me, they are magic, and the cover, it's blue, sky blue, on the cover, you can see the word Phenomenology in bright red letters, like, it's vital, it's alive, it's *urgent*, and under that, the word Existentialism in bright green, and it's the red, the red and green letters, on a blue background, it starts me thinking, meditating, reality, what is real? But then, unfortunately, I open the book and the excitement of the cover is lost, nothing is left now but black specks on a dull greyish paper, not even that, even the black letters are gone now, now there's only a haze in my head, like a smog, concepts, Husserl's quarrel with Kant, Kant's quarrel with Hume, and Hume's quarrel with Descartes, it's so stuffy, they're like lawyers arguing over the meaning of a word, it's not livable, and anyway, the colors of the cover have already defined everything, so I close the book, and *think*, looking at my blue cover, with the bright red and green letters, red and green are the colors of life, red is fire and green is earth, and the blue, well, that's the sky, the universe beyond, the blue background beyond Phenomenology's red and Existentialism's green, Husserl is red and Sartre is green, Husserl said stop and Sartre said go, I'm wishing Existentialism was a movie, I wish they could make a movie of *dasein, existenz*, I'd sit in the front row with this huge image dancing in front of my eyes, drowning in the color, losing myself in the sound and movement. Life is a movie, not a book, it's a Cecil B. DeMille spectacular. Philosophy is in black and white, and reality is in color, living 3-D COLOR!!

Kuhn, Loeb & Co. / July 1

People are walking down the hallway, and I'm trying not to see them, that would be too much, it would be a stimulus too...hyper, it would blow my tubes, so I try not to be aware of them, to me they are not people, they are not...*me*! they are disturbances on my retina, fluctuations in the color field, the angle of light and shadow, disturbances, and they have learned, like me, not to hear the typewriters. They don't think, as they walk down the hall, that *I'm* typing, but such is the reality, it's true, I'm typing. He, the man in the hall, doesn't even go so far as to think, *he's* typing, he doesn't even hear the type-writer! But it's not he, it's me, *I'm* typing. The word HE is a shield we use to protect us from the reality of others, HE is my ego's way of not accepting the other man's centrality in the world, HE is my refusal to see him, to be aware of him, HE is not him, HE is *me*, it's me, I'm walking down the hall.

Down the hall, there's a picture of the sea, the surf breaking on the rocks, and over all this white foam, over all these black rocks, are two dirty strips of Scotch Tape. A hand, suddenly I saw a hand, then it pulled back, as if afraid to be spotted, I guess somebody changed their mind and turned back, and I'm sure he/she doesn't realize that a member of the Typing Pool saw his/her hand stick out, then pull back, doesn't know that a member of the Typing Pool is writing down that strange occurrence, but the same goes for me, I don't know where she was going, or why she turned back, and I don't know what the rest of her looks like, only her hand, our knowledge of the world is necessarily abstract. Think of all the concrete human experience I have not experienced, and will never experience, all the sights, sounds, sensations. What is it we do, when we see faces in the street, what is it we do to blot out the full, mind-blowing reality, the totality, the centrality of what is outside of us? We are thinking our own thoughts, and we don't see the faces, we see our own thoughts, isn't that something, when somebody sees me in the subway, he sees his own thoughts, his problems. When a stock broker sees me in the subway, he doesn't see me, he sees an option on securities, and when I see him, I see poetry. He doesn't see me, I don't see him. This is the only way to survive. Not to see, not to feel. There are too many faces, it's too much.

I'm back from a drink of water. It didn't taste too bad, considering it was New York water. There's nothing to do, and it's nice to see somebody walk-ing by, it's a major event in my afternoon, actually, it's like I'm watching this very dull existential movie, the film of my Existence, and it's dull, and I mean

SUPERDULL, nothing's happening, but every now and then, thank God, somebody walks by in the hallway, and this is a major event in the film, a turning point in the plot. Real human beings are walking down the hall. I am perceived as *he*, if I am perceived at all, I am just a backdrop for their thoughts, the concerns of their job, or their daydreams of being out in the woods, or by the ocean, this is getting hard to take. When I can see IT...the way IT is, I get this strange feeling that I'm going insane, that's why I don't want to see them, I want to shut them out, I'm a typist and they are not there, they are just disturbances on my retina, they are a backdrop for my thoughts, they are the landscape and decor of my own ego. You admit, you accept them just enough not to feel alone, not to feel that sudden dread that you alone exist. Solipsism. All men who thought deeply on life came close to it: solipsism. 3:05. The human, terrestrial way of making time seem understandable. It's very simple and obvious, 3:05, no mystery there, it's 3:05, no problem, hey, there's a black tray, and the upper level says INCOMING, and the lower level says OUTGOING, like us, like the generations, when one generation is INCOMING, the other is OUTGOING...

Kuhn, Loeb & Co. / July 2

I haven't had a hamburger in months, it seems like. I'm becoming a vegetarian. Pretty soon, I'll turn into a vegetable. That would be the ideal existence, to vegetate, I mean, literally, to be a vegetable, then I would have vegetable experience, the existential mind blast of being a vegetable, the earth, the sun, rain, swaying in the wind, being torn out of the ground and eaten. The whole trip. Being a vegetable. The experience of being a vegetable might beat nirvana, it might top satori, it could be the ultimate experience. Don't knock the Vegetable Experience. It could be great. How do we know? Vegetables don't play ego games. Vegetables don't kill other vegetables. Or how about a stone, how about the Stone Experience? What's it like to be a rock? But is there such a thing as the Stone Experience? Why not? If plants can experience their own existence, then why not stones? Down the hall, it's like a freezer, down the hall, they have executive air conditioning, and here, in the Typing Pool, it's hot, here we have clerical air conditioning. If they could arrange it, there would be executive sunshine for them, and clerical sunshine for us. There's those breakers breaking on the same old black rocks, just like yesterday, just like every day here at Kuhn, Loeb & Co., on a pillar, under two dirty strips of Scotch Tape, the ocean is breaking in bursts of white foam, break, break, break, on thy cold grey stones, O sea. I'm at Kuhn, Loeb & Co. and I would that my tongue could utter the thoughts that arise in me. Can you imagine, no, it's inconceivable, all the things that are happening right at this moment, it's 10:50 A.M., July 2, 1974, it was a loaded, a crowded moment in human history. Everybody on earth was busy existing, breathing, all those hearts beating, it's like, we're lost in the storm, the hurricane of physical reality, the sheer size and bulk of the world, and we cling to the life jacket of our abstract concepts, we cling to the driftwood of conceptual thought, wallowing in an indigestible mass of reality. The concrete is too much, it's overwhelming, we seek refuge in abstractions, we cut everything down to size, it becomes almost understandable in the abstract, almost…comfortable.

December 28

I'm testing my new typewriter, which Art and Karen bought me for Christmas, they bought me a typewriter for Christmas! It's not quite the same as my old one, the side letters don't hit hard enough, like the q, what about the A, aaaaa z2*====½½¢//q, strange little machine.

I was sitting on my red canvas chair feeling depressed, and thinking I wanted to write something, nothing, just anything, just to be writing, I don't know, so much of what I write is just writing to keep busy, the Work Ethic, writing because it feels good when you've just written something new. I was lying back in my red canvas chair, and suddenly I wanted to fight, it's OK…that it's hard, I want to fight, and that's what I'm doing here, fighting, fighting for nothing, fighting because I like to fight, or fighting because there's nothing else to do. Of course, I could be watching TV, but that's not fighting, that's just living somebody else's fight, pretending you're fighting somebody els4, hey, els4, somebody els4's fight. *Mary, Queen of Scots* is on TV right now, I could sit and pretend I'm Mary, Queen of Scots, and fight her fight, which is a losing one, even more of a losing one than the one I'm fighting now, if only I could forget Vanessa Redgrave, it's never really Mary, Queen of Scots, for me it's always Vanessa Redgrave playing Mary, Queen of Scots, that's why movies fail me, I want them to be real, I want Mary, Queen of Scots to be Mary, Queen of Scots, I want to be there, in my Scottish armor, riding at her side, I don't want to be here on East 28th St., I want...out! I want to get out of myself, I don't like myself...well, I don't know, sometimes I really do like myself, I like my life, but I can't live with it...all the time, every day, I need a rest, sometimes, from my life, from my...condition, the way things are...for me, sometimes I want to get out...of this fix, this bind, my life, and I'm not very athletic, when I want out, I don't think of surfing in Montauk, I think of Mary, Queen of Scots on Channel 4. I check my TV listings, I look at tonight's movies, hmmm, let's see, who do I want to be tonight? Do I want to be Errol Flynn as Captain Blood? Do I want to see the monster on Channel 9? Do I want to scream in terror at the sight of the beast coming out of the ground like a huge tree? Do I want to be a GI landing on the beaches of Normandy, do I want to leap out of the landing craft and into the shallow water, and hear the shells screaming, why not? I know I'm going to be alive when it's over, I won't be one of the casualties, no matter how many bodies fall, I won't be the one, there's no risk in it for me, I know I'll turn off the TV when it's over, and go to bed, set the alarm for 10 tomorrow, and...but that's just it, it's not real enough, I want to be there, on the beach, it's June 6, 1944, I'm wading through the water, they're shooting at me, the Krauts, it's really happening, that's what I want, I don't want to be here, I don't want to be myself tonight, I don't want to be a poet Xeroxing poems, I want to be a GI on the Normandy beaches tonight, I want to land and be afraid of dying,...but that's just it, it's not real, I'm not there, the movie doesn't make me forget who I am, or where I am, it doesn't really take me away from 223 East 28th St., it doesn't take me out of myself, there's no risk, no danger. I want to be on the beach, I want to be afraid to die, I want to die, I want to die there on the beach and never come back, I don't want to come back, I don't want to find myself sitting in my red canvas chair, when it's over, I'm tired of being Guy Gauthier. But why? Because it's not exciting enough? Because it's not enough like a movie, because it's not enough like landing on the beaches at Normandy? Why? Why am I tired of being myself? Why do I want...out? Why do I want to be on safari with Allan Quatermain, searching for *King Solomon's Mines*? Why do I want to be a pirate in 1492, why? It's always something to do with violence, war, danger, exposure to the elements, anything but sitting here, thinking, typing, anything but this, yet...I wouldn't be doing this, if I didn't really want to do it. The reason I'm here, and not somewhere else, is because I want to be here, nobody's forcing me to be here, typing, so I'm here because I want to be here, I mean, I could have watched

Mary, Queen of Scots, but I'd much rather be Guy Gauthier tonight than Mary, Queen of Scots, I like to be what I am, I like to be myself, but why can't I make a full time job of it, why can't I live with myself all the time? There's always some night when I just don't have it in me, when I find myself checking the TV listings, wondering who I want to be, what dangers I want to confront, some night when I want to fight somebody else's fight, without the risk, but what risk, the man is invincible, nothing can defeat him, he's Errol Flynn in *The Sea Hawks!*

1975

7 A.M., Jan. 21

It's this, this seeing, this feeling, that…will be gone, my hands, I see my hands, they're moving, they're moving, and when they're not moving any more, it's this, this seeing, this…feeling, this sight of…the white wall at 7 A.M., that will be gone, I won't see, I won't hear, it's no great loss, if it's only this…this is no great epic moment, this is no great turning point in human history, it's just a white wall at 7 A.M., a dirty desk littered with paper, Bic ballpoints, it's no great loss, it's just this, it's nothing, it's me, it's being here, seeing, feeling, it isn't much, it's only…my existence, I feel so small, so insignificant, I don't matter, I wanted to matter, when I was 17, I was epic, I was tall, a gigantic figure on the horizon, I cast a lengthy shadow over the 20th century, I was a formidable figure in European history at 17, and now, well, now I'm just looking at this white wall, at 7 A.M., I'm simply seeing it, I'm hearing the keys hit the paper, it's morning and I'm here, I'm breathing, I'm existing, it's an activity…it's something you can't help doing, really, for as long as it lasts, you just exist, you see the white wall, for as long as it's there, and then you don't, then the wall is there, and you're not, it's cold, there's snow on the ground outside, snow on the street, why was I born, was I born so I would be here now, at 7 A.M., looking at the wall, writing these words, was I born so I would die, it's all going by like a flash, I'm a flash, I'm a flashbulb, hey, I can see it now, I can feel, sense my own terrible brevity, now, at 35, I know…I'm short, quick, and it's…THIS, this quiet…existing at 7 in the morning, that will be gone, this loving my mother, praying for my father, water, I hear running water, the

102

sound of water running through a pipe, what a sound, I heard it, I heard it, I'm here, I might as well say it, and say it, I'm here, because, in another moment, I won't be, I won't be, this...being here looking at the white wall...will be over, gone, my mother's asleep, God bless and keep her, and my father's asleep, God bless and keep him, they're sleeping now, in St. Boniface, it's 6 A.M. there, and they're sleeping, God bless and keep them, I'm here...because of them, I'm here writing this...because of them, they gave me...this, this *existenz*, thanks, Mom, thanks, Dad, XXXX, Love, Guy, they gave me this...for what it's worth, this being here, looking at the white wall, they made me, they made Guy Gauthier, and I've made...nothing, I've made no more Gauthiers, nothing, only words, I haven't made another *me*, another moment like this, a 7 A.M. moment with the sound of water running through the pipes, God, my God, *je t'aime, mon Dieu, Dieu de mon enfance, Dieu de mon pere, Dieu!* Karen's...asleep, it's this, this is what...will be...gone, me and my little *existenz*, I want someone, anyone to be reading this 100 years from now! But I'm learning, I'm learning to live in the present, to taste, touch NOW, to taste myself, for as long as it lasts.

Later the same day

Art knocked on the door, it was 6 in the evening, he was on his way home from work, and we went out to a restaurant, he wanted to eat supper, and I wanted to eat breakfast, so we went down 3rd Ave looking for a place to eat, and we finally settled for the Grammercy, though we didn't like the price list in the window, and Art ordered the special, which turned out to be a chicken leg, with rice in a red sauce, and my pancakes were not bad, I had too much syrup, and black coffee. I'm drinking tea now, it's almost midnight, and I'm drinking the second of my many, many cups of tea for the night, and...we were talking about Japan, the economic...scene in Japan, and Art said, as far as I'm concerned, Japan is going to sink into the sea. He still believes in Edgar Cayce's prophecies about Japan sinking out of sight, and California, etc. etc. I used to believe them myself. But around the end of the Roman Empire, the notion that the end of the world was very near became a common thought, and again, on the eve of the year 1,000 A.D., there was panic in Europe, people were afraid that the world was coming to an end, and now, once more, the same mood is spreading through the Western world, many psychics have predicted that...crash! Boom! Crumble! But I like to think that these predictions, these grim prophecies, are some kind of poetry, a very sensitive, *mediumistic* poetry that captures the mood of our time, they are the Zeitgeist, I like to think, here's hoping...that the world...will go on, just simply and wonderfully GO ON, and go on going on...and that, in 2050, people will say, in the 1970's, people in the wealthy, decadent Western countries believed that the U.S. coastlines would sink into the sea, and the earth would be devastated by earthquakes, tidal waves, floods, another Ice Age, it was the mood of the time, and of course, earthquakes did occur in California and Japan at the end of the 20th century, but what is most revealing, in retrospect, is that people in the 1970's were willing and eager to believe in even worse disasters, it was not only a *fin-de-siecle*, it was a *fin-du-monde* atmosphere! And while I was listening to Art, I suddenly felt very small, I was...infinitesimal, when I thought of the world, what the world would be like...in another two hundred years. I could see lights flashing across 3rd Ave., in a big display window across the street, and suddenly, I saw the world in those lights, I saw the next two hundred years, and how small, how infinitesimal my work as a writer was, in this vast 200 year...wow, I can't tell you, but I wasn't there, and the lights were flashing across the street, it was two hundred years later, people were living only for the moment, talking, eating, and I wasn't there, it was good. Art and I paid our checks, and stood in the street talking about continental drift. I wanted to go to our bedroom, and kiss Karen, and say hi. Karen was lying under the blue wool blanket, and I kissed her, and I told her about my sudden glimpses of the cosmos, those... instant...glimpses, like instant coffee, or instant pudding, wow, I told her what I saw, as I was going to sleep, I saw a Daddy Long Legs, it was standing there on its long legs, and behind that Daddy Long Legs, I saw the universe, everything, it was pulsating, vibrating with life, and the Daddy Long Legs was...unspeakably BEAUTIFUL, it was alive, yes, it was so alive, and...I was there too, that's what was so wonderful, I was there looking at this Daddy Long Legs, it was one of the many living creatures in that universe, pulsating, vibrating, wow, I'm so nervous, my hands are trembling, my body's shaking, I feel very strange, like I'm going crazy, I saw the universe, only for an instant, as I was going to sleep. My tea's still warm, I was saying to Karen, I have these moments, these instants...when I see...but it's no help, these visions don't help me to accept my life...as it is, I wish they could help me, I need help, help me, somebody, help me, I'm going crazy, slowly, each day, going crazy, and...I saw the universe, and it was good, it seemed so right, ignore all these words, you'll just have to guess what I'm trying to say, you already know what I'm trying to say, wow, I need a tranquilizer, THE UNIVERSE, it's always there, THE UNI-VERSE, but these instant coffee visions, it's not enough, I don't want to be infinitesimal, I want to be big, I want to be big, huge, enormous, I want my name written on the sky, I want, I want, oh how I want, I WANT THE WORLD! and this wanting, it's so deeply rooted inside me that, though I've tried to tear it out of me, to tear it out at the roots, there's always some part of the root still left inside me, and then slowly, through all my feelings of acceptance of the way things are…Lord, I accept, your will be done, *que votre volonte soit faite!* this broken root starts to grow, it starts to grow again, god-dam it, I want somebody to read this, it's that simple, I want somebody, somewhere, even if it's only one person, to read this when I'm dead, that's why I'm writing it, Karen's in the bedroom, she was there, while I wrote this, another human being was there beside me, she was breathing, existing, play-ing bridge hands against herself, she's there now, her name is Karen, and she exists, she will always be…Karen, seeing the world, seeing *me*, through the eyes of Karen, I'm Guy, she's Karen, she has experienced, since she was born in 1947, a Karen world, and me, I live in the Guy world. Jesus, it's cold. I've poured myself a cup of hot water, I don't want any more tea, my nerves are too hyper, I need a toothpick, oh, the toothpick! When I was talking to Karen, I was looking at the purple rug, all the bits of…what? cat litter? dirt? on the rug, there was a toothpick on the rug, and suddenly, it was…the cosmic tooth-pick, THE UNIVERSAL TOOTHPICK, it was the ETERNAL TOOTH-PICK, I'm warning you, I'm in a cosmic mood tonight, everything I see, Swingline Stapler, it's the cosmos.

2:10 P.M., May 9

I've been sitting here feeling sick inside, my body's just…shuddering, I'm so disgusted with being…me, being the person I am, my body's shuddering, and I thought of doing what Barry did, he jumped in front of a subway train…and now he's under the ground somewhere in Philadelphia, Barry, Barry, I was staring at the page I was writing, I was trying to fix the page I wrote last night, about tea, my cats, the pigeons, I felt sick…inside, sick with myself, but I want to go on living, just to see what happens, who knows, something really good, like the sound of rain outside my window, might happen. There's this really stupid music on the radio, some classical masterpiece, an immortal work by God knows who, and I couldn't care less about your immortal masterpiece, whoever you are, I hate myself, so how can I love your immortal masterpiece, I don't even love myself, the window's rattling, it's the wind, somehow I know I'm going to go on, but that becomes more and more of an achievement, really, it's like, it's an achievement in itself, just to go on, it's a problem that becomes more challenging each year. I'm 36 now, and it's 36 times more challenging now, more difficult than it was when I was born, and next year, I guess, it'll be 37 times more difficult, then 38 times, until you're dead, well, at least that won't be difficult, being dead, it won't require any will power, you don't have to be good at it, you don't have to prove you're better at being dead than anybody else. Well, maybe I feel better now, a bit…better, now that I've…what a lot of bullshit this is! It's me. It's my life. This is it. This is the great adventure, there's not going to be any other.

10:20 P.M., May 10

I have a perception of reality, which is just simply…the way things are, it's so obvious I would feel silly trying to tell somebody what I see, he'd just say, well, yes, of course, everybody knows that, but for me, the obvious is hard to believe, I can't quite believe the way things are, and I was saying to Richard last night, I feel like I'm going crazy, Richard, I can't respond normally any more, my perceptions are just not normal, I've got to narrow down my awareness, I've got to focus, concentrate my attention on a much more narrow range of sensations, because that's my problem, really, I'm seeing, hearing, feeling my sensations, really seeing them, it's too much. Karen wanted to walk home from Dr. Generosity's today, and I said OK, and we did, we walked home, but I said to her, I wish I didn't see them, all the faces, all those human beings, one reason I didn't want to walk home, was, I didn't want to be exposed to all that physical reality, all those faces, those cars, windows, sounds, it's exhausting, it's too much reality, I've lost the art of concentrating on my thoughts, of living inside my ego, concentration, it's necessary for survival, you've got to concentrate, and what does that mean, to concentrate, well, it means that you don't see, hear or feel your sensations, because, note, this is the important thing, we always, at any given moment, have such a torrent, such a hurricane of information passing through our senses it's like we would blow our tubes, we would short-circuit, if we could just see…what we see, you can't live and see what you see, both at the same time, you can't do both, it's too much, but thanks to the art of concentration, which I've lost, which I've got to get back somehow, thanks to concentration, we can go on living.

2:25 P.M., May 11

We've just missed our train, David and Marlene, years ago somebody, presumably David, scratched those names in the wet cement with a stick, but that was years ago, the names are half worn away by human feet, rain, snow, are they still in love, are they still writing David and Marlene in the wet cement? Here comes the train.

7:10 P.M. / Queens

Health is something I had only contempt for in my twenties, but now, at 36, health seems more…like IT, a healthy mind in a healthy body. Riding on the Flushing train, I was looking at the streets of Queens, thinking how concentration is necessary for survival. You have to be able to concentrate on your thoughts, so that what you see (streets, buildings, people) is only an incidental background to your thoughts. Unless you can focus on your *ego*, your self, then your sensations, the trees, people, will overwhelm you, they will become *central*, and your mind will be like the Times Square subway in the rush hour. Looking out of the Flushing train used to be refreshing, *un divertissement*, but now, it wears me out, it's too much physical reality. I'm beginning to experience the whole world as if it was my own ego. I feel so silly trying to put this into words, but I've seen something about reality, something so simple, so obvious, that it doesn't…can't be put into words, or isn't worth saying, it's something I think everyone has seen or experienced, but I'm not sure many people have seen this simple, obvious fact of reality with the same disturbing, frightening intensity I have. It's starting to get dark, and my hand hurts from pressing too hard on the pen, on the Queens train, I said to myself, I won't see you, Queens, I won't see you, I'm going to concentrate on my thoughts, I hear birds, jet airliners to Kennedy airport, I'm going to concentrate, and these streets and buildings will be only pleasant scenery, a backdrop for me and my thoughts, Queens will be like mood music for my self…trip, Queens will be my struggle, Queens will be *me*, Queens will be Guy Gauthier, an aspect of his ego. That's how I used to see the world in my early twenties, I could see myself in the cars going by, I could see my thoughts going by in the street, I looked at the gleaming trunk of a new car and I could see Ionesco, I could see his *Bald Soprano*, his *Rhinoceros* going by in the street, and me, my plays, my achievements, I could see all this in the cars, my thoughts would take the shape of a Buick going by in the street, my thoughts would *be* a Buick going by, I was projecting myself, my ego on the screen of the universe, the idea of myself as a leading Canadian playwright became a Chevy or a Ford, it became branches bending in the wind, even the sound of rain, strangers in the street, became the Canadian theatre, life was a rave review, a published play, the world was me. This is the way we see the world, through the haze of our own egos. We might as well be blind. But now, *I see the cars*, I see the faces in the subway, and the *shocking* reality of those faces…obliterates my thoughts, it's too much, it makes me wish I was living in a small town where I could get to know every face, where I could respond to everyone, talk to them and care…that's why I have to learn to concentrate on my thoughts. Ego boundaries. Without ego boundaries, you can't survive for very long. Our ego boundaries are a line we draw (an *imaginary* line) through our sensations, and we think, what's on this side of the line, like the pressure in my head, or the taste of cherry ice cream (which we had for dessert) is me, and anything on the other side of the line, like the car in the driveway, or the apple tree, is *not me*. Some of my sensations are me, and others are not. That's what it means to have ego boundaries. But it's not just the sensations that come from your body, it's also your car, your favorite records, your job, and the movie you paid $3.50 to see, it's…as Lewis Warsh would say, your "Immediate Surrounding," all this is on your side of the line, it's intensely real, and very important, and what's on the other side of the line is not important, at least not to us, and though we'll certainly admit that it's real, we don't experience its reality with any convincing force. I suppose in a way these ego boundaries are necessary for our survival, because if one of my sensations threatens me, like if a mugger sticks a sharp blade against my throat, I will do what I can to defend my ego boundaries against this sensation. Self defense means that one part of your sensations is defending itself against another part of your sensations. Soon I won't be able to see what I'm writing. It's hard not to hear the…*millions* of sounds coming to me from the city, I've lost my ego boundaries, and it's hard for me to…not hear these sounds, the way I used to not hear them, in my early twenties.

108

7:40 P.M., May 12

I was talking to Karen after dinner, we were drinking orange spice tea, I was telling her...that I think I'm slowly going insane, that...it's the rush hour, the IRT, the Times Square shuttle, all those faces, it's too much, and she said...it was good...that I was having these experiences, the only thing odd was that I thought I was going crazy, she said it was healthy, sane, and I said, I know how I used to see people, through the haze of my thoughts, the neon signs, the red taillights of the cars, it all reflected my thoughts, it was me, it was so *narcissistic*, there's so much narcissism in the way we normally perceive the universe, it's like looking in a mirror and seeing your own image. It's the subway, the rush hour, that's what does it, it's the city, nobody would want to take a vacation in the New York subway, no, they want to take a vacation in Cape Cod, when you're in Cape Cod, you can...see, you can hear, on the beach, looking out at the ocean, you're open to your sensations, but in the city, it's the opposite, we're turtles in the subway, hiding in our shells, we don't want to see, the mind works like the pupil in the eye, the pupil that contracts when the light is too intense, and dilates when the light is too dim, well, that's what city life is like, your awareness is like the pupil in your eye, when you're in the rush hour subway, there's too much reality, too many faces, coming at you, and your consciousness contracts defensively like a pupil, and you just don't see as much, when we get home in our apartments, when I sit in my red canvas chair with a book of poetry, my pupil dilates, but not much. No, but actually, this is what I'm saying, that my pupil won't close, in the subway at 5:30, my pupil won't close, with the result that I'm swamped, deluged with the intense sensation of the reality of the people around me, and it's...they're so real, it's spooky.

Nov. 24

It was midnight when I left Art's place, it was cold, I was walking up 1st Ave, and it felt good to be alive in New York, a black man was walking toward me, he was looking in a store window and walking down the sidewalk toward me, and it felt good to be alive and walking home at midnight in the cold, and as I turned the corner on 10th St, I was snug and cozy inside my thick gray coat, and it felt good to be a poet walking down 10th St, somehow that seemed the most wonderful thing I could think of...at that moment, that I'm a poet, but then...why don't I write poetry? It's become a romantic dream I console myself with, I tell myself I'm a poet and that someday I'll be writing great poems, I'll be sitting comfortably at a window watching the rain outside, I'll be watching the raindrops hit the broken cement outside and writing great poems, and they'll have truth, they'll have depth, but...why don't I do it, why, it's all a dream, a lazy man's daydream, but it felt good, I was shivering as I walked across 13th St, and I thought of my work, I thought of Ego Play, I thought of my Object Poems, and my writing seemed good, it was true, and I was very happy with my writing, somewhere around 18th St, I realized how good it was...good enough for me, and New York was at its ugly best, it was frightening and beautiful, the streets were empty, and full of bad smells, I'm sitting at my typewriter feeling good, feeling good about what I'm writing now, it's worth it, for me, now, to be writing this, to be spending the few moments I have doing this, if only it was always like this, it's late, and the alarm rings at 7 tomorrow, but it feels good to be writing late in the night, knowing I'm going to have trouble getting up in the morning, it feels good, and I'm glad I'm doing it, and my ears are still cold, my ears can still feel the cold wind, and...as I was walking home, shivering and happy, I knew I was alone, God was not there, and it was good to be alone, without God, it was good to exist alone, but this, somehow, seemed to be a religious experience, existence was more magical without God, more like pulling a rabbit out of the hat, the more I know and love you, dear God, the more I come to understand that you do not exist. I'm an atheist, and I love you.

Olivia Dresher

Fragments and Aphorisms:
From Notebooks, 1988–1990

Almost everything I write in my notebooks begins as a chant in my head. The chant builds and grows; I can't contain it. It must come out as words on paper—to bring the disparity between myself and the world into a less disturbing focus. By defining (or "insighting") what I feel and perceive, the words on the page take on a new dimension: they transcend my own individual life and become art.

My notebooks/journals have taken many different forms over the years. Recently they have become more aphoristic and fragmented, although that's not to say that long, detailed entries don't also appear. For this selection, however, I chose to represent the shorter writing styles, because they currently interest me most.

Since my writings begin as an intense thought or impression that I feel I must write down, what happens when a thought actually meets the page? One of two things happens: it either becomes even more condensed, or it starts to develop, taking me to unforeseen conclusions. But whatever form it takes, I do not write unless that intense need is there—which occurs daily.

My journals are the rough draft of the work of my life, notes to myself which give the thoughts not expressed outwardly a forum and definition; they contain the words which have come from the depths of a daily search for truth, and contrast with the prescribed reality we live in.

As I wrote in my journal in October of 1990, "Aphorisms are so much more vulnerable and naked than other forms of writing, because they stand alone, exposed." My own observation reminds me of a quote by Joseph Joubert: "Maxims, because what is isolated can be seen better."

ॐ

The smell of memories.
Daily memories, always fresh.
Memories as hallucinations,
flashbacks more real than now.
A constant hum that can become
a madness or a sweet companion.

* * *

Tenderness is humility.

* * *

Your darkness sets my world on fire,
but still there's no light—
just flames of darkness.

* * *

To be cautious is to circle the self.
To be cautious is to make things familiar,
one level.

* * *

What are the deaf and blind afraid of?

* * *

No passion or truth in niceness.
Adults, politely, lower their eyes,
but the screaming child on the bus today

looked into me for a long time.
I looked back, and thought:
finally, a real face.

* * *

Nostalgia makes us "religious" about our pasts.

* * *

He said that every time he speaks,
his words feel hollow.
He says they are hollow, with an echo.
He *hears* it.

* * *

Only that which comes upon me seems real,
not anything I will, or want, or choose, or hope for.

* * *

Truth reveals itself in consequences.

* * *

How much do people mean what they say?
And how much do they mean their silences?

* * *

We are what we hide.
We are what we're not.
We become what can never be resolved.

* * *

A shadow of a spider on the wall.
The spider radiates self-confidence
to the extreme.
Its purity feels evil.
Its web is an extension of its certainty:
it traps exactly what it needs.

* * *

To be in silence is to be underwater.
But I don't know how
to hold my breath that long.
Words, for me, are air.

* * *

What do we share in social situations?
We share our knowledge of good behavior.

* * *

In the dark everything becomes me,
and I become everything.
(Once exchanged, we merge.)
But the light reveals a separateness.

* * *

Passion is the emotion
of trying to swim upstream.

* * *

How far are we willing to go to tell the truth?
How long are we willing to wait
before we reveal it?

* * *

I am touched by words,
the way I'm touched by the right touch.
To not speak to me is to not touch me.
The celibacy of silence.

* * *

What is stupidity?
Unaware vulnerability.

* * *

Hurt lives where there are differences.
It feeds love, mystery, desire.
It makes love a shadow that doesn't fit.
(If you hurt me, I want to *be* you,
to be able to take the pain.)

* * *

I'm interested in psychological truths,
not psychological health.
I'm interested in sensitivity,
not strength.

* * *

The old abandoned house a few blocks away:
it speaks the dark places of my childhood
(that hiss in the trees is my memory).

* * *

To feel safe, we make life as unreal as possible
and then we call that "reality."

* * *

To understand is to surrender
to what you can't understand,
to become naked and helpless before it.
The whole self must become an unselfish prayer
to what can't be seen, heard, or known.

* * *

In person, we're only puppets of ourselves.

* * *

History reveals our essence.
The present too often obscures it,
as we escape into the future.
In history the past *is* the moment,
just as the moment has now become
the past/history.

* * *

I wish only happiness could kill.

* * *

They say: don't take it personally
if someone doesn't love you.
I say: should I also not take it personally
if someone *does*?

* * *

Consciousness is a silence
of words and memories.

* * *

The holy pastels at sunset
became the mountains
which folded into each other:
slim, elegant, mystical,
reaching out and beyond me,
north, south, west...
I don't want the world to be this beautiful.

* * *

I dreamed the night's stark half-moon
turned epileptic, and tumbled out of the sky.

* * *

Love is god, and god is love.
Mostly because we want both
but can't see or find either one.

* * *

We learn skills
so we can cover up our primal truths.

* * *

If only I could have painted with the color of that first most
brilliant Seattle twilight that I ever saw.

* * *

What's not revealed is a lie. Hence this force in me to attack,
to screw things up, as if *that's* the only way to get to the truth,
to get to the layers and layers under the lies, to at least get
things *revealed*.

* * *

Everyone seems so inhuman
in their human tendency to save themselves.

* * *

Give me intimacy or give me death!

* * *

He said that the only thing we have in common
is that we're so completely opposite from each other.

* * *

Conrad Aiken, as a boy, found his parents dead in their bedroom. His father had shot his mother, then himself.
Of his mother, he wrote, "…her mouth wide open in the act
of screaming." Witnessing that silent scream of his mother's
death, is *that* what made him a poet?

* * *

The silence of secrets kept, growing.
The microscopic world of silence.

* * *

I want to be loved for my darkness,
not in spite of it.
But love is loss—whether you go too far
or not far enough.

* * *

Hope makes people dishonest.

* * *

I can't get used to faces,
like I can't get used to naked bodies.
But a body is a face, too:
eyes all over, in gestures.

* * *

I haven't been sick in years,
but my dreams are fevers:
sleep as sickness, to compensate.

* * *

The journal as a long, secular prayer.

* * *

People follow the religion of contemporary psychology. I watch
them fall into self-help nets (oh, salvation) that hold them over
an abyss of dark truth. I call up from the abyss, but they hear
me only as proof of the road that shouldn't be taken.

* * *

At the College Inn: I'm reading a book about the horrors of
animal experimentation. Next to me are two men eating
lunch together, coldly discussing the results of experiments
done on animals.

* * *

When I'm blind,
it's only because I'm trying to look
through my own fire to see.

* * *

I want to animate those old,
turn-of-the-century photographs.
I want to live in them.

* * *

I hear a whisper screaming.
I'm going deaf, hearing it.

* * *

The smell of things...the essence of a thing in its smell...like
the smell of pine trees, wet grass, a rose...birth, death, hair,
skin...

* * *

His humor is his seriousness, his energy, his lifeline.

* * *

I see suicide as strength.
What courage it must take to give
in to death as if to a lover, to say:
here, death, take me, all of me, I'm yours.
For life is the lover that can never be true.

* * *

To be by myself is a sort of drowning that I'm in control of.

* * *

I asked him if he wanted to see me.
Yes and no, he said.

Why no, I asked.
Because of the yes, he said.

* * *

Solitude is clarity.
Only when I'm alone
can I break all the rules.
Only when I'm alone
can I feel the terrifying fullness of me.

* * *

I pressed on my eyelids. When I opened my eyes, for about
two hours, I felt a white light beyond everything.

* * *

The baby cries for one main reason: it is out of its element.

* * *

It's bigger than words.
I'm learning this from silence,
or the near-silence in the fall
of a golden leaf, the inside-out
sound of birds flying south.
It's so big that whatever is true
is in dreams without interpretation,
in cries so deep
they are all the cries of the past.

* * *

Life says: death is none of your business.

* * *

My sleep is wakefulness.
In the dark eternity ticks.

* * *

Don't be so negative, they say.
(They call it self-pity;
I'd call it vulnerability without walls.)

* * *

No one can swallow the cold, inhuman truth.
So we invent human truths,
warm them up in the oven,
and serve them to everyone to feast on.

* * *

The more I lose faith,
the more intense everything is.

* * *

A "vacation" is a cage of freedom.

* * *

I distrust the truth,
for truth is a lie for the elite.

* * *

The beginning of rage is birth. The womb was our first jail,
our first heaven. We raged to get out, yet we raged to stay in.
Primal ambiguity. Everything we're taught after this first
struggle is meant to mislead us into optimism, health. The
beginning of doubt is the rage for the truth beyond what is

hoped for, the rage for reunion, wanting back that first dark spark of experience.

* * *

Words used just to make a point animate separateness.

* * *

I don't want to be silent
about my private places.
I want you to have the imagination
to want to know.
But only being asked questions
makes me feel wanted.

* * *

He's a monk of darkness.
His laughter is pain,
his silence a voice.

* * *

When I die I'll be so free
I won't even be me.

* * *

"What's *your* problem?" they ask.
Consciousness, I silently reply.

* * *

I want to know how people are in private: how their minds work then, what they do with themselves, their lovers and enemies. I want to know mental and emotional things, before they're censored.

This is all I really want to know,
because it's what I can't know.

＊＊＊

Nothing is more humbling than realizing
you're not really loved,
or that there's no god watching over you.

＊＊＊

Every time I make love I lose my virginity.

＊＊＊

As a child, what I couldn't see burned me.
I've been trying to heal ever since
by *seeing*, but now it's sight that burns
even more than the unseen.

＊＊＊

What do you *do* with your life, they ask.
They might as well ask:
How do you avoid the ultimate truth?

＊＊＊

I throw myself into what I do, totally, when alone:
a wave of me sweeps over me.

＊＊＊

Because we joke about what's wrong between us, it makes
everything right. We fight—without fighting. We fight,
because we *almost* understand each other.

＊＊＊

I write because I cry.
Writing is crying with control.

* * *

Non-being is at the core of my being.
When I break it's because
my existence senses my non-existence.
(Time tries to face eternity.)
The first layer on top of the core is helplessness.
On top of helplessness is everything else
I've ever felt and thought and experienced,
in order of severity.

* * *

I'm suffering from an overdose of wonder.

* * *

My heart tells me everything, but everyone tells me I'm
wrong. I sense lies, half-truths. They say the problem is *me*.
I always believe them, but I keep believing myself, too. What
does one do, believing in *everything*? How can one live,
being pulled in every direction at once?

* * *

There is no terror, no darkness, without an active imagination, without daring, without shedding the skin of social conditioning. Being alone is the most direct route to it, especially after loss.

* * *

Inside of me there's always a siren wailing.

* * *

The most astonishing thing about R. was that he could weep. I remember this as I listen again to the old tape from the summer of 1969. The tape distorts his voice—time has done that to it—and ends incomplete: "I seek peace through the war that I envision between us. And the war is that stern silence of space that refuses to escape from between our touch. We speak many languages, but none the same. The moment is too swift a beast and too professionally cunning to attach any compassion to our brief..."

* * *

Nothing lasts these days
except the garbage we throw away.

* * *

The difference between men and women is the difference between life and death, and why it's so threatening. To fall in love is to profoundly experience this gulf. When the attempt at building a bridge fails, one falls into that gulf.

* * *

I'm just not dead enough
to want or need discipline.

* * *

What's free?
Only thoughts,
as long as we keep them to ourselves.

* * *

Looking back, I can't remember ever seeing A. except when it rained. His letters to me were long suicide notes, without mentioning suicide. The words that his pen

screamed out left impressions (almost holes) on the page,
like Braille.

∗ ∗ ∗

Love is wanting to feel someone else's pain.

∗ ∗ ∗

I love him, even when I hate him.
I love being with him,
even when I long to be alone.

∗ ∗ ∗

To lose everything is to become the universe;
to lose bits and pieces is to be human.

∗ ∗ ∗

The waiter is gracefully awkward.
After the restaurant closes,
he's a dancer as he sweeps the floor.
He won't look at you, but I know
this is the way he sees
and doesn't miss anything.

∗ ∗ ∗

I am slowly losing pieces of strength
so I can end up where I started from.
The self-puzzle will be complete
when all the pieces are lost.

∗ ∗ ∗

He needed me, but in a generic sort of way.

* * *

Reflection is intimate:
the feeling self makes love to the thinking self.

* * *

He's a hummingbird slowed way down,
forced to live without wings.

* * *

Everything I feel now I've always felt;
I was *born into* these feelings.
Except now I'm trying to articulate them
(as if to have control over them).
That's the only real difference
between then and now:
this desire to make words perfect.

* * *

There is no "me." There are only these feelings—and they
are bigger and deeper than any *me*. Identity is an illusion, a
temporary state. Everyone is searching for it, but it's only a
brief reflection in a very shallow pool of time.

* * *

The joyful hopelessness of his irony.

* * *

Don't let the physical world fool you:
underneath that mask, *everything* is intangible.

* * *

Their lack of curiosity is evil.
Everything about them is evil—
because they're "normal".
To be a contemporary person
is to be dull, practical, and bored.
They're becoming the machines they created.
They laugh at the specks of purity which remain,
then quickly dust them away.

* * *

Women feel relationship pain.
Men feel philosophical pain.

* * *

It has become an uninteresting, truthful lie:
this constant desire people have
to feel good about themselves
(the "healthy" way they fool themselves).

* * *

The awful truth of finding out that a man can deeply think,
but be cut off from feeling...
The awful truth of finding out that a woman can deeply feel,
yet be cut off from thinking...
For over 20 years I've been rediscovering these truths in
every man and every woman I've ever known.

* * *

Just the three of us:
His wordy silence,
the cat,
and me.

* * *

What I know best are the things no one can talk about: that primal level prior to learned perception and interpretation, prior to truth.

* * *

The women of his past:
I'm more interested in them than he is.

* * *

Life used to be cheap because it was short.
Now it's cheap because it's long.
It used to be that people believed in sin.
Now it's a sin to believe in sin.

* * *

Hope is like having one last fling.

* * *

I desire to be alone, as if in love.
The thrill and passion of it.
It makes me sleepless.
It makes me whole.
I watch everything more,
now that I'm not a part of anything.
Most of all, I watch love never bloom.

* * *

If you're extremely alive, they'll call you insane.

* * *

Murder, in a beautiful neighborhood
on a beautiful spring day.
What does *that* say?

* * *

I have this knack for turning everything into a nightmare.
(Imagination in a jail, trying wildly to escape.)

* * *

Her fierce desire to be halfway normal is what makes her
halfway insane—that *practicality* that doesn't work is her
madness.

* * *

The nightmares return, feeling prehistoric.

* * *

Psychology has not made us more open—
it has, instead, made us dogmatic
about our self's survival, overly protective
of our hard-won separate identities.

* * *

If you could have just been subtle enough
to stay awake and listen to my heart beat...

* * *

A man of intelligence can fall in love with a stupid woman if
he feels that her *body* has the intelligence of beauty. (Men
admire the intelligence of a woman's body because they feel
their own bodies are stupid.)

* * *

What every child learns: you survive
only if you kill who you really are.

***

If I want to say something important to him,
I'll have to say it without words.

***

No one wants to take away your happiness,
but everyone wants to take away your pain.

***

Because men are split, they can tolerate the cold truth more than
women. (Men embrace the very truths that women find intolerable, incomprehensible.) Women, being closer to their bodies, only
find what's *human* acceptable. The male split would be admirable
if it didn't also lead to violence, rape, war...

***

You think you know the truth. But it's what you can never
know that's the only truth.

***

Trying to get close only makes you realize how impossible it
is, increasing how distant you don't want to feel.

***

People think it's better to be cheerful and not mean it, than to
be unhappy and mean it. To be "normal" is to see the world
as you're *supposed* to see it, not as you really see it.

***

The monologue of his silence.
The self-confidence of his silence.

* * *

We *think* we're communicating with each other. Actually, we're just filling up our own reality. What is possible—and blendable—is what's on the surface. Underneath, there is infinite impossibility.

* * *

Why is it that men take my questions seriously, but women don't? Is it because questions remind women of the burden of children?

* * *

What could be more exciting than to read the intimate thoughts (writings) of someone you *thought* you knew?

* * *

His nakedness doesn't feel truly naked; it feels more like another piece of clothing that he wears.

* * *

Everything holds the possibility of falseness, except tragedy.

* * *

When the horrors rise up, who *really* believes?
True faith is born in concentration camps,
not in church or therapy.

* * *

If *insensitivity* were a crime…

* * *

The torment of words, the intelligent words as well as the abuse of words… So I secretly desire to lose them all, though when alone I turn to them like men turn to pornography, to punish myself with such impossible salvation.

* * *

The trance of long-term relationships.

* * *

I can take people's problems
and even their cruelty.
What I can't take is their deliberate stupidity.

* * *

We become individuals when we learn fear.
Until then, we're one with nature,
the patience and urgency of nature.

* * *

Questions aren't for answers—
just awareness.

* * *

Wonder and doubt are one,
leaves from the same tree.

* * *

Ordinary life is like a bad novel:
clichés everywhere,
and no real character development.

✳ ✳ ✳

I remember the beautiful, painful simplicity of the past: when I read, I was totally transported. When I wrote, I was writing my whole being. I could hear every note of a bird's song, smell every scent of every flower carried in the afternoon breeze. Even the waves of the ocean seemed to roll in slow. I remember the past as a time when I was fully where I was and who I was: child, teenager, young adult... Morning, afternoon, evening... But now I am everything, hence nothing, and nowhere. Adulthood is an exaggeration, a metaphor, a cover-up of something not even there.

✳ ✳ ✳

I have never felt that a man has loved *me*,
but has loved *women* through me.

✳ ✳ ✳

His *pride* makes him silent.

✳ ✳ ✳

He loves too easily;
I love too deeply.

✳ ✳ ✳

Trying to blend in with the technological world is only making me want to run away from it even more. I can't adapt because I can't become machine-like. Slowly my life has come to this: it's not really my life, anymore, but some

135

spirit-killing compromise that has me appearing "mellow"
to some people at work, when really I'm screaming and
kicking inside.
. (Why can't they hear me in my eyes?)

* * *

Every moment we ever love
will become the well
from which we later draw
our discontent with everything
which is not love.

* * *

His words echo in his silence.
Silence is full of now and before—
memory, strain, release.

* * *

I feel invisible.
But not invisible enough.

* * *

Doubt is an intense religious experience, too—
everything intense is.

* * *

An 8:00 a.m. walk in the snow.
Trees and bushes in front of this apartment
are bent to the ground
from the thick, white frosting.
Down the street, a cat cries while birds sing.
The sun tries to peek through.
A dog's orange piss-tracks

lead up to the trunk of a white tree.
The sound of children screaming glee.
The sound of car-skids
and the rhythmic chug of wheels with chains.
My boots sink into high drifts,
and I walk as if under water, not seeing,
just sinking until I hit bottom: the road.
Everyone I pass speaks to me—
all boundaries temporarily broken,
covered by snow.

* * *

The embrace of a whisper in his embrace:
the touch of a rough feather.

* * *

We laugh because we don't want to suffer.
Otherwise, nothing would be funny.

* * *

It's like we're living together,
but we have separate rooms
a couple of miles away from each other.

* * *

What is *not* a daily obligation
is all that ultimately matters.

* * *

This mania for the positive;
this disease of mental health.

* * *

They talk of "alternative consciousness",
as if a dessert they serve
after the main meal of reality.

* * *

Street people have their tricks and lies in order to survive.
Those made safe by money despise those tricks, not admitting that their so-called "business skills" are trickier.

* * *

At noon, during lunch, I watch the children on the playground. This is how I get far away from the mood of work
and offices, and the only way I can get close to wanting
children.

* * *

The home of humor:
glimmers of the heart turn to the mind,
then send them back to the heart.
We laugh when we understand, with relief.
Humor is where the heart is.

* * *

The journal as God:
unquestioned, always there.

* * *

There is no truth;
there is only the *desire* for it.
Truth cannot survive one lie,
and we all live lies.
(To be alive *is* to live a lie.)
Yet I can live with the lies;

it's the dogma of false truth
I can't live with.

***

I woke up at 5:00 this Sunday morning and couldn't go back to sleep. Now it's 3:00 p.m. and the chaotic energy I feel when I'm up all night is driving me. I finally finished Denton Welch's *A Voice Through a Cloud*. I'd read in bed, then get up to turn the heater on, peek outside, write in my journal, get something to drink, pace, then go back to bed. Now the after-glow of the book leaves me with a dignified depression. Welch wrote, "why did I seize on the sights and the sounds that troubled me? I seemed to have lost the happy trick of dis-regarding them.... Nothing else but the sadness of destruc-tion seemed real."

***

The older I get the darker everything gets,
as if the sun is going down,
as if perpetually winter...
But in the dark I feel what the light obscures:
the texture of the unique flaws in everything.

***

Holidays are too soft
(and too loud).

***

My childhood gods were old houses, old trees:
tangible mysteries that took me beyond
what I could see.

***

Most everyone worships the sun,
but I prefer rain, and the moon.

* * *

All he wanted to do was change the world.
Instead, he bought an expensive new car.
(His debt goes right to the heart.)

* * *

The more self-conscious a person is,
the more they'll desire humor.

* * *

The way the sun shifted today, late afternoon:
the nausea of eternity spoke.

* * *

Despair is a sort of ecstasy,
an ecstasy that feels bad.

* * *

Silence is a way of giving up or giving in.
Silence is the flame which has burned out.

* * *

Life is insane; only nonexistence is not.
Trees, flowers, insects, animals—
they're all animated with the insanity of life.
But humans—
they are insane only with their desire for sanity.

* * *

People pay to tell their secrets (by going to a therapist), but
I'd pay to hear them.

* * *

I'm not a man *or* a woman;
I'm the *war* between men and women.

✷✷✷

I've tried to know hundreds of people.
But I keep running into the same person,
over and over again.

✷✷✷

I want kindness, too, but what seduces
is the cruelty behind everything real.

✷✷✷

This hope for the future:
it's the same as nostalgia, really.

✷✷✷

The people who are most real
are the people who don't have friends.

✷✷✷

All I have left are aphorisms, fragments…

✷✷✷

Hushed by the world.

✷✷✷

The darkest night is a light,
compared to eternity.

Kimble James Greenwood

Costumed as in War
(February–August, 1984)

When the call came for journals I was in the process of rereading mine in chronological order—eighty-four volumes, age thirteen to thirty-eight. As the deadline neared, I was immersed in volumes 49–51, age thirty, and so chose several of the more colorful and philosophical entries and sent them in. I wanted to preserve some of the narrative, conflicts, and continuity of my life at that time, while also being true to some of the range and variety of mood, attention, fever, and voice that characterizes my life. All this while keeping the total to a manageable size. I can't say whether this intent has been met or not; subjectivity prevents me.

I am well aware of the desire, if not the need, to patronize or deny the earlier self. It seems as if—in the mania for growth and self-possession—the most insidious challenges and threats lie in the confessions, language, and sincerities unwittingly preserved in the journal or diary entries of our past. How often I've heard of people destroying all earlier documentation, unable to bear proof of their youthful illusions and immaturities, unable to bear the imagined critical eye of others turned on what so deserves criticism—or so retrospection and self-consciousness would hold.

I am guilty of a mania for growth and self-possession. But I hope to allow the earlier selves their integrity, and temper the need to patronize them. Nevertheless, there is a tension in presenting to the eyes of others an earlier self. Added to this is the tension of presenting to the public a private document. Perhaps these tensions are caused by nothing more than taking out of context what so belongs to its context.

Though only eight years separate the 30-year-old from the 38-year-old, they have been years of serious exploration, change, and growth—at least in my own eyes. Suffice to say, I find the 30-year-old Apollonian where I feel myself to have become much more Dionysian in the interim, much more given to mind where I am currently given to soul, and much less feminist than I feel myself to be now. The general tone of this earlier voice feels a bit facile to me now, a bit glib, a bit—dare I say it?—innocent.

Having said as much, let it be. There is good fun here as well.

At times one has only a slender notion. One is only out here in this, whatever it is. Whirl. People disappeared and were said to have died, as in war. Or their contexts changed like stage flats leaving them inappropriately costumed, speaking the wrong line. Some disappeared in place, their skulls hollowed out by corrosive spirits or devoured by parasites.... Just out here. Each one alone. The rest is fantasy.

—Robert Stone

&

February 8, 1984 (Wednesday, 10 P.M.)

Show me how a man deals with his frustration and restlessness and I will tell you how mature or immature he is.

Does he go around shooting pellets at things living or dead with his pellet gun? Does he go to sleep? Does he take a bus downtown and recklessly spend money on himself?

So far as I can tell there are approximately four sources of real joy in this life:

1. Harmonizing with nature, God, or people.

2. Being young and/or healthy.

3. Being honestly and mutually in-love.

4. Work well done.

All else is ersatz. And that's the majority of what we see on the dump around us—ersatz joy, pseudo joy, cover-up, superficial suck-the-sand-and-call-it-shrimp joy. That's not joy, that's excrement. And that's why this is a dump.

When a woman leaves us is it the woman or is it our sudden lack of meaning that we miss?

Tessa dropped by the other day. Found me on the porch and protested that she didn't know I was there. She didn't. She started crying. I pulled her to me. We held hands. She cried. I would have cried if I could. We talked for an hour or two. We kissed. We hugged. Did I love her? I wasn't sure. I tenderly cared for her. But love? No—I had turned that off, like a drippy faucet. One can't love someone one doesn't know. I only knew her position—and even that's questionable. When she left I talked myself into believing I didn't love her at all. I don't know what love is anymore than anyone else does. Coming out of *Broadway Danny* Rose in the central city on a dark Wednesday night, listening to the bland businessmen bluster—talking about flicks as if they were fucks:

"It was a good fuck—didn't you think so?"

"Yeah. Yes, it was a good fuck."

"It was a rollicking good fuck."

"Yeah, I thought so. It was a rollicking good fuck." Blanched smiles that barely cover the bones.

I wander the city streets alone eating delicatessen potato salad. The only thing real and beautiful is the rain. I'm young, I'm healthy, I'm free. I've got no job. My rent was due eight days ago. I've got eighty dollars in the bank. I don't care. Why should I care?

Why should I care about the fat crazies on the bus, muttering insane hatreds and rollicking angers at ghost wires in their heads? or the thin crazies who get on the bus whispering, "I'm sorry. I don't mean to be rude, I need to sit back where there's light."?

Shall I tell you how everyone on the city streets at night is ugly and grotesque? Shall I tell you that Allen's Diane Arbus-East Coast is no different than the Diane Arbus-Pacific Northwest? Grotesques—everyone being eaten alive from inside by their own disease. In certain light the neon shines right through, reveals the gaping holes, the twisting maggots.

It's ironic really. Downtown at the Bon Marché. Big plate windows. The stylized, plastic, young-and-the-free sport their designer duds, letting us know what to spend our money on, the money we make serving Mamon at boring, political, kiss-the-ass-of-assholes jobs that drag on day by week by month by year. But at night, stores closed, when only grotesques seep through the city, what irony, what contrast, what irrelevance! to present your slick fashions to them. Penny postcards for the blind.

We can see it for what it is: a facade. It is all facade, all plate glass, trick glass; cast the light obliquely and it will not show the maggots. Put a Walkman over your ears and you will not hear the scream. Even the beautiful. Tell me how the beautiful are not chimera also and I will call you a liar. The beautiful have their season—and will stink the rest of their lives, stink from their fear of losing beauty thus losing attention thus losing worth thus losing—to pick a sex, pick a scenario—husband, boyfriend, lover, ersatz love (i.e., the love that shoves a bone into the wound, shoots its seed, then passes on, bored again, lunging after the eternal freshness that covers the eternal decay).

Do you need to go back 100 years to find out what's going on? Have you caught up with a 100 years ago yet? Is the Nietzsche on your shelves with your aspidistra plants? If so, go to Nietzsche; *Zarathustra*, chapter "Love of Neighbor", verse 4:

> *You cannot endure yourselves and do not love yourselves enough: now you want to seduce your neighbor to love, and then gild yourselves with his error.*
> *...You invite a witness when you want to speak well of yourselves; and when you have seduced him to think well of you, then you think well of yourselves.*
> *...One man goes to his neighbor because he seeks himself; another because he would lose himself. Your bad love of yourselves turns your solitude into a prison.*

Yes indeedy.

God, it is an ugly, pitiable, malicious, shallow, trite, silly, selfish world out there! I am no different than the rest.

Let's play Nietzsche a moment:

O seekers, shall I tell you the truth that is the cancer of my generation? Shall I reveal to you the fact that fills the unconsciousness of my country, my class, my times? It is this: We have everything and we are nothing.

This is the guilt that breaks our backs and bends our knees. This is the guilt that makes us first petulant then malicious. This is the guilt in whose atonement we gladly invite the whip to keep the wound open and festering all our lives. This is the guilt that underlies all other guilts in this free and prosperous nation, the home of the cowardly, the land of prisoners.

We have everything and we are nothing.

At least one can admire the male, the simple-minded, slow, thick male who knows only to drive himself with this guilt, knows only to lay his body on the grindstone, grit his macho teeth (filled with silver and gold after the sugar-rot has consumed them) and offer himself like Christ, that the bloody attrition of his sacrificial body can grease the bloody cobblestones where his wife and offspring drive in pursuit of their own hollow happiness.

Blessed be the simple male and the simple male's simple role in life: make his woman happy. And what makes her happy? Things! Neat things! *And*, of course, if her kids are happy. And what makes her kids happy? Things! Neat things! *New* neat things!

Or that is what someone is trying to put across. They're doing a good job. The masses have yet to catch the drift, have yet to revolt, to rise up and throw off their oppressors. That's the neat thing about democracy: you can't really throw off your oppressors because you are them. Would a man cut off the one maggoty leg he stands on? A *man* would, yes, but not these Peter Panish baby assholes that claim manhood by virtue of the swinging worms between their legs.

Well, I've spouted off at the pen's mouth long enough.

You know what's eating me? Simple enough: lack of work well done. A day, a week, wasted. Indulgence. Off center. No self respect. Shame.

May 29 (Tuesday, 1:53 A.M.)

Fundamental within me is an extreme reluctance to impose reality on anyone else—or even to presuppose reality.

Since early adolescence I've recognized that I treat each person as if they are conscious, choosing beings, as if they speak and act wholly from their intentions. I have also had an absolute horror of imposing myself or my acts on anyone who does not invite me.

What this has often meant is that I approach people chameleon-like, allowing them and encouraging them to present their reality. I then match them, so far as I am able. I match them up to the point where my *own* reality cries out for expression or validation. I do this honestly, not only seeking to know others and the common universe, but to avoid the reality squabbles that often ensue when people meet.

(For the most part, I don't think I need or ask to have my reality validated by other people—except wherein it concerns them. I am confident enough in my own reality—or my right to it—to not ask for the Other's ratification. People take this confidence for arrogance or smugness. It has infuriated them at times. Understandably. What they often miss, however, is that I extend that same respect to them and their realities. Most people have had their realities denied from the very first and so are starving, it seems to me, to have others validate and accept them.)

This also means that I have taken people at their word. I've always assumed that people speak the truth, that they are intent on knowing and communicating the truth. But as my experience in the world has deepened, and the troubles I've had from this proposition persist, I've learned and am learning secondary shadings.

People invariably express *a* truth; but truth is multiform, conscious and unconscious; irony abounds, intentional and unintentional. I also come up against the fact that many people are very inarticulate when it comes to the inner landscape, and can not find the words to verbalize their emotional states, reasons, or needs to themselves, let alone others. It is simply a language they do not know.

Age has also given me greater cognizance of the natural ambivalence and ambiguities that constitute, perennial beast, the human soul. This wreaked havoc with me as an adolescent—adolescence, the tailspin of childhood with its black-and-white judgments, its need for purity and security. Age teaches me every day that there is more to heaven and earth than is dreamt of in *my* philosophy. Age? I mean experience, my experience of other people, and what I've learned from *their* experiences.

I can't think of anyone who has known the extent to which I respect and grant the realities of other people, the seriousness with which I listen to them, assess what they're saying; the seriousness with which I have *always* taken criticism. This last factor is such a powerful influence that I've done my best to surround myself with good critics—critics serious, sensitive, sincere, intelligent, and subtle. Otherwise I am condemned to answering and defending myself to and from the careless, projecting mood-stuff that characterizes many people's criticism—which, nevertheless, I am compelled to give credence to, extend benefit-of-the-doubt to.

Yes, defend. I *do* defend my reality. It is human to do so. Since my defense is usually so passionate, thought-out and articulated, most people assume there is no reaching me; I'm "always right" or smug. What they fail to see—or I fail to show them—is that the defense is just that, an immediate defensive reaction, an aggressive protective device that is meant to challenge them even as they have challenged me. Most comments, judgments, and assessments stay with me longer and in more serious ways than the critics will often see. They, after all, may be right; their perceptions may be true, true for me. If so, it behooves me to see and act on them. As I couldn't get across to my brother once when he accused me of self-deception: the truth sets me free. I have nothing to lose from the truth but bindings. If I refuse to accept the truth about myself, or anything else, painful consequences will naturally follow.

May 31 (Thursday afternoon)

The challenge these days is not in finding the great secrets/mysteries/truths of the universe, but in communicating them most effectively and freshly to as many people as possible.

As a writer I am constantly obsessed with accuracy of expression—expression first, then communication. For I am convinced that to express something as sincerely, fully, and freely as possible is the first and most important ingredient in communication. In other words, one's first audience is oneself; one's first communication is to oneself.

As writers we are always searching for that context wherein we can write the most freely, deeply, wholly and sincerely. Each foray into form is exploration toward this end.

June 1 (Friday evening)

Who are you?
I am one of the race of men given to see everything for the last time.
What do you mean?
In the morning I come to my room to see the sun streaming through the eastern windows. I disrobe and kneel, naked on the floor so that the sun strikes my exposed genitals. I fondle the shaft which pulls blood to it so that it grows, and grows more sensitive.

This is a metaphor of the mind without sleep. The mind without sleep pulls blood into the body, making it a sensate shaft, a tingling sensor of sensuality.

All noises are loud. All texture astounds. All faces amaze. Yes, the mind full of its own blood becomes a seascape, awash with sensation, perpetually astounded at the images offered to its senses.

I mean I am a metaphysician, preoccupied with the great cycles and their strange turnings. All that I see are instances and variations of the great laws.

It means I am increasingly a stranger on the earth. Surprised, always surprised. Growing ever more into a child—so sensitive a raindrop is a flood, a batting eyelash thunder.

What do you care about?

Beauty and sex. Sex and love. Love and beauty. Youth, Beauty, Death. Sex. Love. Beauty.

Quality and Art. I care about Quality and Art.

Why are you the way you are?

Body type. Ectomorph. Tall and skinny. More bone than skin, I retreated of necessity from the contact sports of active life. Sought instead cerebral brawn, the scholar's light, lucubration.

Who will give you shelter from the storm?

I don't know. I never know. Is that possible? How can that be? Am I not sentenced to be hopeless and forlorn?

Who do you brake for?

I brake for Gandhi.

What else?

Hallucinations.

What hallucinations?

Everything!

Why do you write? Why do you live?

Love, fame, money. Curiosity.

Is life worth living?

What else can you do with it?

June 30 (Saturday, 8:30 A.M.)

Things sneak up on you. To turn your front on one thing means to turn your back on all else. How did it happen? Everyone saying: Have a good day, have a nice day, have a good 'un, have a good one, have a good sleep, enjoy your meal, enjoy!

They either say that or say "Fuck you!" (The youth say, fuck you; the older youth say, have a good one.)

Either way it's a superficial way to touch another human being. Have we become frightened of other human beings, nervous, perennially uncertain and worried? Or do we just never have enough time for anyone else, for the hundred new strangers we see in a day? All this strange palliation going on, talk to sway the intemperate beast, to bog down the monsters from the id in treacle. My brother and I used to yell at each other with gusto. Now we tiptoe, anxious not to offend even as we're brimming with natural offense. (Natural offense? The force of our persons, the strength of our individualities.)

I keep having to remember that I am not catching up to the adult world I saw as a kid. Things have moved even as I have moved. What I couldn't grasp at age five, 1958, I cannot grasp now at thirty. What I saw then will always be what it was then, frozen, unredeemable, unrecoverable in this relentless here-and-now.

Forced out of the womb early, I think this is a theme in my life—for I have spent my life trying to slow down, to step back, catch up, get ready, assimilate, stop the world.

The world will not stop. But I may stop. Someday I'm going to be killed, I really am. Like Billy Pilgrim in *Schlacthof Funf*. I may stop. Isn't disdaining TV and newspapers a way of stopping the world? Isn't isolation a way of stopping the world?

As many lives as I've lived—still, how many lives have died in me! To say I am ever more approximating myself is absurd; I'm ever more approximating a self, at any given time. I ride the bus and look out on the docks and wharves of Lake Washington, the sailboats and motorboats of an early, serene, cloud-wonderful, sunny, Saturday morning. Intimations come to me—fantasies? moods? of summer on the seacoast, and sailing parties, and teenage fun. Theme from a summer place. Happiness and recklessness. Beach boys. Hardy boys. Valences of summertime assault me with such nostalgia that I nearly weep.

What have I given up? What can I never go back to? Innocence and fun. Being young and reckless, simple and free; wearing sneakers and bumming around with friends. I am a cave man to that world—so withdrawn, so deep into my strange introspections, my mental circumspections, that sweet unconsciousness will never be mine again. Was it ever? Yes, it was. But I didn't have the consciousness to know I was so unconscious.

Randall Jarrell looks out at me with those sweet, longing, nostalgic, sensitive eyes. "The lost world!" he proclaims. "It is pain!" he explodes. Beside him Wallace Stevens, controlled to the point of no return, gazes serene and curious, an abstractionist on a merry-go-round, making order of the world he walks, strumming a classical blue guitar.

And I remember one of my original observations of why we write: to release the pressure of our singular memories, to share and recreate those memories in others, to broaden our base, consolidate our love in the world. But it is all vanity and delusion. Words are ultimately inadequate.

Shouldn't it tell me something, that I am much closer to people in my imagination than in person? Isn't this a sublime clue? Does this only mean I'm a writer—rather, of a writer's mind? Is that our conspiracy—a conspiracy of writers dwelling amidst and perpetuating the abstraction of words— because it is there, in the land of the imagination, where we most appropriate the world? Isn't it there we can touch, know, and love each other best? In the exterior world we are too nervous, too trembling to touch anyone but with the cautious hand and its fingertips. We are fingertips of icebergs in the exterior world. We meet and make simple roles among us, regenerating stances of irony. But inside we are the greater iceberg itself: massive, twisted, historical and complex, besieged with so many currents, frozen and liquid, that nothing but the inner eye can begin to do it justice.

Anais Nin: "In all love's beginnings this journey backwards takes place: the desire of every lover to give his loved one all of his different selves, from the beginning." That's part of it.

All of our different selves. And what do we do when we perfect a self? I assume that every self is perfect. Are we not always and only perfectly ourselves? I think of the boy who worked a summer as dishwasher/cook in Riverside, and bussed the 50 miles to L.A. to see the Dodger baseball games on the weekend. Nearly ten years later he is living in L.A., making much more money. Not once, not once did he go to the baseball game. Why not? Because he had perfected that pleasure, had he not? He had perfected that sweet and simple life, that simple pleasure. He had so incorporated, consumed, lived and loved that life that it was his forever. Ah, forever only as exploding cells are forever, drowning in a sea of seemingly infinitely exploding cells.

My impatience drives me forward—as if there is a great unknown, as if there will always be a great unknown, as if there is no end to the great unknown. And yet, I am such a nostalgist—regretting, fearing, aching at the dying of the past. At the same time, such a rage in me for the new, for progression, movement, growth.

It is actually the same circle, you know. I only bear its witness.

July 5 (2:25 A.M.)

The subject is paradigms.

A paradigm is like an assumption. For example, I assume that women, to maintain power among the more physically powerful male and male world, developed other powers, stratagems of the mind and senses, psyche and soul. This is a simple enough assumption, hardly polemical in many circles, current knowledge of the tribe. It is even, perhaps, "self-evident." Because it is self-evident, I do not question it deeper or further. I do not find the *energy* to question it deeper or further. There are more interesting and exigent questions for me to attend to. Thus, I pass over it and build structures upon it.

At some point I *learned* this assumption. I learned it either by articulating what my observations told me, or—more likely—I read or heard someone else articulating it, examined it in light of my experience, found it true, felt its rush as a new idea, and then moved on.

The assumption is a personal paradigm. It is also a cultural paradigm; I needn't go far to find the literature of the time supporting this view. Such overwhelming external support, coupled with my own immediate empirical agreement, works to sanction and reinforce the assumption. I will *not* look at it closer unless I confront the experience, the literature, of someone else looking at it closer, or unless my own experience becomes at odds with it.

This is the danger of paradigms. They are ways of looking at things so agreed upon and reinforced that we are blind or indifferent to other ways. At the same time, assumptions are necessary to utility. Wittgenstein: "In order for the door to turn the hinges must stay put." But the door on its hinges may only be embedded in a much larger door. It is the ever larger door whose turning we may be interested in. To get at the larger doors is such a task! Everything conspires against it.

Another metaphor: it is as if we live in quicksand, quicksand in a fog at night in the winter. The human animal, remarkable for its adaptability, its subjective creating, considers it the norm. We've gotten used to it—built machines to make it easier; built our jokes and self-help books around it; developed stratagems for forgetting or distracting ourselves from the fact.

To get out of the swamp takes considerable motivation, a.k.a. will. Extremisms are employed. Tricks are employed. Disciplines, even unto death, are followed by the explorers, or the willful, among us. Look at Wittgenstein. He epitomizes a man trying to break out of the stifling logico-literal paradigms of the day, of Western philosophy itself; a man who by exerting excruciating mental effort to think, concentrate, focus, and see, confronted and expanded paradigms by sheer force of mental (or psychological) will. The rest of us go about it more haphazardly, less obsessively. Most people, of course, don't bother with the subject at all. They take what's given and make the best of it, routinely bitching along with everyone else when it is appropriate to do so. Many are held within their own personal paradigms, blind to the connections between us all, indifferent to the value of the explorers— whose work to find and open the larger doors sets us all more free.

It is an unending task for me, a two-fold effort: to come to see, know and expand my own paradigms (or else chart my blind spots so well that I can work around them, casting light from other perspectives), and come to see, know and expand the paradigms of the culture, the age, the race. The assumption—the larger door that allows and encourages this activity—is the belief that the expansion of paradigms, the freedom to see, consciousness itself, is *freedom*. Freedom is good. Ever greater freedom is the goal.

But this too may be a false assumption. The purpose may *be* the limiting rules and contexts of the game—the necessity of limits. The breaking of paradigms seems a very Western-male-white preoccupation. Indeed, this is a honing of the task stated above. Thus: it is my never-ending quest to determine what rules and limits are necessary to the game, and what limits are inimical to it. Even a seemingly broad and tolerant view, this too may be a limited paradigm whose hold on me blinds me to all else....

I still think one of the more telling experiences of my life occurred in Denver the summer before I turned five. I was in the kitchen with my grandmother, my mother's mother. She was nearly blind. We were looking for the nipple to my sister's bottle. I saw the nipple but pretended to go on looking. It made for a better game, the continuance of the game. Was there in me the belief that grandma was also choosing blindness to make the game better? I think so. Weren't we both conspirators, doing the same thing for the same reason? And then, was it pity that intervened when it became evident to me that her confusion and pain was real? Or was it boredom at a game no longer fun? It became too real, too sad, to be fun.

July 6 (Friday, 5 P.M.)

As things develop they become more defined, the greater manifolds gain shape, their outline emerges from the fog.

Things get better and better with Tessa. Love flows between us. We lie in bed and talk for hours. Our talk is intelligent; mutual respect for each other's intelligence, opinions, world views. Our greater deficits, I feel, are the past and its necessary positions, the history of pain that has rubbed me so raw. But viscerally. Mentally I know and forgive her—if only, if only she will now love me, and love me consistently.

Love is lying in bed talking with each other for hours.

Love is driving over to his house, even when she knows he isn't there, just to leave a note: *Nagdeo!* I love you!

Love is visiting friends together, that you may all become the same friend. The slow sweet human integration, lives mixing with lives, past mixing with present. The life has been rich, so rich I've abandoned its description and have used my time to develop abstractions instead.

This seems basic and simple: love is the condition best shown by two people spending time together, talking together. If you don't have the time, if you're not talking, where is, what is, love?

But. I can not, I do not live only my own life. Don't you understand? To love is to live the lives of those you love. If you love the world, you live the life of the world. To love is to share the lives, the thoughts and feelings, the *being* of what you love. To love the world is to know and feel its terror, pain, loneliness and confusions no less than to feel its ecstasies, joys and sheer delight.

In other words, my life is not my own. My love is not for her alone. My purpose in life is *not* to create an environment of loving comfort for myself and my mate only, my mate and our children. I care for a greater world. I can not abide the selfishness, the solipsism, of all energies used solely for one's own sustenance and the sustenance of one's offspring.

What I seek in a companion is someone likewise dedicated to relieving the pain and injustices in the world—working, through whatever means possible, to solving or resolving the problems. Working diligently.

Everyone, I imagine, likes to think their lives are not merely selfish and self-serving. The middle class has many mechanisms for banishing its guilt—usually through monetary contributions to worthy causes, or volunteer work. This is all fine. There are levels of involvement. We all rationalize the best we can.

I like what K & D are doing. I greatly admire that activity. K was Tessa's best friend in high school. She and her husband moved to Venezuela and are operating an orphanage there. Very minimal funds. They teach the basics: hygiene and health, farming, reading and writing. But more than anything, they serve as an example, an example of how men and women can treat each other with love and respect, an example of Americans, blessed with fate's opportunities, taking those opportunities southward, into the lives of those less lucky, Americans having given up their high estate to cast their lot with Americans of another estate.

So often I hear people saying, as my good friend M has said, "My problems are great enough for myself; how can I even think about the problems of the world?" There is validity in this. Of course, the first level of responsibility taken for the world is the responsibility taken for your own life. But so many people remain on that level; they wallow and indulge there. In fact, they do not resolve their problems, or deal with them honestly or deeply.

It is one of those strange paradoxical mechanisms: energy for one becomes energy for the other. Attending to the world's problems *is* attending to my problems, and vice versa. The deeper I attend to the world, the deeper I attend to myself. The deeper I attend to myself, the deeper I attend to the world. It is the depth, perhaps, that is the key here. We are the world. And yet the world is always so much more, so much greater than our restrictive, imploded visions can grasp of it or give it credit for.

But the problems, they all wail, are too great. Talent is lacking. Courage is lacking. So, they do what they can. They make things nice. Wallpaper the rubble. Put happy-face stickers on the rape victims. Tell one another obsessively: Have a good one. They watch the mainstream news and read the mainstream newspapers to be informed, to stay buoyant, to float along. They vote for mainstream candidates.

I feel constantly that I am on the road to Ixtlan. I feel like the congressman in *The Ugly American* who visits the war zone of Southeast Asia to gain first-hand knowledge of what is going on. But the self-serving powers take him and glove that hand, glove it with wine, women, and rich foods. The self-serving powers also provide the translators.

Mine is an extremist position. Typically extreme, perhaps. Sorry for that. I would have rather been more natural or easy in a more natural or easier world. I would have rather lived in a world where everyone else was also doing the work so I wouldn't have to be so obsessive in my own strivings to do the work. If I was doing my own work well, I wouldn't be looking around projecting, castigating everyone else. I'm actually doing what everyone does: trying to talk myself out of doing the work. If I only could.

So it comes to Tessa. As loved one, as one with so much lovely power in my life, I turn to her over and over again, asking: whose side are you on? Are you out only to have a good time, only to fill your belly with good foods, to raise your kids and send them to school with ribbons in their hair and clean faces, only to read books for the momentary pleasure they give—sugar reading—only to get by on as little put-out as possible? Etcetera.

Naturally she's offended by such questions. It is never "only" of course. There is a rich mix, many motivations, spheres and cycles of activity and consciousness. I mean no offense. I mean no self-congratulation either. I am not such a hot shot, nor that different from anyone.

But I try. I am obsessed with trying. It is hard for me. I look to make it easier. I look to band together, to join forces, to organize teams. I've been doing this for a lifetime. At age ten it was the "Junior Justice League of America," at age twelve "The Goldfinger Club." And now, the religion of literature, warriors and men of knowledge. Always it has been soulmate, helpmate.

Tessa is coming closest, closer than anyone else has ever come. It is only natural for me to question her so relentlessly, to examine her so closely. Better now than later, after marriage. Better openly that she know my expectations from the first, the better to choose or unchoose them. It is not one-sided. Not at all. She does the same with me. She has her own pictures and expectations; she examines and tests me as well. She is less conscious of them than I am of mine, makes less overt noise than I do, but is no less forceful. We engage in the healthy clash and investigation. Things are gradually becoming simplified—where we have only to consider each other, our feelings, our love, our life-long plans. Whether we choose yea or nay is not so important as that we choose as consciously as possible. But I speak of a future still a long way off. I speak only of possibilities. I mean to be a meteorologist, reading the meanings of the clouds in their winds to determine tomorrow's weather. A difficult task, the winds are always changing.

July 31

It was one of those moments of utmost honesty—or attempt at honesty. It sounded bad, but it had to be said.

"Everyday," he said, "I attempt to create an environment, a space, a quietude where the most subtle moods can be known and fostered. In these moods I hope to learn and feel things that are otherwise lost in the lack of time and space that characterizes these manic times."

"I envy you that," she said. "That's impossible for me. Two kids make that impossible. If I try, the frustration is only greater."

He went on to say that in the interest of his quietude and the concentration it meant to nourish he would like to see her only twice a week. "Please," he said, "don't just stop by indiscriminately."

Three days later when she stopped by indiscriminately she greeted him with, "I hope I haven't destroyed any delicate mood you were building," and smiled at him sardonically. "Of course you have," he replied, "but now that you're here that's no longer important, no longer the point."

The next day when he invited her to drop by she made another reference to his "delicate moods."

"Why," he asked, "do you mock this? Why do you make light of it? As if it didn't sound precious enough, as if it wasn't already too intimate to confess."

She sobered. "I do not mean to mock you for it. Oh no, I do not mean to make light of it at all. I am jealous you see, both for the fact that I haven't the time to do the same, and that your doing so takes away time between us. There is so little I can tease you for."

He looked at her awhile. Admitted a token defeat. Replied, "Tease me for the smallness of my penis."

On the night of lightning he sat at the back of the bus and eavesdropped on a young couple fighting. The young man's voice was thickly drunk. "You doen lissen to me. You doen hear a word I say. You know why? Your dum, thass why. Your dum. You doen unnerstan' the English langwige. Your dum bitch."

The young woman replied in very even, modulated tones. "I've been listening. I understand the English language. I am not dumb. I've been listening to you. But you're trying to blame me for not working, and that just isn't true. You could have taken that job, you..."

"You doen know nothin' I been talkin' about! You doen lissen to me! You talk so all the people on the bus can know our problems!" he yelled.

"I've been listening to you all night," she replied softly. "The bus is where we happen to be."

August 1

Notes:

1. I miss Mary Esplin.

I miss everything I never had, I never knew, I never entered and learned, I never fully experienced. Does one fully experience anything? No. I miss everything.

Love, sex, Art: there is an essential void in me which can never be filled—psychologically.

That's why one calls on the mind and its tempering control and discipline. The mind creates its own laws, its desired forms of behavior, and then enforces them the best it can. The enforcer is called WILL. The mind is repulsed by prodigality, by excess which leads to destructive behavior, by indulgences and spoilings. The world rots; the mind seeks a place above the world, out of the rot.

2. The psyche alone is much more free. We know this. Unpressured, it ranges and reaches, articulates its territories with aplomb. The trick, the quest, is to preserve this state of being, this presence of mind, in environments, situations, and under pressures that squeeze and reduce it, bind and choke it.

I learned, as a boy, that people become free and opened up if accepted. It was always my intent to both free myself and my own articulation, and to free those around me, those talking to me. When people are not free and comfortable, they express defense mechanisms. Or else their words and thoughts spring forth miscarried, bloodied and crippled. The information in such instances is vastly inferior, has considerably less integrity or quality than the person him or herself naturally has.

So I say "Yes!" to people. I say, "I understand." And people blossom and open up. Finding free expression, they "pour out their love," as Miller says. I claim understanding honestly, not meaning to be manipulative or controlling at all. After all, I echo Terence: *nothing human is foreign to me.*

3. In listing the Arts, don't forget that philosophy is meant to be the art of thinking.

4. We were at Alki, the haunt of the young and the free, the party-ers and cruisers. July 4th: clouds of sulfur, music of explosions. Lights. Artillery. Action. On the front. On the beach.

He watched her walk away from him. He longed to touch her, hold her, enter her. He imagined telling her. He imagined her indignant, pressured, "Why do you always…?" He imagined responding, "To be close to you! Don't you see? We are all so distant from each other, so alone in our thoughts, in ourselves, in our worlds. The body tries to do what the spirit wills to do, enter each other, cleave as one, be less dreadfully alone…"

He thought. He observed. He looked at the couples, hand-holding, bored. He looked at the singles—roving packs of girls, roving packs of guys. What do couples do together?

He continued the imaginative monologue: "…or have experiences so strong, as a couple, that you become united to the loved one by virtue of the passion of the experience that captures both of you."

How else to become close to someone?
We have this desire, need, craving, lust to be close to someone.
But then, once achieved, illusory or not—ambivalence be praised!—our will is to break and separate, to go forth strong again in ourselves, all choices open again. Or am I only describing the male sensibility here?
Observations. Valence-hopping. How much energy in the singles, how much boredom in the couples! How much boredom repressed in couples by trumped up lunging after happiness, stimulation, fun!

5.
Ease me gentle into the day.
Consciousness is diamond stone.
I break on it, poor flesh and bone,
Lest you make soft my way.

6. Middle Class health: all that intelligence and no wisdom to do anything with it; all that will being used only for self-preservation, for selfish security. Sleeping intelligence. Maintenance intelligence.

7. The Middle Class makes things *middle*. They tear down the colorful and interesting, the extremes, e.g., turning "anxiety" or "angst" to "fretting" or "going without breakfast," etc. (They're probably right, to a point. But the point points toward the middle, not the edges where the unexplored and interesting lands are.)

8. The thing I'm meaning to say about sugar is that it's an excellent metaphor, a metaphor of horror; it fools the monitors. It offers the rush of pleasure called sweetness and follows with no nourishment. It sets a bad example; I wouldn't want my children hanging around with it. How more dangerous can you get? It's like our president. It's like bad sex.

9. The problem is, you try to construct your life, giving it consistency, a consistency you like.
Here you are—as Thoreau says—an experiment largely untried. You are this pinpoint of consciousness in a sea of unconsciousness. You share the sea with an inexhaustible myriad of other pinpoints of consciousness. And what happens? You are washed, you surge, emotions rage within you and without

you. Things never hold still. An unknown or hardly remembered past accumulates and weights you down, even as an unknown future imposes.

There we are, one small mote of thought inflated in any given present moment by the given present moment. Ridiculous blowfish confronting whales and sharks.

Inflated, always inflated with the present, with thought, with oneself.

10. Kids keep one in contact with reality. What's reality? The will of others, the *indomitable* will of others. (Women's wisdom comes not only from dealing with ego-centric men....)

11. What I both love and hate about external reality is the way it overwhelms and exceeds the imagination.

12. Poetry builds a context of time, time and its rich attention. Poetry takes its time to tell about things; it surrounds things with luxuriant space. It is the space of love, it is the attention of love. Poetry makes love to the world.

13. What others call arrogance in genius, for the most part I call confidence, hunger, and impatience.

14. I get excited when I find male intellect unaccompanied by male ego. This is intellect based on curiosity and humility, as it should be.

15. Wittgenstein to Drury, "I know I'm a freak."
The great souls are misfits—unable to be satisfied with the world as is.
The middle territory holds the most, the middle people, of course. They too are dissatisfied, but able to distract themselves from that dissatisfaction, able to delude themselves into kinds of satisfaction with what's given them (television, sports, sex, alcohol, fashion, wars...). The great souls must effect, must *create*, their satisfaction. We reap the benefits of that creation.
16. How simple the conscious human mind is—how dull and impercipient! Foreverfully mistaking form for content—as if physical beauty alone indicated beauty through and through, as if sexual penetration alone, orgasm alone, were the greatest pleasure, as if millions of dollars, all the time in the world, no death, were all we needed to be happy and satisfied.

I am driven to possess that which, if possessed, would give but ephemeral pleasure before turning to dross. I know this principle as well as I know anything—yet still am driven.

17. It is all such relentless struggling to tell the truth, to be set *free* by the truth. What else am I doing? And all these words I put to page only make things messier. It is endless metaphors. I say the same things over and over, changing metaphors, changing combinations—all to get us to *see*, to admit the truth. Then, no longer contending with the obvious, we can say "So what?" as my friends and I often do, and move on.

These journals testify to how much noise one man can make alone. That has often intrigued me about writing: other than thinking, it is one of the most solitary "inactive" acts possible—but look at the action it inspires, or can inspire.

The noise I make here must be seen, I hope is always seen, together with the immensity of the silence of my being in the world. The noise I make here is counterbalance to the silence. The aim isn't noise, it's music. But music is grace, and falls as it may. Mostly noise. Once the parents recognize my clamor, like any child, I can lower my tone and get on with what I have to say.

It may be, when finally given the floor, I will have forgotten what I had to say.

Sean Bentley

Lake Sutherland and Seattle, 1987–1989

I have kept a journal in one form or another on and off for over half my life. The first diary, the cramped five-year variety, was begun in high school. It wasn't until the mid-Eighties that my perception of the journal changed. I resolved to take note only of "significant" thoughts (albeit not limiting content any further than this) rather than merely setting down a daily and generally dull documentary.

Meanwhile, I was slowly developing a personal philosophy that contained fragments of Zen, pantheism, and Native American philosophy; I spent more time outdoors, in a sort of contemplation. At the same time, I had decided to make a commitment to a certain woman—whom I would soon, it turned out, marry. I believe the quality of my writing improved when the quality of my life did.

I still, of course, set down entries of a non-meditational nature. But the woods, the beach, and the annual pilgrimage to Lake Sutherland on the Olympic Peninsula are where the journal for me comes into its own, as art as well as journalism.

ॐ

9/27/87–10/1/87 (Lake Sutherland)

Robin and I were talking about documentaries. I noted that their nature makes everything appearing onscreen surreal: the normal looks ultranormal, and so parodies itself—and the odd looks so odd that it looks invented. Therefore there is a flattening of the spectrum: everything looks objective and out-of-place as in Magritte's paintings. Now, if I could achieve that in poetry.... How to present the everyday detail to make it stand out from the background in 3-D? I think juxtaposition of images is required to accent the *beingness*.

Thinking of a series of lake poems for a chapbook. After all, Monet spent years on waterlilies. The lake holds so many purely visual images for me, and ones that are extrapolated beyond the lake itself. Alas, some are pathetic fallacies or cute at best.

The lake emits a fractured light like a video screen gone to snow, late, after the anthems and the last used-car spot have died away, the viewer asleep in a lazy-boy, socks off. Some claim that alien messages are beamed in through that static, subliminal as the "sex" in scotch-rocks ads. Some claim they can read fluttering messages in the dotted code on TV, or the lake—messages some great power transmits to whoever is listening. The crackpots find their stumps and try to let the blinkered world in on the cosmic data. Alas, the *Enquirer* is where each message eventually surfaces, like mold on a once-pure glass of milk.

But today again I sit by this screen, blue depths blue as the deep sky, and try my hand at translation. What are these dash-dot-dash gibbers across the wind-blown surface? There is the current, pulling itself along like a baby tooth towards freedom, towards least resistance. It is the accent that tinges the message. There is a patch of gust-ripple, like a smear or erasure on the page. This gust forms ink-blot shapes and teases the message into stenciled forms.

This wilderness is not much quieter than our city house: motorboats, log trucks on the highway across the lake shifting down as they climb and drop over the hill, the stream like a uniformly busy road pushes under the trees that rustle in the cool updraft and autumn breeze.

Dogs the shape of wolves stroll next door. The power cruiser has left a wake that sends waves rolling like an indicator toward our shore, whacking the stony beach as though to slap us out of our trance. All around us the soup of sound roils; the trucks are far away and nature is on our side for now.

Robin reads on the grass looking debonair in *faux*-Italian shades. On the same ecliptic, Bootie, the neighbor's mutt, snoozes on the dock, looking like a lost sweater.

It's very warm but there's that fall bite in the air, and the sun is as high at noon as it was at 8 A.M. this summer. The lake is a lot smoother from lack of ski boats. We can hear birds instead of engines. Three ducks traverse the clear air above the lake, like the belt of Orion. Three points of moving light on the still tapestry of greens. Above this all is the distant rumble of a jet—an ominous reminder of how much a veneer this rustic vacation is.

Beside me is a fallen maple leaf, brown except for spots of blight which have mysteriously kept little corrals of green around them, perhaps providing them with a continual source of energy after the death of the leaf as a whole.

The dock: How many years since those trees were cut and nailed in place? The wood is white and gently warped, rough with winters. Two fresh boards are orange with recent life. Across the runway reaching out to the lake, yellow leaves have blown. They lie out of their element like children fallen on the bones of their fathers. Next to them lies a scattered still-life of kindling, laid out to dry in the autumn sun; arcs of bark and wedges of heartwood hunker together like aborted visions of dockdom, draped in sphagnum and platoons of sowbugs and spiders with guts big as starving infants. These critters feel as at home in the lopped limbs as on the living tree, if not more so. Their cousins clamber in the hidden belly of the dock, feeding, in their webs, from captured midges and mosquito fledglings. The dock resembles an exploded view of a tree designed by a brilliant but depraved cubist/mathematician. It appears to grow as naturally out of the grassy bank as its living relatives. It has been here long and will be here long, one supposes.

I will not, I think, climb the ladder into the water. Winter is just over the hill.

Night. Most of the lights on the opposite shore that I see in summer are not there tonight. This makes for a vivid blackness starting with the hill below the Big Dipper and ending at the lake at my feet. Depth of field is lost visually, though intellectually I know the distances involved. But personal space dissolves effortlessly to cosmic space without those far porch lights.

I'm writing, later, at the kitchen table, looking out the window at (what must be) the lake. Our porch light is on and I see, beyond my reflected face and illuminated room, the deck rail and furniture—but beyond is the same pure black, punctuated now by only two crosslake lamps. What I dread is for some creature—human or not—to come up from the dark into my light.

I feel like a bug under a magnifying glass. Close the curtains? Still, I like to look at a black void rather than stare point blank at a curtain.

The sky is faultless, blue as a crayon. It reminds me of my "class" in fourth grade with Mrs. Perry. That summer, she and I, Elaine, and Stewie would explore the city from her house in Wallingford. We'd walk the rail-road tracks collecting spikes and odd rusted machine parts, we walked to Green Lake where I had my first hot bakery-fresh bread. We played in the dirt and concrete pilings where the new I-5 was being built—where years later my girlfriend lived not fifty feet away. I don't know where else we went—I'd guess the Locks, or Eastlake, the Showboat Theater, or the Columns. But even now as I sit beneath the blue without anything on my schedule, or in town as I drive the freeway and see the city skyline spread before me filled with its busy construction and bustling traffic, I get a flutter in my gut as if to say, *Chuck it all and go explore. Go to Volunteer Park, go to Shilshole, walk a street you've never walked before, climb on some school's jungle gym...*the gut feeling of freedom and challenge. It's been a long time since I had truly no place I had to be, nothing I had to do, no one I had to be responsible to. Including myself.

I'm in the canoe, mid-lake. Though clear, the air is hazy enough that the hills—only a mile or two distant—fade nearly into invisibility. Smog or autumn haze? The latter, I hope. The wind and current have made for tough paddling. I aimed to go to the east end of the lake but it would take me all day, round trip, at this rate. I'm settling for a quiet midlake doldrum.

Light from the tops of wavelets sparks against the green like stars in the sea of night. It's clear from that one image how the idea of starships came about. I am suspended in some kind of field that clings to the side of the globe. Patterns telegraph across its dark surface, mapping energy. Objects as disparate as catkin and canoe adhere to it and to the surface of the globe, which hangs above a depthless eye-blue void. It's a long way out. Only the occasional duck escapes the pull of the lake. I want to stay here until something approaches from that void and completes the empty half of the frame. Unfinished Picture.

In another sense I see a strip of land, of subject, between the blank canvas of the sky and the merely primed canvas of the lake, where I sit like a misplaced blob of pigment.

There is of course the sun, which burns to the south, unwatchable. What good is this portrait when the viewer is blinded by it? Perhaps it serves as a repelling magnet to sway one's vision to what ought to be examined. After all, the sun and what it lies in are probably too large and arcane to bear our examination anyway. They need not be analyzed—they are the muse, which is sacred and inviolable. Analyze the gross production perhaps, but not the inspiration. (What malarkey.)

Under the dock the countless minnows, which scatter at every move I make. They can see me as well as I can them. Dizzy the cat crouches at the edge of the water, lapping the fresh lake. She will drink out of the tap at home—just so long as her water is fresh! She does not see the fish, does not know enough to think something might be beneath the water. She understands that a duck can sit on the lake and be unreachable, but not that there is a world under the surface. So she laps unseeing. The minnows, meanwhile, are browsing for food, and are attracted to the sound Dizzy's tongue makes in the water. They are not courageous, though, and refuse to enter water that's too shallow. But they follow her as she edges her way down the shore, sampling water from several spots. The potential prey and the potential hunter, ignorant of each other.

The drop-off. Here where the waving weeds are stunted nubs, where minnows leave the way to fingerlings, a ladder enters Sutherland like a syringe into flesh. Down it one can slide into the cold serum and stroke away across the green and placid surface. Close in, the vegetation tangles in the feet and rubbish on the bottom makes white faces from bones and other waste. Only here can you see what you are getting into. Farther out perhaps the mud is laced as well with old shoes, weeds, and hooks. But beyond the drop-off, feet will seldom rummage in those oddments, they mill the cool water and shuffle like minnows between each other's wake.

5/30/88 (Seattle)

Songbirds astir in the ravine. A sound either of droplets falling from the trees or of caterpillars falling from the trees. A herd of the latter explore the rim of a large peat planter pot which sits at the tip of the driveway. Just beyond is all the vegetation the little guys could want, but they are intent on their patrol. Small groups lie somnolent on upturned leaves of a young maple, or crawl on the logs laid unceremoniously at the yard's edge. Caterpillars also ascend the wooden deck railings as high as the roof. None have made it inside the window yet, but they are omnipresent as a plague outside. This is our first spring in this apartment and it is a pleasure to be able to get close to nature by just opening the back door—and I am not referring to caterpillars alone as "nature." There is, despite the traffic noise filtering through the trees, a wide selection of bird life and at least the appearance of wilderness complete with squirrels. We are shielded in back from view of all neighbors.

Have been walking around the lake with Robin a lot. We can walk around the neighborhood too, but it isn't as inviting as our old neighborhood. I find myself bored by the circuit of the lake despite the endless supply of new faces, ducks, etc. I guess it makes me feel a little like a rat on a treadmill. A prescribed route. Apart from that, the condition of being in motion—walking versus standing, driving versus walking—decreases the quality of reflection possible for me. I get more out of sitting watching the lake than walking around it—exercise aside.

So I sit in the tiny grassy spot we call our back yard, and watch the trees sway. It is like layers of clouds moving against each other—some left, some right, depending on elevation—which wind they find themselves in and whether they are bounding or rebounding from the buffets. Bees of various kinds, flies, gnats, and moths go about their business among the money-plant and nettle. The caterpillars undulate like heartbeats on countless oscilloscopes in their foraging. Small planes, here as in the Herb Garden thirty-four years ago, buzz over the trees. The sky, blue and grey, folds all these ingredients into its cool crust.

You look at a small caterpillar probing along an upper twig of a young fir tree and you cannot but think about the inexorability, the dumb determination of attaining that height—how long it has taken to get that high, and how little reward.

The play of light and dark in the leaves and shadows; the play of silence and birdcall; of air and substance, air and foliage; of stillness and motion, the quiet leaf bending with the breeze, the sudden fall of a caterpillar orange as a spark, in a stripe of sunlight, before it hits a leaf. I too need a balance between inner and outer forces, between generating—creating—writing—and listening, paying attention to the world or to others. Perhaps it's all going over the same material again, and perhaps not, but the reflective mood is essential for well-being. Reading, watching TV, talking to others is all outer focus, and hard work. Reflection is hard too, but cleansing.

7/30/88 (Lake Sutherland)

Still the mystery. I canoe into the lagoon and stare at the tiny bugs who scoot along the mucky bottom. They are searching for the same things we are. Who sits in a huge canoe above our mucky world unbeknownst to us?

The rooster keeps crowing downlake though day is hours old. This A.M. four young she-ducks nibbled at my fingers. Could they tell I was inedible? From here the ducks are invisible but I can see Robin, Kathryn, and Susan pulling out the flotation devices on the yard. Soon the lake will be full of us. Specks of sunlight start off the wavelets like stars in a choppy night. The drift, as it must be, is shoreward, since the shore corrals the lake. What heavenly configuration parallels our shoreline? On what beach do the universe's waves break?

There are ripples within each wavelet that correspond to fingerprints. I sit on the flesh of the lake. It pulses beneath me.

10/2/88 (Seattle)

Last week I looked out my office window at Madrona Publishers into the back yard—it was about 10 A.M. The moon was up above the pear trees. It shone pearly in the muted blue, and the lower right portion of it was obscured in blue. I considered the sun shining on the moon from out in space. I shifted my eyes down to the pear tree, and sure enough the shadows on the fruit were just like the shadow on the moon. It gave me the certainty of our floating in space—just like the moon—and of the enormity. Because the sun was so far away, there was virtually no difference between the two smaller bodies, moon and pear.

Meanwhile, I skimmed through Stephen Hawkings' book last night, which deals with such things. What caught my attention was a photo of a distant galaxy which was supposedly what our own looks like from several billion miles away. Again I was struck with the incomprehensible enormity of everything outside earth. Still, to the hornets that circle me at the picnic table, the world—the city—is incomprehensible enough. Beyond a certain point, wonder at the universe is too much to grapple with.

11/19/89

All I can recall from a dream last night: When asked how I wrote—how I chose the words—I replied, "I don't choose the words, they choose me." There was more, of course, but I had no handy pen and paper at 3 A.M., so fell back asleep and forgot the rest.

Ja Luoma

Selections from Three Journals

The Regular Journal
1985–1990

I like to use a number of journals for different purposes. It's interesting that I call this one "The Regular Journal," such a banal title for the journal with an alchemical purpose. The alchemy of The Regular Journal is to meld together four things: environment, daily occurrence, thought, and dream reflection. I have learned from making bread that "rest" is an essential ingredient in all recipes, all processes. "Rest" is the pot the four things stew in, and perhaps why I give the banal title of "The Regular Journal." By calling it that, it is fair to doodle in the margins or on whole pages, list books I'm reading, movies I'm seeing, songs or music I like, shopping lists, project lists. Lists and doodles are my ways of resting. The Regular Journal also has a built-in function of rest: I do not necessarily try to pull together the four categories of writing to make a statement, a singular meaning, or explain how I've come to understand something through recorded interactions. I rarely need to, because the moving together of the ideas, by writing, accomplishes a feeling of understanding in me.

Journals reach into the blind spots. The thing about a blind spot is that it can't be seen until you have reached an understanding about it. Growth occurs that moves you beyond the blind spot, and there it is—no longer a blind spot. The writing of journals is a progression, a movement toward understanding. The writing itself is the movement, not a statement of what is understood; the movement coalesces in understanding. But the learning of what a period of time was all about occurs only after reading a past journal, after you have already made the journey to a point of understanding.

I like to begin every writing session for my regular journal by deeply relaxing as soon as the notebook and pen are in my hands. Then I sit very still and listen. I listen very closely to the environment. I may be sitting in the laundromat or my truck, a coffee house or at work during a break, but I begin the same way—listening as if I've never been there before so all the sounds are new. I might write about what I'm hearing, maybe to wonder if the birds with the strange gravelly call are "afternoon birds" because I never hear this call at night or in the morning. I always listen first; it is the more subtle sense, the one forgotten easily in observations and daydreams. To attend to what I am hearing around me pulls me into a deeper frame of reference. Once I am deeply involved in listening while relaxed, I go on to looking and describing (if something compels me) what I see around me. My purpose is not to record what I hear and see every day, but to launch myself into the state of reverie, the mood of observation. I try to include at least a few sentences directly concerning environment from the listening state, although it may not be what is heard or seen at all. To listen is to capture mood.

What I mean by environment as one of the four elements in The Regular Journal is not the events, people, and interactions of the day, but very literally a sort of "mood photograph" of my immediate surroundings. The interplay between environment and all other stimuli is primary. It can reflect me, or take the place of my character or someone else's character entirely. Later, when I reread a journal from a point of understanding, I can often find very interesting connections between my observation of environment, my thoughts, and the events of that time—as if some part of me had been aware all along, able to read in the wind what the meaning of "happenings" were. Almost as if environment plays images to you, as a dream does, to metaphorically size up the inner state.

Besides dating a day's writing, I like to title it according to the mood of the listening state. Usually, and this fascinates me, I won't title days as I go along, but only in retrospect, as if I need to feel like that day has coalesced into an understanding; I'll go back a week in the journal, or whatever distance it takes, and give the titles. In another notebook, where I keep only dream titles with a brief statement, I can juxtapose day titles. A sort of personal computer system of reference. A title that applies

*directly to the mood-photograph rivets my memory to the day instantly,
like a familiar smell.*

&

Summer 1985 / A Clean Clutter is the Canyon

Restless baby, breathing the breaths of sleep. Beyond, rumpled blanket,
clothes. Beyond, shelf. Super structure, the shelf, with a pair of infant socks
never worn. Jar, clutter, unused. The yellow plastic window overlooking the
pond between canyon walls is dusty, dirty; a tattered moth is hanging from
one weak wing—the spider's triumph. Further yet, beyond horizontal beam
structure, brightness on a young maple, shadows on foreground, berry bushes. Clean clutter unnamable, the white leaning alder central in the sun. Green
spray of new branch and leaf streaming outward low on its trunk. The ferns
lean to it. The baby snores. Ah! How easy to put the baby to sleep by emptying the mind of all but observation.

Harmonies, various tonal bees are near me now as I sit on a pile of cedar in
the yard. Candyflower, berry blossom, pea vetch, who could ask for more?
Sparrow on the wheel, CHPPPing. Blue-jay as usual looking haughty and suspicious, head cocking vigorously, squawking and screeching in the compost
pile. The water falls, falls and runs constant. The children in the house talk
and hoot. The breeze moves leaves.

An uprooted buttercup catches my eye. In my mind, I hear Aemmer's voice
say "Ranunculus." Why? Inwardly I am straining at "WHY?", a long
anguishing wail, it might as well be. The breeze flutters leaves. Does the
breeze, then, make a flutter noise or does it make/*have* no noise? Can the
leaves sound like flutter alone?

Are all meanings interdependent. Are we alone or all-one.
That's not a question.
I am alone I said.
Sentimentality said it was an insult.

I wish to interrupt for a moment and explain that at the time of this writing I was in a very difficult relationship with a man; living with him imposed certain rules, such as never voicing my dissatisfactions. He often read my journals without invitation, and then accused me of writing negatively, or having nothing but complaints in reference to him. My writings often reflect the inhibitions imposed. But even though I've disguised my anxieties and troubles with the man/relationship, understanding the feelings in my journal is not out of reach. Inside, while putting the baby to sleep (although it is subtle), I am actually mourning to some degree the inability to raise our standard of living above squalor. I probably feel like the moth hanging from a tattered wing. I try to focus outside on the natural order and cleanliness of nature, the potential hope of sun shining on a singular tree. I fear to name why I am wailing "why?" inwardly, but I mention the breeze, or perhaps time and the certainty of change. The always-falling water, my desperation over a changeless situation, the questions: are my turmoils caused by the partner, like the breeze causing leaves to have sound, or is the turmoil inherent within me?

In the next selection, my outward observation steps in to deliver an interesting message.

October 1987 / Blue Lips

I am sitting in the yard in the sun. I'm thinking about the dream I had last night. It was Halloween. I kept searching for a costume. One woman had a pile of blueberries in front of her on the table. She dipped her head down into them. It was magic. Her head went right through the table. Then her head rose up through the blueberries as if she were coming out of an immersion in water. The berries had turned into marbles and made a nice sound tumbling away from her face. When she came up, the marbles were attached to her face as part of her costume, but especially pronounced were her lips of solid blue marbles.

M. jokes about me having tight, blue lips, or that he will buy me blue lipstick because he thinks my lips would look more natural if they were blue. It is his image for what he feels is a narrow, conservative nature in me because I "disallow" him to behave in the ways he wants to behave (actually, it's because I am not able to stifle hurt feelings and a look of disapproval regarding his relationships with other women). I do not disagree that it is an apt image for me, but I see the image as one expressing my silence, passivity, and inability to express myself, especially with M. I feel that my mouth is constricted, that I don't move my lips very much when I talk. When I speak I am self-conscious about my mouth, it feels tight and dry.

A bee just came by and deposited a strange-looking worm on my notebook. Air-delivery...but I don't see what it has to do with this particular writing. As I examine the worm I see it is paralyzed, but not stiff, cold or dead. And the humming bee, with its warm vibrato, is assuring me of this. The worm is an inch worm. I can possibly inch my way out of my crypt of silence slowly and smally, sneaking out. Why else would a bee come and drop a worm on me if it is not to be used?

M. refers to me as a "psychological" person. I *am* psychological. But what does that mean? For me it is that I have a drive to understand how another person comes to know or understand things—the individual process of grasping the essence of a meaning. Having my own visualization of how I see another person's inner process is my psychological nature. In order to understand things, I need to look at them long and carefully, what appears to be staring. This "staring" seems to be an absorbing. Even with books, I cannot just go along from one word to the next, connecting them all into a meaning, but I must also stare at the whole page awhile, or a few words, or one paragraph, dwelling, mulling, staring until it comes to birth. I know other people by staring at them, absorbing them. My "psychological nature" is not to take models and cheap power words and create an empire from them. It is to know people, things, and situations from their own deeper structures of process. Sometimes I even inwardly hold my body in the form that another person holds theirs, to try to feel how they feel to themselves.

M. is dominant in his voice and postures and opinions. He is overpowering, to put it mildly. His volume is loud and persuasive, insistent. When mastery is what he wishes, not merely the point where he actually stands, all the words and meanings coming from him are only to underline his mastered opinion, to enhance the figure of himself as something to respect. This powerful type of personality that needs a superior, knowledge-containing position is hard to talk to. He is not allowed to hear what a lesser opiner (me) tries to offer. Nothing penetrates the thick hide that is already thinking about what his counter-opinion will be. In his own words, he told me, "I do not TOLERATE sloppy language. I EXPECT people to make sense of what they say. Yes, I AM hard on people who cannot define their words."

Is "hard on" sexual terminology? When he demands that another's language be whipped into a shape that will satisfy him, is he not possibly raping the other's sense/way of knowing, with this hard-on approach? He's like a big Shelob spider coming down his tunnel to devour the meaning out of my words by demanding that I change my mode of expression or my choice of words, or that I continue to define them until he is satiated. That is, until I have defined away the soul essence, the love of the meaning that I chose the words to clothe, and ended with naked words with no soul, but which please Shelob because they are then empirically sensible in his structure. How can I maintain my soul and meaning as he tries to spin Shelob's web with only his specifics?

This strict language requirement is confining and altering. It does not allow my meanings passage. A barrier is erected. The Shelob nature has me analyzing every word I might utter with fear before letting it pass through the rictus of my forbidding lips. In the dream, the marbles made a sensually nice sound as the woman's head rose up out of their depths. I was looking for a costume, a way to represent myself, or disguise myself. A mouth made of blue marbles (blue associated with my passionate self) is a playful metaphor. Play at speech. Learning how to speak, the psychology of articulation. A costume of pretending I can speak articulately. A one-time game, Halloween, takes the focus off the fear of "I can't."

19 September 1990 / Traveler

The day is sharp and clean, and I too. A late, hot sun for September. I am pleased when I and my companions face the day with open, satisfied minds. T. is driving; we're taking my sons to the dentist.

Going past Center, it crosses my mind: how to stay a traveler in your own town, your every day after day routine where it all tends to banality? Take Center—the hub of nowhere. Now if I were in Mexico, and hopped off the bus in an enchantingly named place like "Center", only to discover that the crossroads led four ways into nothing, centered at a long-abandoned store that once sold only the most heinous of pretend foodstuffs at wildly swollen prices, I would find it very funny. One town is eight miles away to the south, the other twelve miles to the north; the other two roads meander through cow-fields and rural residences.

I thought of it on this bright day when I feel brand new as we pass Center in the car, and outside the empty Center store is a very well-dressed woman in nylons and heels, her hair sprayed and face made up. I imagine that she just stepped off the Greyhound. She's from France, traveling America by bus. She says, "Oh Center! I must step out and see this bit of Washington." Ha ha.

T. and I talk about movies and books. I say how successful Margaret Atwood is with *The Handmaid's Tale* because I can't stand to read it, it repels me. Not because of the idea, or plot necessarily, but because the atmosphere is so successfully bleak. T. asks if *1984* bothered me, or *Eraserhead*. No, they didn't. Atwood's bleak is much too much like my own internal bleak. T. mentions how affected he was by the movie *Under the Volcano*. I ask if reading *The Handmaid's Tale* ever came back to haunt him. He says no, it did not bother him that much. Then I recall enjoying *Under the Volcano*, but not finding it emotionally, or disturbingly affecting, whereas I couldn't get beyond page thirty in *The Handmaid's Tale*. I realize then that T. and I have been most affected by what we identify with. He was a drinking man when he first saw *Under the Volcano*. When I feel grim and down, the world is a gray, bleak, collapsing ugliness.

With Yeti at the dentist. He is so exuberant, so happy. I can't remember him being so light and cheery. He just loves his first year in school. I am enjoying watching and listening to him. I have missed him...missed living with him, being his mother in the daily sense.

I am the Mexican in Port Townsend today, sitting on this bench waiting for Yeti to see the dentist, watching passers-by as if seeing them for the first time, perhaps with tons of "Hamacas" strung over their shoulders, or brightly colored dresses swirling around the ankles of the women, babies tucked in their shawls.

24 September 1990 / Superstition

The witch was here today.

I'm suspicious now. She asked if I will have another baby. Although my mouth says lightly, "I'm not planning on it!," I feel like a liar. I can't help noticing that a dark corner of my mind darts over to the fact that my period is a little late... "A little late," I say to myself, "only ten days, she says...she who is as regular as clockwork." Up to now I've allowed the lateness to be shrugged into the background; I've been too careful to consider pregnancy as more than a very thin possibility. But *she* asked me, and she touches awake my most superstitious reactions. The very last time I connected with her for at least as long as today, things were right on the edge with M.; I had just clarified to myself that I definitely must leave him, when she called me on the phone. My adrenaline whooped up; I was fascinated with wonder that I lied my way through the entire conversation: everything was fine, we were all getting along perfectly well. It was only a matter of three or four months after that call that I made my move. All of this glares in my mind. I can no longer avoid imagining the possibility of pregnancy.

30 September 1990 / Working With What I Have

There is an acute state of observation that allows me to be confirmed and corrected by the environment immediately around me. It is tied into something I'm very good at: working with what I have. These thoughts circulated while I built a porch today—a spontaneous launching-into, accomplished in one hour. While I built it I remembered the porch I built two years ago, and how I moved only a few weeks after building it and had to tear it down. And now, when I am actively planning on a move, soon, I build one anyway because I want one today. It affirms that I am working with what I have—not only the punk materials I used (firewood blocks and ancient naily two-by-fours), but that I can't demand success in moving, can't insist on finding the right and affordable place, and can't count on it being soon at all. If I must stay here, I'll have to work with what I have anyway.

When I woke up at 7:30 P.M. my period had begun. Part of the certainty that I would have to move soon was the suspicion of possible pregnancy; having built the porch today, perhaps, was a sign of my body knowing I was not, and I would have enough time here for using a porch. I was imagining how to tell T. when he arrived for his 8 P.M. lunch break. I got as far as "Guess what..." and had repeated only that much a few times in my imagination. When T. arrived, even as he was still stepping through the door, he said, "Guess what? Evil is afoot, red tide!" Of course he meant at the oyster hatchery we both work at...but imagine how I took it? I could have used that very same sentence to say my period had started, and we no longer need to consider a surprise pregnancy.

How do I feel? Strangely, very interested. Interested in the week when I was convinced I must be pregnant, and the way T. and I adjusted to that probability. Wondering what purpose there might be for that week of living in a complete state of certainty. There is a lot of power in being able to accept truth and reality just as it comes to me. I went through the fears, insecurities, and vulnerabilities of thinking I was pregnant, and then moved on to acceptance and some degree of pleasure. Now there is some disappointment, but also an equal measure of relief. I'm very interested in the equal ease I have had adjusting to either truth. Freedom is knowing I can accept whatever gets thrown my way. The porch says to take things one day at a time, work with what I have, take things as they really are. Thoughts of pregnancy give rise to an expression of the feminine, not easily expressed by me.

1 October 1990 / Night Ghosts

It is the hour of three in the morning...lunch break in the hatchery. When I sit in the break room, the hatchery seems so much louder, OUT THERE, when I am no longer an integrated, moving part of the water flows, boilers, buzzing lights, food pumps kicking on and off.

There are ghosts tonight. A shouting ghost within twenty feet of me. I had an armful of larvae screens, slowly lowering myself at the knees to set them down by #L6, when the high-pitched "Hi!" sounded. Not the hi of a hello, but a very surprised, step-on-the-cat sort of hi. I looked around a bit, thinking Pam might have come down. Not a soul. I even went to glance in the parking lot to see if any cars were there. Eric was busy in the algae lab, and he's not sneaky enough to have fooled me anyway.

Outside, the moon is stretching out. At the rate it's going it will be full by morning. The temperature has really dropped this week. The setting tanks that are twenty-seven degrees centigrade are steaming into the night. When I passed the dip tank on the bulkhead, I knocked against the side of it like I often knock the tanks, and it knocked back after I'd passed. I turned to look. Nothing.

The moon reminds me again that my period has begun, reminding me of the dream last night of "Priming the Goat." Goats are being taken out of violin and guitar cases. They seem to be two-dimensional, but when they are set up with their instruments, they are alive, three-dimensional musicians. I step inadvertently on one of the cases to see how the goats are placed inside, to see how they can possibly survive this way if they are real. A female goat holds her jaw up against a table, waiting passively for me to pour a whole gallon of water down her excessively long and skinny throat, as I am directed to do. In the background a woman's voice says, "that goat was flayed at the vagina, you know, and is looking up at you out of her own vagina." Although the dream does not really show or say so, I had some glimmering feeling when I woke up that I was supposed to reach down through that throat and pick something golden and circular out of the stomach of the goat. The whole process seems violent and somehow pains me, makes me queasy, but I'm supposed to do it, and so I do.

How have I been looking out through my hormones during the week? All the premenstrual alias pregnant illusions. The goat is animal, is a nursing-mother mammal, has communicative, feeling eyes, personality, vulnerabilities. The stomach is to digest and assimilate, and the womb, too, is located nearby. It may have been the womb. Prime the mammal and remove the message? To prime something is to get it flowing again, it assumes what normally flows freely has been blocked and now does not have enough of its own natural fluid to begin flowing on its own. It's no mystery that my feminine expression does not flow freely.

Why were the goats taken out of musical instrument cases? They were both prop/tool/instrument and living beings. What is "encased" may or may not be real. In what way is my feminine nature contained to keep it in a static, two-dimensional state, as the goats are when in their cases? When they are taken out, they can play music and sing. I am also reminded of the portrait I drew awhile back: a woman pregnant with a rather malicious-looking centaur. It was supposed to represent how I feel about my feminine qualities being oppressed by a troublesome Animus. Is the Animus the thing to be plucked out of the stomach, freeing me to "flow" with some natural, uninhibited female characteristics? The stomach digests and assimilates, separates poisons and allocates the direction to send nutrients. Is the Animus a poison to pluck out once I have primed the feminine? If he is a golden circle then he must have his value. Mentioning the Animus, I remember there were three sections to the dream.

First I am in my childhood town of Astoria. I am to meet T. for dinner. When I come out of the store I'm shopping in, it is unexpectedly dark outside. The streets are empty, all the stores are closed and dark, and it feels threatening. I decide to try to get to the library since it is only three blocks away and might be open. I see a man across the street, only from the knees down, but he wears black jeans and ominous black-and-chain pointy toe boots. This is definitely an atmosphere as bleak as Atwood's book. This is the premenstrual paranoia, threatening atmosphere, the worst of gloomy fears and negative expectations enveloping me.

In the second part of the dream, I am given a gift from a woman. It is a long and narrow book about Tarot cards called *The Golden Phoenix*. T. asks why it should cost nine dollars, it is old and wrinkled, and not such great content. Somehow the woman has my driver's license and other personal effects of mine between the pages that she is returning. I try to look grateful and pleased because it is a gift, but the book seems superficial to me, too. I tell T. it is full of platitudes, silly and sentimental. When I open the book to a page, it shows a horse falling from the sky, his testicles exposed…a card representing something masculine made vulnerable.

The book is long and narrow, like the goat's throat. It is a gift from a woman whom I "identify" with...she has my personal identification. Golden reappears as a book title. But excitedly, I notice the horse (Centaur/Animus?) is made vulnerable. Not exactly silly, sentimental, platitudinal work, this. T. may represent in the dream how easily I agree with the masculine point of view, even though a careful look at the book belies my response. Also, the phoenix is a bird of rebirth and transformational powers. A very loud clarion to make me note the week of submersion into things wholly feminine.

If the goats were packed into instrument cases and only taken out for a gig, then might I think of my own feminine nature as something of a prop that I only pull out on occasion, like motherhood? When I went to look into the cases to see how the goats were packed in, I had to step on the case and it made me feel queasy. Pregnancy, and the thought of pregnancy, makes me feel queasy. What contains the feminine may be pregnancy. What inhibits the feminine may be the Animus/Centaur depicted in the womb of the drawing.

I am always compelled to tighten up the finishing thoughts about a dream and its connections to living. But the truth is that the dream is never truly done but always in movement. The questions and airing-out of all the potential angles is the only importance...dancing with it. The night of ghosts at the hatchery confirms me. Intuitively I know better than to hunt for them. I looked a bit just to acknowledge their hoots and knocks were not lost on me. The answer is to glimpse scantly. To end up with more questions than answers is...what? Glimpse scantly; it moves.

The Phenomenologic Journals
1984–1988

Phenomenologic attention is to track inwardly the meandering thoughts, fantasies, daydreams, and visions passing through your mind, while outwardly noticing what your body is doing at the time of the thoughts. It is to note what other people's gestures, bodies, faces and voices are doing, recollecting what shifts in mood and thought occur in you while interacting, as well as any reaction to signals from the environment. It takes a disciplined attention, a choice, to follow these movements. Most often, they are movements we make all the time, but they are interpreted instantly, hence the movement itself is forgotten.

While compiling notebook selections for the Phenomenological Journal study, the work shaped itself into the story of a relationship. This relationship and the conflict inherent in it is what inspired, or demanded, the phenomenologic attention in me to begin with; focus on the relationship through this attention was primary for a few years. I have cooperated with the story that wants to be told, so some of the following writing does not strictly adhere to phenomenology in order not to disturb the flow. The relationship was one of continual struggle and conflict. To say it was a struggle does not say it was devoid of love, or without good work done...good work centered on the raising of six children. In many ways the relationship was largely responsible for helping me develop integrity, values, a sense of competence, and responsibility for myself. Although I have represented the partner in some hard tones, it is not my intent to judge the man described. Only he can judge himself from the vantage point of his personal vision, which I was never able to fully comprehend or share. The following pages are from my point of view, with all my weaknesses, emptiness, and struggle exposed. It was a relationship of fire, and I have gratitude for the iron forged in my soul from that period of time.

Following, the journal speaks for itself without interruption.

ℬ

7 November 1984

There are vivid visual earth energies today. A powerful wind, not terribly strong, but intense and ever-present. Yellow maple leaves are thrown everywhere, and they fly around my head in spirals. I am down in a hole. The toilet hole I'm digging is four feet deep. Of course my notebook is down here with me. The yellow leaves over my head, the silence of the woods...and by silence I mean no human noise, I guess, because there are multitudes of delicate sounds. When I hear the kids playing across the canyon from here, as I'm down in my hole, I feel so removed, so secretly animal. I imagine this is what it is like when a coyote, raccoon, deer, or quail happen by, cock their heads toward our human noises in a frozen moment. I feel like that, and guarded, when outside...hidden in nature by being part of it. The sky is platinum, slate gray. A muted rainbow has been splashed against it...a kid painted it there when the paints were still wet, it's all so hazy, ready to run and spread shapelessly.

The pick was stabbing into the hardpan. A good swing to bite into it, first the four corners of my square hole, then work toward the center standing first at one side then the other, as deep as possible into the clay. Then shovel out all the loose stuff until I have a nice clean floor to start picking again. I stopped to write when I suddenly attended to the flow of my thoughts while picking and shoveling. I was thinking about the current dilemma, the relationship between M. and Elsid becoming complex with her pregnancy. I am trying to pick and shovel my mind for a solution, a solution for my own hard feelings. Thinking: as long as the "I" who has problems that need change is the same "I" who is planning the change, and the "I" putting the change into being—then no change at all is going to occur. The "I" itself must change. No plan for detailed behaviors will succeed unless I can miraculously change "I"—the root.

Standing down in this hole, I wasn't really aware of this sentence going on of its own dialogic energy. Actually, I was remembering a day on the playground in Astoria when I was five or six. I was staring into the huge cedar tree in the corner of the playground, wondering what I would be like when I was "old" (mid-twenties). I was aware, then, of the "root". I can trace the feel of that root and know how everything begins and ends with it. Unless that basic core is free of its structures-that-define, it cannot change. I need to look at the core that I began with, remember that aware and complex child, instead of looking at the artifact of the structure currently around me, instead of the definition of myself through circumstance. The pleasure and humor of the memory as I question in the way I did as the child, who could feel herself as "serious" or "introspective" without knowing the words, the meaning, no self-conscious explanation or conception that *others* perceived me by these terms…I simply *felt* that way, no words. How did this child shape me? This me at twenty-six who can still *feel* the same feeling of "serious and introspective" that defines me, now that I have words, and have the mirroring humanity defining me. The feeling of comradeship I feel toward that child, laughing with her as past meets present: we pass one another, patting each other on the shoulder in recognition. Yes, child, I acknowledge and answer your beseeching question sent out into the future…and here I am. I am "different". Remember? With all of your intensity, you made an oath to that cedar tree to be different…but it is not what you expected, is it? Or did you have any expectation? Why such a fierce oath, child? What have you gotten me into? That lonely child who demanded something different…and I keep beginning to learn how I might possibly fulfill it. It reminds me to listen attentively to my children whom I underestimate with the handicap of being an adult—to remember that they also have strong identities, and full, complete perceptions and awareness. Nothing is lost. Everything is all-important, going into their building memories, shaping perception. There are no dull edges in children.

I have a dilemma. M. asked that the three of us discuss how we should regard Elsid's pregnancy. But the two of them have already discussed it yesterday while I was away, have come to agreements and decisions. Today would be a remouthing to achieve my consent, and probably a rewording to make it sound agreeable to me. M. is a master at creating a different version of a reality for every different person in order to get them to cooperate with a plan he already intends to implement. I know I have no real choice, so I am out here with my hands in the dirt, down in the hole, voiceless, refusing to cooperate in the only way I can…withdrawal. To stand out here in this hole in the rain long enough to forget my name and humanity, start walking into the woods, keep walking, climbing, eating earth, until my clothes rot off and my hide thickens to tolerate the weathers. How I long for that! To not have any memory of being connected to things that bring me back into the structure of my personality: family, house interiors, keeping warm, cups of coffee and food. If a child yelled for me right now from across the canyon, I would laugh silently to myself and secretly not answer; gone, dissolved into a leafy hole, just another bit of organic material out in the woods. If I could do this—dissolve the connecting structure that makes me Ja, a mother, a partner, the cook and cleaner, and on to the deeper attachments of being inwardly complex and motivated for deep study...would there be no more me? Therefore, solution? M.'s meeting is a prop, not a sincere and truthful approach to me. So I am out here working on a toilet (a place to put all his shit), daydreaming about being part of these wordless, wild woods. Helplessly, I know I have to come out of this, back to verbal manipulations. I will be driven back by my own paranoia, by my wanting to know what is going on; my voice will strive to interject that I can't live with a second wife-type being pregnant in the house where I am the mother. I want a new structure for myself to be able to deal with this. I will label it "fanaticism" and leave it at that, because I understand what that means. And, honesty by the minute. But, my doubts about the success of this are as deep as this toilet hole I'm standing in and will soon be just as full of shit.

15 December 1984

I'm high because the winter sky is high, because the frozen landlock is more full of life than the rotting fall. When I feel really good like this my eyes turn to the earth. I breathe differently, as if the air was the magical essence responsible for my at-one-ness. It's my birthday, the time of assessment. My focus— to be satisfied. "Compost is god," is the way I phrased it when I walked through the frozen garden this morning. Compost is god means to be satisfied with the real as the real really is. I breathed the air and stared at the compost, I was god and that was that. There is a synchronicity alive in writing a letter recently, explaining to a friend that my birth name had been "Janet", which stood for Ja and Nyet and the balance of the yes and no. I've been Nyet all my life, and now is the time for the Ja. When Usana and Eressea were toddlers they named me *Ja*, for their own reasons, perhaps being much more perceptive to future changes than the rest of us. I recall the birthyear focus last year. I visualized a very demanding conscious challenge—and it came about almost immediately after my birthday. I feel so overwhelmingly as if I failed it—Elsid is the epitome of that challenge. Not Elsid herself, but the relationship between her and M., and really, the challenge of communicating honestly about it with M. I know I failed the challenge because what I expected of myself was not what my action really was. I'll find out about Ja this year, eh? The way out of failure is through Ja, through compost, satisfaction toward what I expect of myself rather than what M. expects. I will live up to my stringent need of what *I* can admire in myself.

21 December 1984

I'm lying in bed, very tired, but it's only ten. M. is in the sauna with a bottle of wine, celebrating the equinox alone. It's been a hard month…since he made an oath not to have sex with Elsid anymore, and yet she lives in our home…great tension. He also hasn't had sex with me, and I haven't missed it. I think I often screwed him to keep him from going to her, only… Elsid comes into the house with clean clothes…to take a sauna. "That is allowed," M. said with great wrath yesterday, though I hadn't said anything. "Phony vanity over nudity," he said. "A person I had a child with, we shouldn't be condemned about seeing each other nude." I've never disagreed with M. when he uses his voice of wrath, of demand, of insistence…it is a voice that says THIS IS THE WAY IT'S GOING TO BE!!!!!! I was almost asleep, but now I am strainingly awake. I am straining at the feelings of doubt, mistrust. I am supposed to trust M.—the greatest sin in his eyes is to call him a liar by doubting him. I am straining at listening hard…I can't hear anything anyway, but can't help myself. A half hour has passed, and still I listen. But now a terrible adrenaline has come into my chest…I might have a heart attack, I am breathing so shakily, so poisoned by adrenaline. I intuitively feel that they are screwing in the sauna. Of course I don't believe myself—M. has promised, and that would be insane while I am right above the sauna in bed. But I can't shake it, and the adrenaline still pumps after ten minutes of trying to rationalize it away. Finally, against every tendency of mine in the history of this relationship, I actually intend to go right down and go into the sauna. I can always pretend I woke up and decided to take a sauna with them if I am wrong, but I have to know, I can't stand not knowing anymore. Why else would I have this crazy adrenaline. I go down very quietly. There are no voices, and I realize this is what seemed so suspect. I open the curtain and walk right in. Elsid is straddling M. and they are in a very intense moment of heated activity. I stand and look directly at them, calmly, until they both look at me. I am not a prude. I am not emotional or angry, and I want them to look long at me because this event means something else far more important than caring about their sexual interludes. They look at me and freeze, they look down. M. says an "oh no" sort of thing, and his mouth makes a face of frustration, of misfortune. Elsid hurriedly climbs off him looking shamed. I leave the room and wait in the outer room. And then I cry, but not for the reasons they obviously think. I cry because inwardly something is collapsing that is so painful, so crushing, and I know it can never again be erected. M. comes out and insists that Elsid will have to leave, not live here anymore. Let's all go to bed and not discuss it, and she will find somewhere else to live as soon as she's back from Christmas at her parent's home. No, I say, we will talk now, talk while my feelings are immediate, real, and justified, talk while Elsid is witness; yes, Elsid must leave, not because they have had sex, but because the relationship between M. and me is up in the air and we need the space to find out if we're going to make it or end it…something we can't do with the continual distraction of Elsid's presence that causes a sideline of unending tension. I tell M. I cry because I have walked through the tarot card "The Tower" just now, and the edifice that is thrown and crumbling is my image of him, our relationship based on the past image that has just met its death. I tell him I cry because he cannot make it change by saying he is sorry, that nothing can change the effects of this that I finally have: proof. Proof, his demand that I supply it to support my "negative" feelings. Proof that he can lie, can be dishonest, can sneak about saying one thing and doing another. His only excuse is that it is not a lie because he was going to tell me tomorrow. I give him the wilting look he deserves. But I am not against either of them. The crushing pain I feel is loss of image, a tremendous fear that I am not going to like M. now that the image that made him special to me has been whisked away. It is so shocking to be without it.

January 1985

I have to begin to look at M. and myself realistically. Humanly. I have to come to terms with the thing that carries this relationship, the fear and idolization of M. when I was a teenager; my impulsive pregnancy that trapped me with my born and bred tendency to loyalty, which in these days is becoming as senseless as anything can be. My self-imposed slavery and meekness in the face of his emotional demands, let alone household demands, is bordering on the insane. When I try to tell M. anything...my feelings, my sense of injustice about the division of labor and money for household needs, he somehow always convinces me I'm wrong, talks his way out of having anything to do with it, demands proof that my "accusations" are correct. Somehow he carries it on and on, one proof further away until it's in the realm of the unprovable. I walk away in disgust and giving up, a dark fog rolling off my back as I walk away...the fog is the feeling of giving up, pouring off me like tears I can't muster, like the screams I can't open my throat for. And somehow, I *am* convinced he is right because I don't have empirical proofs of the kind he asks; I am walking away to await a moment of pure proof that will be so directly in his hands he won't be able to deny it. And at that point, years of unprovables will tumble off the burden on my back into his lap. He will be guilty of all.

6 April 1985

I have my head on your chest. You are talking into the dark. I can see in my mind the pained expression on your face, customary to this type of monologue. Sincerity=Pain? Your voice in your chest...the feelingness of the topic causes half of each sentence to come out in a breathy way, as if enclosed in a yawn. I am listening as much to this tenor, to your voice as the ancient music I have known for years, as the words. The comfort, the meaning of love perhaps, to feel I know you because this voice is so deep in my knowledge patterns. You're talking about Elsid. When I finally venture out with a suggestion, a defensiveness returns. You don't want to know any ways out, not from me...I could say so many things. Offer ways of neutrality. But you are trapped and can't accept them, afraid to know them. And myself, I am getting stronger in my position. I hear that in you and withdraw. At the moment, a suggestion was in order. The moment passed and I let it go—a great achievement. To let go of the expectation of results. Results from you. From anyone else. This is what I'm working on: not expecting anything from anyone, focusing on finding out what I want, how I can achieve it, and making the moves. I do not want to be concerned about the results of your actions, I do not desire control.

15 April 1985

I can feel you (down in Olympia, my fantasies of you with Elsid. She moved there one week before you started school there, and that fact is not lost on me, though you talk of "rights to move wherever a person wishes to live"). You teach me not to trust feelings like this. You rage against my imaginings, even though they have been borne out a dozen times…and the one provable time. If there is any assault on me by you, the most grievous is that you have taught me to doubt myself, mistrust my intuitions…the intuitions and insight that truly reside in my feet, the way I know the world and walk through life. If I can't trust the knowledge of my intuition then I am a cripple, relying on you to tell me what everything means. I am gloomy, melancholy. I can see my intuition turning green with decay. It needs my trust. It is my primal function and I throw it away for you. You can lose people without leaving them or them leaving you, you know. You can lose me without separation. That is what is happening, and I am horrified that you can't even see it, so busy trying to straddle the line with Elsid, trying to maintain a picture for me that I will approve of, though I tell you I can't trust you anymore and it doesn't matter what you tell or don't. Thinking that if you adhere to "my rules" about a relationship with her it will be enough, even if you are not actively relating with quality to me and our children. There are subtleties, you know? You're too busy to notice. Hidden behind your evening beer and saunas, behind constant study. Being home is what you count as time with us, even if you are not involved with us in any way. With Elsid you take an hour off and give her direct attention, rationalizing that she only gets a few hours of your time a week. That's a few hours a week more than this family gets. You don't notice or care what is lacking in this relationship. My trust is rebelling, my trust knows intuition is waiting with the direct truth you don't offer. Every day that I open up the intuitive window is another day of strength, another day that the gulf between us widens. If you can't hear me, or see it for yourself, I cannot help you to reclaim the lost ground. One day I'll be too far away to call back. In my mind we are still freshly from the sauna incident, we are building the possible future…therefore we are in a serious quick decline because you've already forgotten—you think you have done, and are doing, enough.

2 June 1985

When M. met me he was overwhelmed by his own swiftly branching philosophy. The movement of it was "love". It created a certain personality in him. Right now he is similarly overwhelmed by his growing expanding philosophy. However, now the movement of it is conflict. The pain, the frustration, the feelings of failure in the Elsid situation, have contributed to the driving force in the all-encompassing present philosophy. Pain is where his energy arises from, and from failure.

That I cannot disassociate my role in that failure and pain, and that his overall philosophy centers where his vision has failed, locks me into a difficult self image. All of his current expressions center around pain. I'm in a "giving-up" feeling because that is a focus on my failure as well—by disallowing him to handle the Elsid situation...by means of having the feelings I really have.

This expression of failure has pushed him and created the axis of his present life. Everything turns on it. Likewise, it turns on my failure. What I did to M. by not-doing. It's like living every day being grieved that his relationship with Elsid wasn't a success. The only avenue of success available was a two-wife situation, and three people in bed...which I tried more than once. His main focus now is at direct odds with *me*, by my honest position of not being able to provide this. I am antagonist; he makes no other role available for me in the way his play is written. I am the dark area, the sin, the insane... How can he ignore and deny the position I'm trapped into, and doesn't he see I won't be able to live with it long? He thinks he can just say to me, "that's not true!" in a demanding voice and I will be appeased. Somehow it doesn't work.

4 August 1987

We are trying to find common footing in a long-term disagreement. I am attempting to explain how I see, how I understand, thinking if I give my language some structure and connection points it would help. I get excited. I tell M. that being introspective and processing information in an intuitive way is different from his approach. I have convoluted mazes where I absorb a wholeness of what is understood, and then simply feel that "I know", but cannot define it in the structured language he demands. He asks me where intuition fits in, in terms of long-term memory, the unconscious, and awareness. I don't know how to explain it to him other than that it's a tone that resonates into understanding. He says—insists, rather—that intuition does not exist because if a thing has one foot in the unconscious it can't exist: unconscious=unreal.

The conversation falls through here. I feel the reality of intuition in my way of understanding. I get defensive, my brow heats up, and I do not want to be convinced that my thinking does not exist since much of it is an open door to the unconscious realm. I watch the physical changes. I drop the subject, lighten up, say something humorous, put my hand on his knee. I am not going to listen to a lecture that attempts to correct my view of understanding myself. I am breathing in a way that relieves my frustration at feeling unrespected. This is the message of my body language. M.'s breathing is deeper. The exhales are deeper and louder than the inhalations. He swivels away from me, back turned, shoulders hunched, eyes squeezed closer together. He is frustrated, bordering on anger. He isn't going to let go of it. He rejects me by physical removal. I glance at him, feel disappointed that he doesn't recognize the impasse and let it go. I turn away too, talk to a friend nearby, covering up disappointment with banter. I don't want the friend to catch the mood of tension. (Later the friend asks M. what he is having a temper tantrum over, what he is sulking about. "I am not sulking!" he snarls, and goes to talk to someone across the room. Later I listen for an hour about what a total asshole this friend is.)

5 August 1987

We are sitting on M.'s bed, his hand on my chest under my shirt. The conversation shifts to my ideas about Tarot. He asks, "What are you searching for? Where does the information come from? That's not your unconscious, that's your ego...ego gratification is the only purpose for your use of Tarot...." His voice is rising in authority tones. My answers are inadequate, and make him affect a lecture voice. His hand on me at this point is suddenly repelling; I feel nauseous. I watch this shift in my emotions with interest. I had been feeling very mellow, casually talking…and then the sudden shifting, feeling the pull of my own room, wanting to go study, not wanting his touch, his proximity. I never feel M. is "right" or "wrong", or that I am either, simply that I understand differently and want the right of my own beliefs. He seems to be saying that once I begin to think like him I will have "real" knowledge. Why else would he be angered by my not agreeing with him?

7 August 1987

Last night M. and I were finishing up some french fries in the tavern. Kim came by to pick up our baskets, so I hurriedly threw in all the crumpled napkins on the table, and my two empty sour cream containers. M. still had some fries. Kim left. M. stared at me, bristling. "Why did you do that?" he asks in a seething, hissing voice.
"What?"
"Throw *my* sour cream away! I'm not done!"
I remembered for sure that I'd thrown napkins away, one being near his sour cream, and believed I saw Kim pick it up. But he said he SAW me pick it up intentionally and throw it away. He puts ketchup in his basket and angrily jabs his fries into it. On the way home I feel angered and disappointed that he would be such an asshole over such a trivial event, so I don't speak to him.

He speaks to me and I answer that I can't believe he could get so worked up over missing sour cream. He accuses me of hanging on to such mickey mouse bullshit and starts to drive very fast, hunched over the steering wheel, breathing loudly through his nose. My hands tighten on my seat, I stare out the dark window and feel sick to my stomach…I shake my head as though shrugging off the stupidity of this life. I accuse him of being mickey mouse to begin with instead of just getting more sour cream, and who cares who or if someone is at fault; is it worth introducing such anger into the environment? He says, "NO! You are being mickey mouse to have to talk about it." I give up. I make a long breath of giving up. If only my heritage didn't include "giving up" as a nearly suicidal shrug of complete apathy that makes every last coal grow cold.

11 August 1987

M. and I are riding in the car to the beach. I am completely gone, absorbed, looking out the window.

M.: Why are you frowning?

Me: I am not frowning, I'm thinking.

He: You are definitely frowning.

Me: (Snappish.) Frowning and thinking are the same!!

The impatient and snappy tone of voice is out of place, combined with the emphatic statement made. It is true, but I wonder why after I say it. Thinking for me is a visual process, an internal scanning of a plane of existence. I have to concentrate, squint inwardly to observe the movements there. It roves through time, colors, dreams and feeling blobs that mean some-thing…and then, I am also a stickler for minute, or more appropriately true, microscopic detail.

14 August 1987

M. jokingly calls up to my room, "what will happen during the convergence?"

Me: I don't know.

He: Don't you think you should consult your Tarot cards and find out?

Me: No. I don't have any interest in that.

He: (Smarmy, patronizing voice.) You should know what's happening at the end of the world.

Me: If it were a real energy shift, society might change its priorities and then there will be a place in the world for people like me…an appreciation for those who think and feel as I do, whose projects and studies would be valued and needed. Maybe then I would be completely normal.

Up to now I have been humoring him with a banal, sarcastic-jokingness…because he tries to make me out as a conformist, now in the "New Age" movement. I believe strongly in following only myself—compost and I are god is my belief. He knows it. He is lying in his bed 2½ floors down, and I sit at my desk at the top of the house—we're calling back and forth to each other. After I answer, he begins a typical response, and I automatically shift into listening to the punctuating words and the song of his voice:

"You will NEVER be a psychologist, you will NEVER be a counselor of ANY kind, you'd be NOGOOD at that whatsoever…BUSINESS MANAGE-MENT, BUSINESS MANAGEMENT is what YOU COULD DO really well you'd be REALLY GOOD at that. I THINK you should go into BUSINESS MANAGEMENT."

When he talks like this I involuntarily make silent noises of the familiar beat of his voice, my face taking on an unpleasantly mocking expression. Each sentence looks like large square blocks descending into smaller squares, cycling over and over again—a beating by verbal squares. I tell myself how awful it is for me to imitate him in the secrecy of my room. The respectful female tells the self-centered female how awful this is, and the self-centered female giggles wildly. She has the upper hand these days, thinking only that she must protect the fledgling beginnings of *her own viewpoint* as valid, by blocking out the constant opinions of this loud and dominating man. The gig-gling one believes that this, in the long run, is healthier.

I call out, "Calm down! Calm down!" because once his pattern of lecture gets underway you can't fit a word in, you certainly can't talk above it; you can wait and listen, or run away. I make my voice calm and tinged with pleasant amusement (exactly replicating how he interrupts me…I am "matronizing"), a signal that I'm not mad or defensive, but calling for attention to my words: I'm focused right now in pursuing my ideals in my activities. I don't think there is anything wrong with finding a place for my passions first. If that doesn't work, I'll turn elsewhere. I am not going to drop my studies and embrace business management right now when I don't love it, and only like it as an occasional tool.

I think about the respectful and self-centered females, and as soon as I do they begin to move, and expose other sides that live in this relationship. The Dutiful Self…M. would call this one appropriately respectful of him, but respect seems to mean "do it and think it his way"…. The dutiful self does one or more of several things: shuts up, changes choices to appease him, reads the subtle signs of disapproval to base behavior on, listens and agrees even when listening has become a burden and a chore, compromises with a strongly stated viewpoint, goes outward toward him to comfort him, repress-ing her own feelings and thoughts. The Self-Centered Self tunes him out, argues viciously, tries to stay rational but avoids areas where contest is important to strongly held beliefs where she is sure to lose the rational battle, agrees with her voice but keeps secret her differing views if under attack, avoids topics or avoids M.

When I am really overwhelmed and negative and the voice music from M. is unbearably oppressive, the Self-Centered Self suggests I don't live with him anymore. The Mother Self leaps up in defense crying "Impossible!" and throws visions of deep love and intimate moments with the children, touching scenes between siblings who might lose one another. The Robotic Inner Self, tough as nails survivor, and head as thick as concrete in its tolerating abilities, tells me to wait calmly, to work on it, and it will protect my inner brightness while M. and I work on striking some balance. My Impulsive Angry Self prances around saying "that's too bad!," compulsively throwing clothes in a bag and driving off in a fury, screams back to shut up, refuses to talk about controversial subjects. The Hopeful Self visualizes some areas that might be good again and shows where they can be strengthened. That I can be strong in my viewpoint, listen to his respectfully, reiterating my own viewpoint rationally and unyieldingly without giving a fig whether he's able to take it that way or not. The Sentimental Self recalls a chain of good points that brought about union, and the growth since. The Pragmatic Self balances pros and cons of working with things just the way they are, recognizing the value of difficulty, the shaping of myself with, or in spite of, the negative pressure. It reminds me also that I do not strive for constant happiness or expect it. In fact, my Happy Peaceful Self reminds me over the top of Pragmatic's voice that I am happy. Happy is simply to be in a state of inner peace and connection with the earth, with no expectations, curious and open to anything that occurs as a signpost of direction. She is the most prevalent, at least always present on the inside observing, watching languidly and without terrible concern. She's content with living as it *really* comes across. At this point Fear and Near-Tears Upset Self pipes in and says, "What about me? The car quit running again yesterday and threw me into an uproar about having no money to fix it or the gas to drive the other breaking-down-car—I might not get to class at all this month! Three broken down cars, and only M. to fix one of them. Ha! How does the Content Self deal with that? She didn't invade me with peace and unconcern!" As soon as I write this, the Content Self comes in and passively settles over and suffocates the Near-Tears Self. "Yes, I will accept that too, who knows what adventure car troubles will lead me to. Everything is life and everything I do leads somewhere else and everywhere has value for me," she believes. The mulling over, staring out the window. The Disgusted Self reaches over and infects me with poisonous feelings of dislike for M. She can't even stand his smell anymore. His superiority, his disdain of humanity, his two-faced way of taking advantage of "friends" (and family for that matter). She sees that in his mad rush to teach me values, integrity and competence, he forgot to save any for himself. He's as sleazy as the worst of the people he puts down constantly. Inconveniently, she sends waves of negative feeling through me at most times these days, interfering with any friendly relationship. Sex has not existed for months. She imitates his self-important stance and makes faces behind his back. I try to counsel her into openness, respect, letting others be themselves, but she is dangerous to have around. She has her own opinion of her value, and doesn't think she has to take any shit. She has a hard time inspiring herself to show a love she no longer has. She paints an ogre's face over M.'s. The Smart Self tries to inject herself here, quietly. She shows me little tricks, like having a demeanor that *lends* rationality when I know I can't make my words compete with a logician. She keeps my demeanor cool, so the logician in M. seems to be ranting. Then she can walk away smoothly as if untouched, maintaining detached intelligence that does not seep down into a feeling center. She does some pretty good work...but she's weak and doesn't take a true stand, just defends. She's not as likely to jump in the fray as one of the others. The Baby Self pouts over being oppressed in conversation. She is sure she can never compete in the big time of the word-exchange. She's inexperienced at high level competition. She'll lapse into personal criticism, drag the conversation out of the logical realm and assert what she's feeling and interpreting. She is always easily slapped away by "you're wrong!" Too bad baby is so strong.

17 August 1987

Yesterday M. and I had such an honest, listening talk about how we relate, about how he offends me into secrecy and quiet, how paralyzed I had become around him because of his criticism, raucous laughter at my beliefs, sternly overriding my conversations, calling my ideas invalid, and making demeaning remarks hidden in a patronizing voice or his language itself a disguise for insult. As has happened so often before, I truly believe he has finally understood me and now things will be better! I believe I have finally found the right words and all our problems will be solved with the magic key of some words he can relate logically to.

Now I am studying in my room. M. comes up and lies on my bed and starts leafing through my dream journal. I feel instantly apprehensive. Moments later he is laughing raucously.

I stare at him fixedly. My heart sinks. I am saying in my mind, "please don't put me down, please don't criticize me today, please don't say anything insensitive when I am feeling good about you."

He rereads aloud what he laughed at. I feel very ashamed, invaded, as if it is stupid. In fact, it has something of spiritual content for me, although the language of it may be archaically corny, as active imagination experiences sometimes come across in dialogue.

M. is really laughing about a line he's just read to me. I am offended especially because we just talked about this very thing yesterday. It was exactly this condescending, invalidating, raping and exposing of my most personal center.

As if to console me—I am icily silent and staring at him in disbelief—he starts telling me I should be a writer (as if I'm not), that this is the stuff for great fiction or romance novels or mysteries (the commune with my soul—a romance novel!). I am shriveling up with a burning wrath for him. What a hopeless state of communication, or relationship! Toleration is the only blood left in this system, and my pump is breaking down.

Staring blankly. I am sitting nude in my herb garden in the sun, staring toward the kitchen-house, listening to Yeti laugh at cats. I am hurt and blank. Listening to M.'s music coming from the living room-house. The big mullein and mallow plants tower in my vision. A fly is on my spine. Conscious of myself in the same blurred way as the plants being "there" in my vision. I feel melancholy shifting into emptiness and melding with the mullein and mallow. I am wondering if M.'s tendency in his own inner thought, inner dialogue, is to cut off his emotion—to condemn it. He always accuses everyone of condemning him: his mother, his previous partner, me, even Elsid now. How he so perfectly mirrors his fear of condemnation, his hatred of it, onto me when it is I he is condemning...he just can't see this. Does his constant depression and dissatisfaction have to do with being self-condemned? Does he analyze, block out, and disallow his feeling? I am amused now, because sitting here so completely absorbed has apparently rendered me invisible. Eressea walks right past me and into the house and calls out for me toward my room. No answer, so she calls down to M. asking where I am.

Awhile ago I read to M. from a book, still trying to find the right words to prove to him that my way of thinking is valid, about hypnogogic phenomena being the antithesis to ego, that ego is not present during that stimulus. I do so because he keeps telling me that my interest in dreams, active imagination, and the rest of "my work" are all from my ego—that they make me feel important.

When I read the item he pulls away from me abruptly. He begins an authoritative lecture on why hypnogogic visions come directly from ego. I ask him after several minutes if he knows what hypnogogic phenomena is...because some of what he is saying simply has nothing to do with hypnogogia. He is terribly offended, and lectures and rants, and shows me definitely that he has no idea, but he has to be the authority so therefore I must be wrong. He is much too important to not know what a hypnogogic vision is.

While he goes on and on my train of thought has entirely left the station. I am thinking about all the years before Elsid when our relationship was smooth, if not really happy. I realize it was because I was still imitating my mother. The man is the boss. If I don't agree, I shut up. If we disagree, he is right. I was sensitive to approval and disapproval and acted on them to keep peace. Such as, when he pulls away physically it means disapproval and I should shut up, stop, I am using a dangerous approach or the topic is dangerous. I used to stop and shut up. Because of Elsid, because my image of him came crashing down, because I no longer idolize and idealize him, he is no longer the estimable boss.

A Phenomenological Framework of what is happening in conversations when mutually frustrated. My experience:

—Lips get tight
—Breathing gets more pronounced, labored
—Feel heat in my brow
—Eyes squint half way, feel pain emanating out of them
—A give-up feeling, like sweat springing out of my head
—Constriction in solar plexus
—Outward gasps of emotion…like throwing heart up through throat, beseeching him to not be so far out of reach
—Capacity to listen becomes short and shallow
—Desire to understand and absorb opinion becomes sparse
—My voice gets concise, mechanical, clipped, with downward emphases on ending words…wanting to end or close
—Black, deadening mood overwhelms me; I shut down, a voluntary catatonia
—Sometimes my voice becomes pleading, soothing
—Feeling of effort: to find words that will offer fitting explanation to lead to understanding
—Inwardly I am pleading…for an end, for an understanding, escape

Frustration observed in M.:

—Outward exhalations heavy and pronounced; inhalations unheard
—Shoulders hunched up and forward, and set
—Turns away, yanks body parts out of proximity
—Lips bunch up
—Eyebrows hunch down over eyes
—Eyes look snapping and blazing
—Nods head as if saying he expected as much from me, like I've schemed to anger him
—Voice sounds angry. Each word a huff and ending clip, volume rises, tone is lecture, amount of words increases and speeds up as if to overwhelm, convince, prove. Ending sentence a closed-door, last-word ending, dramatic emphasis, spit out, with which the body parts make a final backturning jerk. If possible he goes out a door and slams it, or walks away.

25 August 1987

I wake up. I'm looking over at the chair at my desk trying to wake up. Clothes are thrown into the chair. Between the rungs on the back of the chair, a bunched up wrinkle of my shirt has formed perfectly the onion-shaped face of an old Russian woman wearing a Babushka. Or she could be a Finnish ancestor of mine—my grandmother who always wore scarves around her big doughy face. Her eyes are closed. She is very plain, or homely; she leans her head out over the chair rung as if she's seasick. Or maybe, like the strange dream of my mother, she is praying. Why do I see the old oatmeal head in my chair this morning? What about my old Finnish grandmother I never knew? I think of the dream of my mother, who is normally very secretive about her beliefs, unnaturally referring to "the Lord" and being very religious. If I ever saw her like that I'd believe she was close to death. Is the Millie in me—the passive, silent, bitter, martyr-victim, suffering-silently type—dying? The one who claims to be too stupid to do and know anything? She's seasick and has to get off the boat (out of the relationship?). My mother talks about her mother in a very restricted tone of voice..."my mother," as if it were scary and sacred ground...caution and respect of an elder rather than a comforting mother. My mother's story is that she was put in a cardboard box under the bed at birth and called "baby" until six years old. She, the result of the thirteenth pregnancy to an old mother. How do I feel nameless and insignificant? I can't imagine this 200 pound woman standing in front of a camera in Finland seventy years ago...her identical sisters in long black dresses flanking her, all with oatmeal heads, their solid legs planted in the dry leaves, faces as stern and legs as strong as a never-resting plow horse.

I'm staring at a bunch of these photos on my desk now. My face is leaning on my fists—just like my mother does to hide her double chin...her alcohol-loosened skin melting around her hands...that thought is enough to get my hands off my face.

Why is Oatmeal Head sick?
Why is she praying?
Why do I see her at all?
What old lady wants me to attend to her?

In what way am I being unusually sentimental or "religious"? All kinds of notebooks I keep, charts of cycles, etc. All the jars of huckleberries I canned were done poorly and weren't sealed in my dream last night. Maybe I'm not paying enough attention to the household and the children in order to focus on my inner dimension and paper work. M. said recently that I was just like Kay, religious like her. I became offended because Kay is a narrow fundamentalist, she won't even read a newspaper...she has no living that resembles being involved with reality. Everyone not adhering to the faith has a demon problem. My concept of "God" has been solid and permeable since before M.'s time...but he likes to take credit for any of the good or intelligent sides of me. Recently, I remember, Kristin said to me, "Religion is anything you feel passionately about." I agree with that, and so find grounds for understanding the truth of what M. says...I am fanatic in my inner focus just as Kay is fanatic in her new-Christian framework. Passion is my religion. If passion calls the shots it must be right, I always think, it must be for the soul and for the soul's need. And, in that sense, nothing I've done has been wrong...behind all the confusion I'll find value in this relationship with M. as well.

31 August 1987

An examination:

1) I played excellent pool.
2) M. became moody and angry.
3) When he quit in disgust after I won, I asked someone else to play.
4) He said, "Ja, we're leaving as soon as I finish this beer!" He guzzles down a full schooner on the spot.
5) I make a choice not to behave dependently on his approval/disapproval system, and continue to play (maybe the first time I've done this so obviously).
6) He goes and sits in the car for the twenty minutes it takes me to play the game, until I come out.

In the car. The radio is loud. I have never defied him in this way, to the point where I ignore his exodus to the car and not obediently follow him out. I am a little scared, excited, curious. I have the keys and it is my car; I get in and drive. He breathes heavily all the way home, through his nose. He says, "it all boils down to the fact that I don't like you."

Actually, opposed to how I should feel, I am ecstatically happy because he is being honest and direct for a change. (And because secretly I don't like him either, but I wouldn't want to hurt his feelings...I am hoping he'll hate me enough to kick me out so I never have to say, "I don't want you.") I think I pretend to myself most of the time that all is well. In fact, I think for months now we both have been very lost...we have no relationship, but don't know how to confront *the fact* that we don't. We maintain a public front as if we are still really together, but no bonds remain in private. Anyway, I admire his sentence and tell him so. The fact is that I cannot go back to behaving robotically for his approval, answering to his constant desire to control me. I'm glad it's out in the open that I don't intend to, and if he can't bear it, then we should discuss what to do about that. I tell him this, and tell him I believe he only likes a woman who can passively accept his authority, as I had always done in the past...at least a long-term woman he has to put up with in his home. No, that is not me anymore.

3 September 1987

M. traps me under his arm. He is on his side, so he seems to tower over me as we lie on his bed; I am trapped in a cave between his arm and body, and he tells me what introspection means. Something about being in the past. If I am introspective, I live in the past. He wants me to learn to live in the present. "Intro" means "comes before," he says, "in the past." I say that I take it to mean "the inner substance," the framework for why the outer events are occurring. He says, "INTROduction, a way to say *comes before*." I say, "That could be intro: inward, as in 'introjection', which is to shoot something *into* the middle, of a sentence for instance, and duction: deducing. Deducing the inner substance of what is coming up: what is between the covers of a book, what the inner story of a play or movie could be about—speculation about the inner meaning." Anyway, what I say spoils the language lecture he had designed for me tonight to tell me all my work lives in the past. He releases me with a disgusted noise and turns away.

I am in my study. He comes up to my room. He talks talks talks too much. I'm not even listening, enraptured by his tongue moving inside his steadily flapping mouth. I am saying to myself, almost mantra-like, "his tongue is dead." This comes to me because he has been drinking vodka out of the bottle, and it made his tongue whitish and swollen. It looks like a fat and deathly white worm. I remember Elsid once told M. he should learn one of the dead languages. I commented to her, "he already has one mastered." Or maybe I am too too too too quiet. He has to fill any and all empty space with blather. I have to create a huge net of silence around me to seal myself in. I don't have anything to answer, so he leaves the room.

"It's 10:36 and do you know where your husband is?" "In the noise void," I answer. He laughs and I tell him I visualized it. He tells me visualization—all of it—is fragmentation (so? unholy?). We're yelling between our floors, as usual. He's yelling up now that I take reality so seriously...that he just can't.

Do I take it seriously?

I take it...deeply. I take reality as the meaning it has within from one moment to another.

25 September 1987

Have I ever been able to really listen to and understand M.? Will I ever want to again? The struggle of the first six years to really hear and understand, and still he is melancholy over being misunderstood. Now the last five years of active conflict. I don't have the energy or the desire to work up the energy for it anymore. I am returning to an older self-set pattern of extreme silence, and comfortable solitude. I am invaded in this relationship. Did I ever make a commitment to him? Too horrifying to ask this after ten years. What is the purpose? Any purpose. Everything is change. I feel like it has all been a dream. An image supported it. The image collapsed and I cannot blow new life into it, so I fail to find the purpose in it anymore. Years of effort to erect the image. As soon as it completes itself I drop it and let it crash. What is the meaning? Where am I headed?

3 June 1988

I have been living in the other house since November, and telling M. he is free, I am free, I doubt things can be revived, ever. I stay on the land, here, as mother, but have not been "his woman" for several months in any way. Yet he speaks and behaves as if I am just taking a break, and will soon snap out of it. I try not to think of it, because I fear leaving…knowing he will take control of the children, that I will lose everything. I am dragging my heels and it is making me sick…I can't help fearing that I will cause myself serious disease. Because I feel dis-ease.

I woke to the sound of the kitten this morning. The kitten that is diseased…it has strange fits and is out of control of its body. It howls in pain and races all over the yard and up walls. Frightening and sickening. I hate for Yeti to see it. Hearing the kitten in my sleep, I thought, "this is it, I can't take it anymore." I decided to kill it myself. Realizing the expense of a vet, I convinced myself that I should be able to kill a kitten. It went very badly…a half hour ordeal, and the kitten wouldn't die, but I couldn't quit because I'd already seriously hurt it. I was out there in the pre-light morning before the kids awoke, sobbing loudly as I had to try method after method before it would die. I was horrified. When M. got up, he asked what was wrong. But first, he tells me about a frightening dream he had of a cat lying on his face, smothering him: he screams and tries to throw an arm up to get the cat off. Then he thinks he feels me touch him and screams. He hears water running then, and goes to look in the sauna; when he woke up, he was very sure that I must be in there taking a bath.

5 June 1988

Last night I slept with a friend. I was nervous, partly because although I have not been intimate with M. for months and have told him that I am free for other relationships and do not live with him, I have not actually done anything physically that goes against his comforts. Somehow, M. stopped at the friend's house, being acquainted with the man himself, on his way home from Olympia. He said he knew I would be there. He stood in the doorway staring at me. I ignored him, with the obvious tension that I have an interest in the friend; M. was standing there with all his quills out. Finally, after the friend and I both ignore him, he says, "I'm leaving! Are you coming home?" I ignore him and he leaves. But I stayed, I stayed all night. Especially because of this scene, perhaps. I am angered, I feel victimized that he steps freely into my business.

I come home very early…feeling guilty I'm sure, feeling terrified about M.'s reaction. He actually came to the friend's house…what else might he do? When I got home he threw a fit. Either get in bed with him naked or he would commit himself. So now he is in the hospital. All day I did not *allow* it to penetrate my consciousness…I even happily described to Aemmer how very wonderful and healthy it had seemed to be with the other friend. I had remembered what a healthy relationship could be…it was so friendly, I kept saying. I was washing and waxing my Volkswagen. Full muscular effort, bringing it to a high shine. I worked three hours at it, talking to Aemmer all the while in a most cheerful way. Simply "forgetting" about M. being in the hospital. Now the blackness, the implications sink in. I lie on my bed and begin to sob and cry. About my entrapment, not poor M. I maybe realize for the very first time that the real point is that still living here makes me remain his possession.

I pick up my notebook and write without thought. The actions of trying to break the kitten's neck, twisting it, and then trying to crush its skull with the splitting mall, and finally drowning it, are re-played on the paper. On paper, the kitten spoke to me in the sobbing redescription of that mutual agony. Telling me that it was a lesson I chose for myself. Some part of me had the vision that a sick cat was an opportunity, and that I took it…I put my hands into it and followed through even though it was a torture. I was not a detached witness but a participant…that was the crucial factor. I needed to put my hands into it and carry out the most devastating act. The kitten says I have a diseased, twisted, dying, incurably painful relationship with M. I cannot kill it by gently and passively bumping and twisting it…I must immerse it into a final death with choice, with the strength of my hands (real action). It is not going to heal and I must end it. What to do now? Be strong in what you have, the kitten says. Follow the kitten…step by step, never giving up no matter how horrifying it gets.

M. returned from the hospital three days later, all demands and threats. I had all of my belongings moved into a small trailer I had bought; the moving into true separation began.

Ja Luoma

The Gray Area Journals
1989–1990

My Gray Area Journals are journals written in retrospect. The "Gray Area" is what occupies the mind while staring off into space, preoccupied with another task, or a daydream-thought that gets censored before consciously considered. My passion for journal keeping has traveled between the covers of forty or fifty notebooks, and half as many purposes, styles and titles. That none of them were satisfying enough was the feeling that led me to want to begin the Gray Area Journals. I wanted to capture and then admit the secrets, the things that might shame me—things maybe "too petty" to be written down, too banal. Often I have to really concentrate to remember what I was thinking; many times in the course of a day I stop and ask myself where I was during the last blank. Yes, sometimes it is banal, but often it is a surprising reflection that completes the puzzle of the day, clarifies a dream fragment, pinpoints how I feel about a yes-no decision. But mainly I keep the journal of the Gray Area because it is another good avenue to finding the root of my passion. Unburying that root is what motivates me as an individual, is my purpose in all the journals written.

☙

6 April 1989

I just spent half an hour trying to learn the words to "Wildwood Flower." The image: next time T. plays the song for my dad I would surprise all of them by singing the words. The fear is to sing imperfectly, or maybe even to sing awfully, for the ears of T. who sings so delightfully. But then I persisted, thinking that the more I do what is the most difficult for me, the more I come in touch with the multifaceted self that I really am. I want to experience fear, embarrassment, but then do it anyway.

While singing I was thinking about being sick the last two days, how it made my mind weak so I couldn't even think of writing. When I spoke to

Jonathan I avoided any topic I truly felt anything about, stuck to "safe", unfeeling topics.

My emotions…when hurt, I stifle them. I suspect T. of hiding hurts…and I do so myself. How can I tell him: please lay out your hurts for me and I will hold you and protect you, when I, myself, conceal my hurts? The night air is spring and summer and tasty.

7 April 1989

Gray morning, feeling lousy before work, sitting in the car. All diaries are essentially lies. They're all lies because you lie to yourself and only realign them with the truth some day in retrospect when you can stand to. For years I kept insisting to myself that I loved M. and tried to make it right…when actually I barely even liked him the last six years or so. I long for the godawful, gray and bloated, stinking truth now and every now, to be stabbed with it constantly so I don't have to waste my time rediscovering how I really feel and believe.

11 April 1989

A moodiness while washing dishes. It is summerlike, sunny—in a town—I don't know how to immerse myself—the whole trickery of women and wearing little patches over their sex spots. These images and half sentences flashed through my mind—mood flashes. I'm having a sexist tantrum. Washing dishes. T. is lying in the sun—I don't know how. I am self-conscious because women wearing bikinis is so artificial…little scraps of material hung on the secret parts. I dread summer because last year and the nine before it I was allowed to garden, walk, sit or lie around totally nude, and living in this public place I am required to participate in artifice…. I actually am embarrassed to walk outside with contrived modesties. It is more shocking to me than what full nudity in front of a stranger would be. Maybe I'll get used to it. For now I hide in a sink full of dishes, at the same time not admitting that I am feeling resentful of T. lying out there for hours, ignoring housework in his freedom and comfort of being accustomed to sunning beside the trailer with only a bright cloth clutching his groin. And I feel fat. Hayfever and fat go together.

Fat doesn't exist if I can fully expose myself naturally, but it is appalling when bound by little cloths of properness. I am also disturbed over my lack of contribution to my school work. I don't have time; yet I am not at work either.... My car is only half-running. What else? I feel sorrowful that T.'s exxie called on her birthday to complain to him about some income tax thing from their past marriage, and it hurt him.... Why hurt other people? When you no longer have the passion, you go ahead and slap them.

Night. Maybe merely the Doppelganger. Well, that's not the right word, but I cannot find the right word. The mood was the foreshadowing of the egregiousness to come, perhaps. What has gone through my mind in the now several hours of tears? Harbinger, T. says. That must be the word. Anyway. Tears over what?

I got the papers in the mail ordering me to pay M. child support; pay the man who has stolen my children, stolen my home, my land, years of tools and investments, my hundred different wild herbs carefully collected and cultivated, not to mention all the work put into it all. His reason—because he was forced to break up; he did not want to, I did, therefore I must pay for all and come out with nothing. The bottomless unfairness of it! I hate him virulently. This child support thing is the final straw.... T. and I sat on a mattress in the driveway in front of his trailer drinking more than half a bottle of Wild Turkey while I endlessly wept on him. New thoughts kept intruding...they have my social security number so I can't work and hide also. I can't get out of the trailer and can't get out of this trailer park because the amount I pay in support is that much less I can save to get out of here. I can't sell my land for money to move because M. scares buyers away, and threatens my life and peace of mind if I dare even think of it. I am all tied up, painted into the corner. How neatly M. has made it impossible for my sons to live with me, because I don't have a home and no money to create one. I am supporting M.'s being a leech. I realize I have always supported him, while *my* needs have been ignored, unthinkable, who cares. I was trying to get out of M.'s living style; I have a job, trying to improve my own situation, live somewhat more straightly...and now a slap in the face, it's just like welfare, having to report and make support payments...God, I wail...all because M. has to make another buck off someone else so he doesn't have to work. He gets it all; and I, who am trying to do it right, who has made all the sacrifices, lose again, lose it all...even the right to make my own life what I want without his interference.

12 April 1989

The emotions have receded, but not the unfairness cutting into me like a newly sharpened blade.

I have been sitting on a bench, waiting in the weak morning sun for the city bus to come and take me to Brinnon to work. My car really won't make it and I have been skipping work for days now...first really a bit sick, now the emotional crisis keeping me home yesterday. I walked facing the sun, blind with sleep. My focus was on the first small steps. I focus on my need to establish integrity with my employer in Brinnon. Focus there and let the rest of life take its course...I can't afford to think of anything else. It's so hard to go to work, but I must...they could easily see me as sleazy and unreliable, in fact calling them with my excuses I believe it myself.

Spoke to Kay last night. I called her with the desperate notion of being saved. She and M., side by side, the substitute insane parents of my past. Again my mind reels away in doubt because she is just as influential as M., and neither of them contains the answer of how I find life for myself....

The Wheel of Fortune is the sun I stare into, these thoughts and moods wheeling through me and into and out of the sun.

The "parents" push on me in two opposing ways and I am the third party and will go my own weird, combined way. May the Wheel protect T. from my turmoil and dilemma, let it not leak upon him like a pissing dog. My one bright moment of living as an adult with some real mind is my time with T.

Kay says, "hear God speak through M.'s disease." Well, I've done that all my life. I didn't have to relearn it like she did. God is psyche is Self, not some detachable icon to murmur at and cajole. And I follow my own voice. I go through the panic, I collect maximum input from all sources, and then I step bravely into small, seemingly unrelated steps. But they are *not* unrelated. First step: establish integrity. Show and tell that I'm not just skipping out of work, that I have a disturbance to deal with, whatever it takes. I will not patriotically put work ahead of life.

I'll go on, do the paperwork toward support payments, go to the hearing, let M. have custody (since I don't have a home for them)…but don't protect him with lies as I have always done; let honesty, total open-book honesty about the kind of man he's been and is, take me where it will. If I end up with the sons only because he runs from a failed scam and lets his "precious" family sink, showing his true me-first attribute, then I will find a way. I am gripped by this event and must meet it.

The giant orange-red ball of the sun is gone, turned into normal light. I've been sitting here putting to ink everything circulating in my mind while I walked…but now I realize how long it's been; obviously, I speculate, I have missed the bus or it never came or the schedule is changed. I didn't expect to be helped to avoid work by the great Wheel so smoothly, yet must now face my feeling of draining integrity in the face of having to call in, missing yet another day at work.

14 April 1989

I feel seized up. Night darkness, a half hour brood, and something like the fear to move an inch. Caution? Open eyes? The Trumps of Doom? Papers and moneys that the dogs rip at, biting deeply into the throat? Disappointment.

Let's just say no one human can share vision, share views, with another all the way down. The ideals. For the first time my heart is not hanging on the line, offering its last drop of blood. So? What next?

At the final deluge, say worse comes to worst, I can still pack a little knapsack and walk on down the road like the real Fool trump, and that may be the answer. Do not fear—be the Fool. One small step at a time, I will do what I need to do, as a fool, without fear.

Maybe this small withdrawal of disappointment is good. I've hung for some time; hanging never draws the opposite soul. As I learned while T. was in Spain: focus on Self. As self-centered as I can be, so will the globe turn more freely in its natural orbit. The psyche has to rest too, a writer has times of waiting. The other half of writing is hours of mindless walking down the road, slobbering into a beer, lazy sloughing around, making lists and phone calls, reading comic pages in the newspaper. All of life has the element of the slow down, of no action...REST. All things have their coasting moment.

17 April 1989, 3:45 A.M.

Have I been to sleep yet, I wonder? So much tension and adrenaline in my chest, I fear a heart attack if I stay in bed one more sleepless minute worrying about providing receipts for every little expense in my life to the state, for them to determine how much to rob me of on M.'s behalf, should I change title on the truck.... I don't even have a home. I leave the fearful bed, full of these circulations. Sitting in the living room in T.'s trailer, while he sleeps; sweating, relaxing. I remember the dream I had a couple of nights ago. In the end, I was carrying an eyeball through a tunnel. I reenter that scene. I carry the eyeball in a bowl—it is really like a blue-yoked egg, the yolk a clear, blue eye. The tunnel is damp and blue. Then I am carrying a large Tupperware box with the bowl containing the eyeball balanced on top of it. I put down the box with the bowl on it, and heap other things around it. Then I notice that the bowl now has an infant boy in it. My word on the dream right now—I am definitely in a passage. Something brand new is emerging, it is delicate and I am juggling it pretty awkwardly. I'm emotionally crushed. I am adrenaline-ill. I could puke or cry.

M. never gave me a moment to panic and fear, or to become totally emotionally distressed like this. He would *cause* distress, but *then* he would surround me with his securities—like a goddamn I.V. I'd die without. So tonight I flounder and am left to it.... T. sleeps steadily in the bedroom; he sensed my angst and kept to the opposite edge of the bed. How many times must I flounder alone before I know how to save myself? Did M. weaken me? Intentionally? My perceptions have narrowed down to such a pinprick of nobody-ness. I need to find some strength, some self. I'm floundering and need to be saved, around and around in my image-thought goes this sentence, until now I am curled in a ball on the couch under the light, under a quilt, sick to my stomach, staring at Grandma Tedford's rocking chair, thinking how human and comforting it looks. Its arms stretched out as if it has its hands on its knees. So personified. Looking into the fact that I don't have a home. I have nothing of my own that is personified and comforts me. Grandma Tedford belongs to T. This is his trailer, nothing of mine is even in here…I can't stand my own trailer. I borrow T.'s comforts and personifications, and maybe he doesn't want to share. I am rolled up like a fetus. Like an eyeball in a bowl. The tears well, roll, and recede. The stomach adrenaline persists. The rooster crows.

6:15 A.M.

I am reading Jung's *Visions Seminars* when T. calls from the bedroom asking if I am OK. The tears run; the floodgates open even though I am basically OK now night is over, but I cry when anyone near me expresses care and concern. I feel groundless. I return to the sentence in the book that set me to dreaming off, reading it over and over as if I haven't yet: "People are more afraid to lose their money than their God. The idea of God has become unreal, abstract." Reading it, M. flashed through, his manic claims to union with God…not nearly so close as I've come to God because of the mere fact that I have lost everything (without even a fight) except the basic fiber of myself, and even that seems to be shaky. I brush close to the exposed area where the curtain of psyche flaps open and I can't help but stare at myself. I have traveled to the point of the smallest, lowest common denominator point of existing. I literally do not have a home or anything of my own, even a few spoons. All that's fucking left is God. While M. grasps desperately at every last tatter of material security and cocoons it around himself, greedy and shut down tight in case any force might try to pull away one small strip of his ample flesh. That holy mouth of his speaks words, only words. The more he flaps his mouth with his holy words, the further away he is from his own soul, God.

12 June 1989

My favorite time of day. It's 4:30 A.M. at the hatchery job; summer on the bay, the sky pulls out its colors at this hour, a sleeve of amber crosses the water, and the blues are as blue as can be, the herons are at rest. A song on the radio causes me to look out at the quiet morning hour and wonder about love, me, others. How enraptured I become. I gaze at T., daydream, get such a strong, deep sense of him and am so impassioned by love. I know he doesn't have that—who does really? It's me and maybe not an easy trait to live with—for myself or for the receptor. Is he sometimes uneasy under the ocean blanket of my love? While I dream of the deepest intimacy, he thinks about solitary wanders. It's just me.

27 June 1989

It happened unexpectedly today when T. offered me space in his trailer for my clothes. I laughed a laugh of enlightenment and freedom. If he or anyone else had heard the laugh they would have thought it a dangerous, malicious laugh of reckless abandon. But I was alone, putting my few things into drawers. When one finds oneself free, and completely alone, one can afford a malicious laugh. It is ironic. I am supposed to take the offering of space as a concession from T. that we live together. And somehow, while I participate in the symbol, I am ricocheted into sudden insight in another realm...I see that I am alone!

What did M. say to me so recently, the man with the manacles of false device who once pulled my strings to make me dance like a puppet? That I had failed to complete the movement toward what psyche wanted of me by leaving him, by moving into the relationship with T. Instinctively I shrugged. I didn't worry about his opinion.

1 July 1989

It is a November-like wind and rain. I am not displeased. The weekend was full of awkward moods, and with the wind a fresh peace seems to blow in. I am looking out the window into it, seeing it, and am reminded—like a daydream—of T. coming to me in the morning when I woke up. To be shown love is irreplaceable. He does not reach out that often to touch, and sometimes I sit quietly watching him secretly, curious at how unaware, unneedful, he is about his own lack of initiative in touch. I long for it. I want it as badly as I need to give it. So when he comes to me that way, for some minutes of contact, touch, nonsexual but intimately warm, I feel like one does in the presence of a wild bird who graces you with enough trust to alight very near. I kind of hold my breath, hoping that no word or movement startles him away. Oh women, so easy to please and so hard for men to do the simple, sharing things; to reach.

13 July 1989

T. and I are drinking Wild Turkey. He sits on the porch hunkered like a lover over his guitar, singing Jerry Lee Lewis, "There Stands the Glass." His brown ankles are crossed, his red high-tops tapping while he plays. I am sitting in an old armchair covered with thick fabric, black with fat gray roses on it. Neighbors pass us around the circular trailer park driveway and wave. I am smiling, fondly watching and listening to T., thinking how soft and gentle he is all the way through. Abruptly I realize I have been sitting here fondling the memory of an insight I've had so very recently, a shocking one. I have only just grasped that M. is not a gentle person. I have a year behind me now after leaving him, but it has taken this long for that old—indeed, original—image to face judgment. I am shocked at the knowledge. M. is a violent person and he violated me, for the most part with my participation. You are either with M. or on the outside...the outside is insane. To be with him on any terms, you must breathe the very air he breathes, see his visions, live every premise from his lips. Gentleness was merely what he wanted me to see.

19 August 1989, 2:10 A.M.

The moon is melting like a blob of cheese. It changes after I take the temperatures of every two blue tanks at work. Take two, look, take two, look. The first look showed only a perfect blot of black cloud nearly the same shape as the moon, covering only the moon. Next look it grew oblong and covered half the moon. Next look—clear moon. Next look a big ink stain over the moon and spilling across the sky. All in a night's work.

While I watch the ink stains, I alert myself to what I had been thinking. I was remembering the feeling I had after having seen M. today. I felt filthy and grimy, covered by his sleaze. Trying to tell T. a fraction of how it was, it came out more like I was barfing, I felt like I was lying…a sort of filth. Gave me a great headache, I felt stuffed with garbage. I went to have a float in the bay. It cleansed and renewed me, returned me to myself, washing M. away from me.

20 August 1989

Sometimes it's just good to brood deeply. I am interested that there is nothing to complain of and yet the brooding is as steady and blank as slate, and the night swallows me up as I walk down the blue bulkhead at work, the rhythm of the grates comforting and familiar under my feet. It is a quiet and peaceful brooding. Maybe the brood is the mind at total rest. I've bitched my fill over M., had my vomitous ejection of anger, hatred, and hurt over him and give up utterly.… Had my night tears over children lost, had my dull ache of emotion…my body still lacking and longing to hold Yeti close, the baby. See no immediate solution, let it go. Felt my guilt, faced all the mutual acquaintances who can't understand how I can let my children go.… I can't explain my corners and leg traps to every other human, none of whom can or will follow my life every move down the line to full understanding. When it all gets enough to overwhelm me, just let it push me down into the earth, and there at the bottom of the grave it seems to dissolve—so evil I'm finally left in peace. Maybe at that moment a door opens somewhere else, but then the fight is over and I no longer feel saved or blessed by the door. I merely pass through.… Brooding used to mean sadness, brooding was always turned to disharmonies. Now there are none. Brooding is quiet.

I am sitting on top of a ladder just watching the water rise in an algae tank I am filling. Looking at the lights over the growing algae in other tanks, the golden bubbles.…

26 August 1989

2:20 A.M. Less than a sulk, more than a brood. But what in hell it is I can't decide. I had a good name for it earlier, but now forget. The word starts with an H. And then a wrenching dream of killing something I'd gone to a lot of work to rescue and get to a protected place.

The prison of myself. Might be that locked-in self-consciousness. This "mood" of self-consciousness is worse than ever. Watching T. play his guitar last night...I was afraid to go into the room while he played, but loving to look. Kept feeling out of place, watched, ugly, grudging. Grudging makes it all that more intense. I grudged over bunches of things lately, but didn't ask for help, as usual.

2 March 1990

I should live in my own trailer, I know I *should*, but the idea even of the disruption of the relationship between T. and me distresses me, and I do nothing day after day.

Today I was fantasizing again about using my own five acres. I suggested my fantasy to M., and he said "I probably won't bother you anymore"...probably isn't good enough. No, not yet. While I was splitting kindling today I was chanting, "I want to live alone" over and over, but was not aware of it until T. happened by and I became embarrassed, felt guilty. The chant was silent and secret, I was unaware of it really, until then. And then I was befuddled...do I really feel that way?

16 March 1990

Sitting in T.'s trailer reading. When I looked up and around at the lack of sunlight, the lack of windows, not one thing of my own around me...it was a gray dismal shock. I went back to my book but was overwhelmed by a mood, a mood with words that went something like this: I really think I need to make the step and live alone.

18 March 1990

Somehow I have just opened my mouth and spoken to T. about my need to make my own trailer my home...and for us to just feel out what our relationship is when I am doing things as I really want to, being most truly myself. He is happy because I have been so tense and disconsolate for weeks. Suddenly we are both in the lightest of moods, energized, and openly laugh and love.

But later, after a long day working over my trailer to make it livable, waking in an alien place…a place more camp still than home…I have shadows in my mind, fears. What do I really want here? I need to fill it with my own quiet first, then my own noise. Both somehow are experiences I need. I reflect that in T.'s trailer it was always his…I was not "home". I need to develop home for myself. The gray fears are that I have no home, no being, alone. I need to feel my own hunger before I eat rather than eat because it is T.'s hour to eat. To have no false enthusiasms, no phantom longings, but see clearly my own work, areas about myself to make clear.

I hear the sound of frogs out the open front door, the meager sounds of the fire burning in the woodstove, the smell of coffee, fresh air from the door and windows.

19 March 1990

Even my own kind of smell is with me, I notice. Waking, the air is fresher and less stuffy than T.'s electric heat. The faint smell of yesterday's fire. Cool floors of morning. I live for these things. These are things that were calling to me…and no attempt to put it into words made it clear.

24 March 1990

I watched in fascination as an unwieldy dark and exaggerated cloud of anger grasped me, and I attacked Eric at work over some petty irritation. He made a demand, putting himself in charge, making a stupid (uninformed) decision, in the process patronizing me. The hatchery calls it an algae bloom when a sudden natural growth of algae develops in the water supply from the bay. I call it an animus bloom when, with no warning—like a sudden fog—the sort of man I hate awakes in me.

25 March 1990

Sitting at my desk typing. I looked out and got the awful mood, looking out at the mountains, the sun gleaming on them. What are the words for that mood, that ache I felt wanting to grow into anger?

Hiding not from the great, but the possible.... Movement, sorting, shuffling. I am an empty carcass that only stuffs its face, zombie. The sun on distant hills, nothing like sun to make me want to be doing something with somebody somewhere else. Something splendid and poetic.

27 August 1990

The few hours to myself before work I am in a wave of mood. The lights are different. I have completed a drawing that seems to clarify a dream, exciting me. I write a letter to Leo because I feel so good. And then I even take a few photographs, self-portraits, something I do only when full of self. The thought: I'm getting self-satisfied. I don't know why or how. I create my own humor. I laugh silently to myself, alone and smug. I look at my little ink scratchings, a portrait of Franz Kafka finding a new vagina between his legs, and tape it to my curtain in front of the desk—and my wild side, the bachelor, laughs.

S. Afzal Haider

Incomplete Conversations
(From a Day's Entry)

I've been keeping a journal for almost 30 years. I write about day-to-day happenings as well as major mood swings and the incidents that precipitated those feelings. My journal is not written to achieve a personal resolution by therapeutic expression, but to go into those things that are not fully understood, explained, or resolved. Later, when I re-read my journal, I can re-experience the freshness of an encounter, like the feeling of a déjà vu—the excitement of time and place, the sounds and smells, or a feeling of loss become immediate and in the present. The idea that the past is not totally lost and gone forever is the joy of keeping a journal.

৪১

September 7, 1983

Today is Adam's first day of kindergarten. I wake up with a dream of my mother. In my dream, I walk to my mother's room. I stand in the doorway. I watch her sitting on her knees on her prayer rug after *Fajr* prayers. She has a rosary in her hand and her green embroidered shawl is over her head and shoulders. She looks so serene and saintly. The cool morning breeze moves the shawl around her face. She asks me if I had prayed that morning. I wanted to say yes, but I reply, "No, Mother, I have not prayed in ages. I no longer pray." She replies, "One needs to pray to calm the soul, to attain an internal peace." I walk toward her and sit down in front of her on her prayer rug. I am a young boy now, four or maybe five, and I am wearing my grayish-blue pajamas. She puts her rosary beside her on the rug and massages my head. The music her bangles make is soothing. I lay my head on her lap and close my eyes. She asks me if I would recite *Sura Al-Fatiha* for her. With my eyes closed I can see her radiant face, and I recite:

IN THE NAME OF ALLAH
THE COMPASSIONATE
THE MERCIFUL
Praise be to Allah, Lord of creation,
The compassionate, the merciful.
King of the Judgment Day.
You alone we worship, and to you alone
we pray for help.

Guide us to the straight path.
The path of those whom you have favored,
not of those who have incurred your wrath,
not of those who have gone astray.

I open my eyes. My mother is smiling at me. I close my eyes again. She kisses my forehead, my eyes, my nose and my cheeks, but not my lips. She whispers to me, as she did when she was putting me to sleep, that I am a good boy and that she loves me very much. She covers me with her shawl and I fall asleep.

Today is Adam's first day of school, a half day. I wake up with a dream of my mother. I get out of bed, shower, and put on clean jeans. I pick up the paper from the front door of the house. The White Sox lost again last night. I sit in the kitchen reading the morning paper, drinking coffee. I am on my third cup of coffee when I hear Adam call from his room. I walk upstairs. He is still in bed, under his red and blue Marimekko quilt with the cars all over it.

"I don't want to go to school," he says. He looks nice and rested.

"I don't want you to go either," I say, feeling his loneliness. I take his grey wide-wale corduroy pants and blue oxford shirt out of his closet.

"Oh goody," he says. "I don't have to go." He covers his face with the quilt.

"What you want to do and what you need to do are two different things, young man," I say as I uncover his face.

"I understand that," he says, "but I am still too shy and I am afraid."

"I am shy as well," I say, "but I am not afraid."

"Neither am I," he says, throwing the quilt off with his feet. "But I am so shy that I get scared."

"You have to be strong and brave about it," I say, throwing his underwear and socks toward him on his bed.

"I can't. I don't know how," he says. He sits up in his bed.

"You are, and you will be," I say.

He gets out of his bed and goes to the bathroom. When I hear him brush his teeth, I walk into the washroom and comb his hair. Later I help him get dressed. He looks so big and preppy. With a proper cap he could go to an English boarding school. I take out the leather flight jacket Susanna found for him at St. Peter's church rummage sale before he was born. I ask him to put it on.

"I don't like this," he says. "Why can't I wear my baseball jacket?"

"It's a very special jacket," I say. I shouldn't have said that. I didn't want to burden him with the guilt of not liking a great jacket that his mother found for him.

"What's so special about it?" he asks.

"Your mother bought it for you at a rummage sale before you were born."

"It looks fifty years old," he says.

"That's the beauty of it; it's one of a kind."

"I don't like it," he says, "but I'll wear it if you want me to."

"Thank you, most kind sir," I say, laughing.

I brush his hair one more time before we walk downstairs for breakfast. During his breakfast he says he is not hungry, and that his tummy is hurting and he doesn't want to go to school. I keep repeating that he should be strong.

Adam lets my hand go once we arrive at the school gate. I walk him to his classroom, give him a kiss and open the classroom door for him. I am ready to leave when I hear Mrs. Colangelo say that he should wait outside at the kindergarten building in line with the other kids for room 101. This way he'll learn the entire routine.

We walk outside. There is a chill in the autumn air. Lines are being formed for each classroom. Parents are smiling at each other and the children are whispering whatever to their parents. I wish Susanna were here. Adam keeps saying that he doesn't want to go. I only listen. I don't even say that he has to be brave and strong. The lines begin to move. I give him a kiss, he kisses me back. He moves briskly, he walks straight. I wait for him to enter the school building. He doesn't look back. I thought he would.

At 11:40 I am back at the school waiting for Adam to get out of his class. Other people are around, mostly mothers. I see an attractive face, she is wearing a short grey jacket and white pants. She looks very suburban. I keep looking in her direction, hoping to make eye contact. It is difficult. She is wearing dark sunglasses.

The school bell rings, and boys and girls begin to come out. Adam is the last one out from the kindergarten building. He is carrying his bomber jacket in his hand. He sees me and comes running. I pick him up and hold him in my arms. He kisses me on the neck. "How was it?" I ask.

"It was all right," he says in a low voice. He puts his head on my shoulder. "Are we walking home?" he asks.

"No, we have our car." I kiss his head; his hair smells nice. I put him down. "What did you do today?" I ask, looking toward the attractive face. She has her glasses off. She is talking to another woman. I can't catch her eyes.

"Nothing," says Adam. He sees the car and runs toward it.

I change my pace and catch up with him. "How could you do nothing for three hours?" I ask, unlocking the car door.

Adam gets in the front and throws his jacket in the rear seat. "I don't know," he says, as I get in on the other side.

"And where is your cap?" I ask, putting the keys in the ignition.

"What cap?"

"The cap that makes you look like a kid going to an English boarding school."

"Are we talking make-believe?" he asks.

"No, I am talking I don't know."

"Ah, I see," Adam says. "Yes. I like my school. Mrs. Colangelo is all right, and the cap that I never had is on my head. Maybe you need your reading glasses to see it." He makes his clown face.

I laugh. Looking in the rear view mirror, I watch the attractive face get into a blue station wagon.

"What are we going to do today?" asks Adam.

"It's about noon now," I say. "If you want we can go to Bill's or Peter Lo's for lunch and afterwards to the Lincoln Park Zoo."

"I don't like zoos," he says. The attractive face drives by. She's in a Buick, and the license plate reads WAW 420. She has her dark glasses on again. I don't think she ever noticed me. "I am not hungry and I don't want to miss 'Inspector Gadget'."

"That does not come on until 4:00 P.M. We can go home and play catch for awhile," I offer. "Then when you are hungry, I'll make you a cheese taco."

"Can we go to our graveyard," he asks, "not the one by our house?"

"If you like," I say, starting the car.

"But I don't want to miss my cartoon."

"We can go to the graveyard for a short while and on the way back we can stop by Mama's for lunch."

"Do you promise I won't miss 'Inspector Gadget'?"

"Of course."

We drive in silence for a little while. I think about what life is and what it is not. Adam is self-absorbed. I wonder what he is thinking.

"Can we listen to some music?" Adam asks.

"Sure."

He picks up a couple of tapes from the glove compartment. "Bruce or Beatles?" he asks.

I glance over. He is holding Springsteen's *Nebraska*, and the Beatles' *Rubber Soul* in his hand. "Nebraska is perfect to listen to on the way to a graveyard," I say.

"I knew you'd pick Springsteen. You don't like the Beatles anymore."

"That's not true," I say. "I was just hearing 'My Father's House' in my head when you asked."

He says nothing and puts the cassette in the tape deck. When we arrive at the graveyard, Bruce is singing 'Well I guess everything dies baby, that's a fact.' We sit in the car listening. The song ends. I turn the cassette off. I get out of the car, walk around and open the door for Adam. "Curbside service to your favorite grave, sir," I say. Adam gets out of the car. He says nothing. "It's a bit cool. You should put your jacket on," I say, picking it up from the back seat and handing it to him.

"I hate this jacket," he says, and puts it on. It's a beautiful day, cool in the shade, and the sun feels warm. "Why do people come to graveyards?" he asks.

"I don't know."

"Why do you come to the graveyards?"

"I am glad you asked me that question, Master Adam. I was just thinking about it…"

"Well?" he says.

"Well what?" I say, composing my thoughts.

"Why do you come to graveyards?" he repeats.

"I come to graveyards to be quiet," I say in a low voice, "I come to remember. I come to say a silent prayer. I come to cry. I come to burn incense."

I don't know if Adam heard all I said or if it made sense to him. He is ahead, skipping from gravestone to gravestone as if he were playing hopscotch. In the Ivy section the gravestones are laid flat as opposed to the erect ones in other sections.

Adams stops, looks back and asks, "Where is my mommy's grave?"

"It is under that large oak tree," I point.

We walk to the grave, and Adam manages to read his mother's name. "What does it say?" he asks.

I read it to him:

> *So we'll go no more a roving*
> *So late into the night...*
> *Though the heart be still as loving*
> *and the moon be still as bright.*

"How do they know what to say?" he asks, jumping over to Deratzian's, the gravestone next to his mother's.

"They didn't know what to say. I arranged for someone to put that stone here and for it to say what it says."

"Does my mommy like it?" he asks, stepping off Deratzian.

"I don't know."

"Do you think so?"

"I'd like to think so. She loved Byron."

"You said she loved you," says Adam, looking at me with a clown face. I smile at him and say nothing. We stay by the grave for a few moments. I look up to the large oak tree. Most of the leaves are still green. Adam walks around the tombstone.

"Do you remember the time we came here and ran around catching the falling leaves?"

"Yes," says Adam, "but I was very sad that day."

"Why were you sad?"

"Because I could not catch any leaves."

"You did, too."

"No," he says in a protesting voice. "I picked those up from the ground."

"I saw you catching."

"I just ran around. *You* caught a lot," he says.

He looks sad; I kiss his head. "You're very young," I say. "You need more practice." There is silence.

"What can we do now?" Adam asks.

"We can walk to the pond and watch the ducks."

"Let's!" he says, walking ahead.

I see a pile of dirt in the Hemlock section. "Look over there," I say. "They have dug a new grave."

"Can we see it?" he asks.

"Why not?"

I've found a thing of interest for him, I think, walking toward the grave. The equipment they use to lower the coffin is sitting on the other side of the dirt. The grave is still open. A glittering copper-gold coffin is sitting in the grave. 'George Jay Calihan' is written on the coffin in large letters.

"What's that?" asks Adam.

"That is a coffin," I say. Why did they write George's name on it, I wondered.

"Why did they put it here?" he asks.

"The deceased is in it and they have lowered the coffin," I say, smelling the freshly cut flowers lying on the dirt.

"Daddy," says Adam in a loud voice, "now you are talking like a grown-up and not making any sense."

I am uncomfortable, afraid that people working on closing George Jay's grave, or a family member, may come back and we will look out of place.

"Are you going to explain?' asks Adam.

"Yes," I say, moving away from the grave. "When someone dies, they put the body in a box, dig a hole in the ground, and bury the box." I wanted to add that some folks burn their dead and spread the ashes around, but it wasn't the time for details.

"Is someone in there?" asks Adam, still standing by the grave and looking at the coffin.

"Yes, I believe so." I think about poor George. It must be very claustrophobic. I wonder how George looks.

"Can we look in it?" asks Adam.

"No," I say, walking away. Adam follows.

"Why did they leave him alone?"

"That's what we do with our dead ones, I guess."

We walk together without saying anything. I think how I would like to be buried: without a box, wrapped in a white cotton sheet with my face left unwrapped, with a skylight over my grave. This way friends could come and see me rot and I could smile at them. Adam stops and sits down on a large tombstone. 'Massey' it reads.

"I don't want to die," says Adam in a low voice.

"Hopefully you don't have to worry about it for awhile."

"But children do die," he says in his regular voice.

"Yes, I know." I remember my brother Iqbal.

At the pond we watch the ducks.

"Do these ducks go south for the winter?" Adam asks.

"I don't think so."

"They have to or else they'll die."

"I don't know," I say. Somehow I don't care.

Adam walks around and sits down on a bench in front of a grave. I walk over and sit next to him. Adam reads "BONES" out loud, a name that is etched on the gravestone. I see a skeleton inside the grave smiling at me. Why do skeletons always appear to be smiling? I laugh and repeat "BONES". Adam starts laughing, too. I wonder what he saw.

We sit on the bench reading last names engraved on the tombstones. We laugh at names we find funny and the names that we can't read or pronounce. "There is a Voss, a Boyle, a Butz. I see a Drop, and there is a Walker," I say.

"Does he walk a lot?" Adam says.

"Not anymore."

There is a moment of quiet. Adam puts his head on my lap and closes his eyes. I comb his hair with my fingers, and massage his head. A sunny day is turning partly sunny. It may rain yet.

"Can we catch some leaves now?" asks Adam, opening his eyes.

"It's too early in the season for leaves to be dry enough to fall," I say.

Adam sits up and says, "I want to do something."

I thought he had had enough of the graveyard for the day. "This is not an amusement park," I say. "We can leave now, if you want."

Adam gets off the bench, walks to a water faucet on the lawn, and says, "Daddy, you're not listening." He turns the water on.

"I don't mind just talking to myself and listening to the trees," I say.

"Maybe we should have gone to the zoo." He turns the water off, looks at me smiling, and shakes his head like he does not know what to say. I smile back. "Can we blow bubbles?" he asks, turning the faucet back on.

"We don't have any bubbles to blow."

He turns the water off again and asks, "Who uses this faucet when I am not playing with it?"

"The people who work here," I say. I get up from the bench.

"What do they do?"

"Water the lawn, cut the grass, rake the leaves and…"

"And?"

"And dig the graves, lower the coffins, and bury the dead."

"I don't want to work in a graveyard," says Adam. "Do you?"

"I would not mind being a night guard in a graveyard," I say, stretching my right arm. It's hurting.

"Like in *The Empire Strikes Back*."

I didn't know what he meant, but I say, "Yeah," still stretching my arm.

"Is your arm hurting?" he asks.

"It's always hurting, sometimes more than others." It is no longer a sunny day.

"Can we go back to my mommy's grave?" he asks.

"Yes." I turn away from Adam and walk toward the Ivy section. It feels like autumn, but most of the leaves are still green. There are a few leaves on the ground.

"Daddy, don't leave me," he calls out.

"I won't." I turn back toward Adam and wait for him. We walk slowly in silence, holding hands.

By the oak tree Adam lets go of my hand, walks to his mother's grave, and sits down beside it. "I want my mommy, I want my mommy," he says in a whisper. I hear the wind. He calls "Mommy, my mommy," loudly. I say nothing. He is not talking to me, I think to myself, leaning against the oak tree. It is cloudy. "Mommy, mommy!" screams Adam, tears rolling down his cheeks. He's crying for his mother and there is nothing I can do. My mother used to say the only thing you don't lose is what you don't have. Adam lies down on the grave, kicking his legs in the air. He is sobbing and screaming, "I want my mommy, I want my mommy." I can no longer stand to see him this way. I pick him up and hold him in my arms. I kiss his hair, his forehead, his cheeks and his neck, but he continues to sob.

"Let's go to our car," I say, "and take some incense sticks out and light them." One needs a distraction from pain. Go on telling me lies, but hold me tight. I move toward the car with Adam in my arms. I keep kissing his head and his neck.

"Why do you always kiss me when I am sad and crying?" he asks.

I kiss his head and say, "I kiss to say I care. I kiss to say I am sad when you are sad." I kiss him again and add, "I kiss to say I don't know what else to do."

"But I am crying for someone else," says Adam.

"So am I, so am I," I say, controlling a sob.

Adams puts his head over my shoulder. I kiss his neck. "If I had my mommy," he whispers to himself, "then I would have my mommy when my daddy dies."

"That is correct," I say, with much energy.

"I am talking to myself," he says. "I want my mommy, I want my mommy," he whispers.

I put my face on his head and whisper, "I want my mommy, I want my mommy, and I want your mommy." I kiss his hair. Adam smiles and kisses my cheek. I hold him for a moment, kiss his head again, and release him from my arms.

Adam runs ahead to the car. I get in from the other side. He already has the incense tube out of the glove compartment. "Can I light?" he asks.

"No," I say, picking up a matchbook from the dashboard. "But you can hold them while I light."

"How many shall we light?" he asks, opening the tube of incense.

"Five," I say, removing a match stick from a box from Berghoff's.

"Why five?" he asks.

"One for my mommy and one for yours," I say. "One for John Lennon and one for all the others who are dead." I pause. "And one for all of us who are living…"

"And will be dead," Adam adds. He takes out five incense sticks from the tube and puts the tube back in the glove compartment.

"Are we ready?" I ask.

"Five," he says.

The incense burns with a flame until I blow it out. The smell of smoke and sandalwood fills the car.

"Can I put these on my mommy's grave?" he asks.

"If you like."

"I'll be right back."

Adam gets out of the car, closes the door, and walks away. The sun is gone now. In the grayness of an early afternoon before cartoons, from a tinted car window in a far away land, I see a little boy walking in a graveyard, wearing a bomber jacket and grey pants. The wind is blowing the incense smoke around his face. He looks like a warrior who has lost his ship. He puts the incense sticks on the grave, by the tombstone, one at a time. He walks around them and then stands in front of them for a moment. He comes running back and gets inside the car. His cheeks are red from the cold, his eyes moist from running in the wind. I comb his hair.

"Shall we go?" I ask.

Adam nods his head silently. I start the car. I turn on the windshield wipers, and ask Adam if he would play *Rubber Soul*. "I'd like to listen to 'In My Life'," I say.

Adam puts the cassette in, sits back in his seat. Before the music starts he asks, "Why did someone kill John Lennon?"

C. F. Asmusson

Apprehension's Chopsticks
(From Logbooks: 1989–1990)

These excerpts from recent logbooks are meant ultimately to be placed in their complete context. The literary universe has always had sufficient room to show the individual finished products of a person's thought (letters, essays, stories, poems). What has not yet occurred is a record of the ongoing real-life context which supports and makes necessary these more finished portions. Despite the continuing need to press for a complete picture, the pieces included in this publication comprise only a portion of the peculiarly irregular process of being alive; I have omitted many details that might violate the privacy of friends, and others in order to retain my own anonymity, feeling that the freedom to say exactly what one thinks is otherwise too easily restrained by compassion.

ॐ

January 21, 1989

If the translation of a work into another language is never entirely possible—since each work's particular strong effect comes in part from the fact that it is a new statement of something and, if the work is well-made, it also partakes of its writer's own definite interior contours—then that's not so bad: life will go on without Dante in Cle Elum. But the impossibility of full translation also means that people (who translate themselves to each other to find out what they mean) will never really succeed in empathy, and also that no writer will ever fully succeed in translating the wordless stuff only spun off from their own nervous system. One can never hope to translate all of one's real self into

239

something else or to someone else, or to oneself. The love songs the radio plays mark this point, although they don't know why; they still propose the possibility of a full translation, fusion of meaning; the *other* is usually to blame for the incomplete translation, for the broken heart! Yet most translations work: I obtain my apples, my cabbage...; its only when someone says they've "got" one of my ideas that I am certain of my suspicion.

February 4, 1989

A robin looks about on the ground and finds sustenance. I go out and can't—I need architecture, agriculture, mechanics. A robin remains a robin. I must become builder, farmer, technician—in addition to myself, or acquire others with these skills, as if they were artificial limbs. My mechanic may be cheerful and well-adjusted, but this does not ease my uneasy dependence on machines.

The difficulty in learning how to speak is that one enters a forbidden trade. It's clear when I need the mechanic's work; but the mechanic is unaware—must be unaware, for comfort—of what necessity speech answers to. The world of action does not want to submit itself to analysis: like MacDonald, it wishes to make love and not talk about it. The world of action knows that to speak is to destroy unawareness. To speak from the core or even to hear such speech is too painful—the discomfort blunts the ability to act. Comfort nearly always has something to hide—Benjamin says, "comfort isolates—; on the other hand, it brings those enjoying it closer to mechanization." (*Illuminations*.) Comfort does not want to be known the sacrifices that support it. It wishes neither to know where its food originates, nor that it must, however expensively, go to the toilet. Comfort remains an infant. Comfort retains the person at the species level. A man appears, the woman has children—all speechless as mice. Only the speaker knows what wall lies between.

The speaker says, there are rules to things that are not visible, and this is what they are. The rules that are not visible are not securely written down, and will change. No church securely houses them—it's those who enter churches who abandon hope and settle for mechanics.

March 2, 1989

.... Then to come home and read literary essays. These well-wrought cara-paces! One must have a fixed point of view to argue powerfully from, and turn one's softer parts so that the antique is protecting them. It must be because it has been. Or one stands facing the past, waiting for something con-temporary to emerge from it—nothing quite measures up. It is as if one watched a laborer carefully place pavers edge to edge, covering a typical green lawn. Yes the paving is coherent, so far as it goes—there are no gaps between the paving stones, they cover the subject perfectly. Only the lawn finds itself in eclipse. Most explanations are equivalent to this.

March 19, 1989

I continue to suppose that I have another self—a predatory one, an eager, aggressive debater; sharp, acute, inconsiderate; active, grasping, combative, judgmental, passionate in intellect and feeling—one capable of strong anger, hate, contempt, a person of more agile, able intelligence, of greater depth of feeling—and that something in me is walling that self and its energy (with unfairness and cruelty) off from me. Of course one cannot calmly at any time have anywhere full access to oneself; it is as if one is necessarily weakened or narrowed in proportion to the achievement of one's individual perspective. The nerves speechlessly select what they must have first—they are the pred-ators of one's imagined independence; after they're done, the final product, coherent or not, mourns the apparent loss of passion—the passion the nerves employed en route to something—oneself—that they desired more hotly still. But what were they about?

April 11, 1989

It's curious to read—much like typing a manuscript, or typesetting. There's never any assurance that anything has been firmly taken in by one's sensibil-ity; even the most striking observations, the darkest, the most private, the richest—not much stops one short. Meanwhile, one comes to the end of the writing having been engaged with something other than oneself, but not real-ly sufficiently personally. A part of me has met a part of them. Why aren't I all there? How can I get more of them from the portion I can read? The closest I can come still finds me interposing my sensibility between, merely in order to translate the words into something I can comprehend. From this location, reading doesn't make sense. One should stick to translating oneself, to alphabet? Yet the most striking moments, reading, are when the author sounds like oneself—one finds oneself "out there"—no matter that that self can no more be held in the hand and looked at than the contents of one's own nerves. The memory net attempts to map itself in order to both remain the same and change. One chases after oneself either reading or writing, like a belt route around a city too jammed with traffic to enter directly.

June 17, 1989

Just these fortifications one arranges in one's interior—that timbering, those shorings against collapse—that begin as temporary means permitting one to exist on one's own, sleep separate, dine without company, see without touch—just when these embattlements against the siege of being on one's own begin to look like considered architecture—that's when the voice that offers observation says, all this would have to be abandoned if partnership became possible again. (Or, a partner must be something different now from a shoring against collapse.) And one says, I'd rather live this way, in what I've built, than leave off what I'm building for mere entertainments. The building has become oneself—one no longer longs to be unbuilt. Only exchange now makes any sense. And how is that done?

July 2, 1989

The whole point of writing is to obtain—to bring into reach—that particular quality which gives the most fierce enjoyment. The taste for this quality comes from one's own unmet appetites, the original ones, and also those pointed and squared against what others have written—appetites that are frustrated by the rules of comportment generally operating in conversation. In conversation, one must respect the speed at which the other may absorb what may be said; in writing, there is no such closing time. In conversation one does not prey on the other; in writing one can't. Conversation is seldom ecstatic—it is a working network that at best gives pliability to one's prejudices. But it seldom flies—not for both parties at once (unless in romance), and if it does, nothing remains of it, unless a machine is present. Living by oneself, fed and clothed and housed, able to obtain almost anything marketed, the entire library available to plunder too, one wants something else—that will fascinate and warm, something into which one may pour one's attention and be fully absorbed, fully active, fully unfurled. This quality of appetite—if it is for joy—can be met only by the one inspecting it. If the appetite exists, then who has it—if they are fortunate—may find for themselves where it points, and begin to go there.

September 8, 1989

Language can't be disassembled in the same way that one can disassemble a bicycle—with the expectation of reassembly. It has no table of elements, or if it has, something happens to them in use, as the items comprising a pie change once baked and then again (differently) once eaten. What one reads no more retains its own shape in one's mind than the shapes of foods eaten can be recovered from the body at work.

What a poem may do is add to or carefully refinish or remodel the personal—the sense of an interior from which one looks out at oneself and everything else. There's no control over what offers itself to be taken into that interior, nor what forms the interior aggregates to relieve itself—but the aggregate can be as real as what went into it, and can bring out, sometimes, a new piece of solid floor where more than a single person can securely stand. One's bones don't have any idea of what's upright about them—they are simply a result of the profound momentum of the personal, of earlier "poems"; we are now engaged in building a less fugitive floor in the dance-hall of the nerves, not by disassembly but by adding to the limits of dance and the music it recalls.

September 15, 1989

My sensibility keeps being there steadily. I begin to comprehend its consistency the more I recognize it discarding what was foreign to me. It took itself to what enlivened it and brought me along. I supposed I must live correctly—it absorbed correctness entirely and when wrung out just it and I were left.

September 20, 1989

Description is insufficient for the same reason that the extravagantly detailed memory one person brings from a shared past is not necessarily proof of affection, but instead usually a form of vengeance on the other, the one who seems to have cared insufficiently to remember in equal detail. When Parkway comes to town he speaks at length to Rolanda of minute details of their former partnership and travels. Rolanda doesn't recall a fraction of it— she lived it without saving it. So careful to recollect, was he as present as she was then? Was her forgetting an aspect of his unlimited adhesion?

The insufficiency of description is that it's my description. I wish to document that I was there, I saw, I felt, I remembered. You can't see the scene without me and my narration—my description is my vengeance, like an empty billboard in a remote landscape. The landscape can't speak for itself, apparently, but the billboard is not only inarticulate in what it documents, but covers up what it's said to show, and somehow also delights in doing so.

Dream descriptions are like this—they "go nowhere" unless I can see them as something else too. One cannot compliment oneself on the ability to describe dreams in detail because anyone can. One records them as aspects of oneself as yet without meaning, expecting perhaps to reclaim them in hindsight. But they are worth little until reclaimed if one values intentions as evidence of consciousness, of knowledge, of mastery—perhaps of art.

September 23, 1989

Art as a protest against "unwonder"—but not a protest with signs, not an argument, no more than bloom on plums is an argument; if poems are art, they come from alignment with amazement—and amazement is not a commodity. Amazement, a lostness that calls for respect, a fascination that absorbs all one's attention—amazement just arrives—it all depends on who is there to greet it. The bet the adult poet makes is that their wonder will not wear out, that it is sufficiently intrinsic and sharp to continue disposing of the unwonderful so what's amazing can be clearly seen. In this way, art itself makes the persons it requires to ground wonder in, in whoever it finds waiting appropriately on the riverbank; that is, the electrical quality of amazement must be grounded in a sensibility that respects it and is willing to restructure itself in order to take shape as itself. The sensibility—*which* individual sensibility—is not as important as that sensibility's ability to disregard unwonder. In a poet we are interested in the clearing away; we will settle for those fractions of uniqueness impossible to dispose of, but we want to see for ourselves that the writer is capable of wonder at the wonderful, not as a commodity, but as an inevitability, and even if the wonderful is terrible.

October 8, 1989

Beauty is apprehended—apprehension's chopsticks bring it close. From the gorgeous, contained smoothness of one's blood going its rounds to the coloring trees set off by a light October fog, to the elegance of a well-realized idea, it's a matter of sensibility. But one can't use such words anymore as if they were airtight—the fifteen year old speeding on a skateboard apprehends something very intensely too, and must have it. The only excuse is that the skateboarder is an innocent and is probably not going to grill me in order to find out what I do that's equivalent—while given the chance I would certainly interrogate him.

October 10, 1989

It's the segmentation that one must watch out for—the segmenting the bacterium must take on, as it leaves behind its little global self with mixed anticipation and regret, if it wishes to continue its evolutionary rise to wormhood. But the hours banded off and marked for work, as if there were a real division—that segmenting of activities to slots—that's an illness that has no boundaries.

October 15, 1989

The person has a sensibility of great depth, but will probably not harness it in art or literature until they are forced to sublimate their warmth and sexual energy by failure in human relationships. One hopes until the very end to escape art or writing through satisfactory exchange with another person. The other person is the museum in which one places one's rarest collections, and if the curator is acute and passionate, then life wins and art is not needed, or not essential for survival.

October 19, 1989

An acute person can be open to another on such a large front that it's difficult to settle on any smaller area without feeling you are defrauding the other of something they might care for better. And yet one does not want to offer little ready-made boilerplate opinions on platters.

October 30, 1989

Anger as gaiety—or the fierce gaiety of anger—anyhow, the savage ungluedness that lets light out from the opening the imagined knife has made, the opening in what appears to be the case but is usually a shade in front of something personal.

November 22, 1989

In the small, contained society of the bus, where everyone's face and body and mannerisms are plainly there to see, I keep looking for a point of attraction, for a sign of lively thought being restrained only by adherence to public demeanor. Instead, fatigue, resignation, pretension, and that pervasive, stereotypical "self-confidence" that takes the place of reason, aesthetics, empathy, originality and innocence. People capable of apprehending extremely technical activities (law, statistics, mechanics) remind me of molds into which desserts are poured—from one side, fullness, completion; from the other, a territory in which nothing appears to have been pressed deeply enough not to fall out easily again. And the physical richness of comfort, looseness, touch, ease—where is it?

December 16, 1989

There is a sea-change that occurs when the body reaches the limits of its concrete appetites and yet the sensibility knows it wants more, and sets about making another world beyond the limited, billiard-ball-like meeting of objects and bodies. The sea-change comes when one is at sea in oneself, sailing toward the origin of sensation, toward the origin of language. This sort of traveling is usually made unnecessary thanks to the business of life, and those who are busy with their lives don't see themselves *agreeing* to disappointment. A bad kiss is set off by a good meal soon after, and one forgets one's life as the price for richly living it. And this sort of rich living is extremely careful to protect itself from sea-change; all around it is a guardian wish, a potpourri of swords in the form of rosebuds. Cross that sweetness and you will learn something.

January 21, 1990

I was waiting for them to expose their art, seeing them as I saw myself, as sheltering something too tender yet to expose. I waited for them as I waited for myself; if I *had* gone first, beating them to it, then there would be no need to shelter them and I might see they were not sheltering any art, but only a befuddled and half-strangled survival, which no one could assist apart from their own courage.

Waiting for them was an excuse I used to extend the time I had to wait myself. How could I go first? They must go first, before I could safely go, and when they couldn't go, I couldn't. I needed something in them to be going first, to give me space to go myself. If I went first, then all they'd do was follow, and follow too close. But I had to go even so, and nevertheless, and went, but sideways, always where it couldn't count.

One can't accord Conrad and the most accomplished embroiderer the same respect. But the embroiderer is better than the delinquent; the embroiderer saves their life, as do the gardener and the editor.

January 30, 1990

Watching a bit of "The Last Waltz"—and I sharply recall it was Robertson and Neil Young and Dylan at whom I first caught fire—and overnight made my companions (most of them) pedestrian. That tremendous decapitated movement, when at least for awhile the head was in place and the body danced! To be stuck then among folks feeling nothing but intoxication strongly—overcome and thunderstruck at what was being accomplished and despairing to know what I would have to do to become a part of it. The channels to get there so narrow, so ecstatic no one could say anything helpful about it. And to find I was the only one to violently care. Perhaps there is indeed a horn that wakes people from the dead—or a guitar.

February 24, 1990

In fact, in this latest book (*Vineland*) one senses even more strongly Pynchon's own voice in the thoughts and feelings of his characters. Perhaps this is not the classic novel, with its formal plot and individually developing speakers, but closer to an autobiography; if so, the author's care to protect his private life has permitted him to speak most candidly, without having to pay the now intolerable price of being "interviewed" and "promoted." By remaining out of the picture, and holding his friends secret as well, the author gains in authentic feeling, and in the ability to more generously hand over, in public form, quantities of unmediated perceptions originating in real life. One feels the author has in fact been living an actual life, not a literary business; and when I am privileged to be let in a bit on this life, I feel oddly comforted. Such directness is rare, and infinitely valuable in this country where generalities are nearly always supposed to be—and are presented as being—sufficient to satisfy the hunger for truth. The strength of this one life, as an actual life, can't help but carry the book to its real readers, who are not *litterateurs* so much as survivors; after all, one does not want to "know" very much except what is personal to an author's sensibility—the generalities will take care of themselves. And without the personal one can't be healed from the illness of the predictable.

May 26, 1990

In creating literature, in criticizing it, one inhabits a situation where value operates inescapably: one must do or read something worth doing or reading. As a poet it may be impossible to know what this might be, because—especially in our society—poetry is a product with insignificant monetary value, and nearly as insignificant scientific value. This places it within the area of the philosophical, the psychological, or sheerly human value, a foggy place having little "material" consequence where I may argue that *my* feelings of value are supreme, knowing that it would be impossible to prove otherwise outside the vagaries of language. Yet there are differences in value; if I happen to prize Emily Dickinson above Jane Kenyon, that's a fact—but how do I do it? It is another kind of fact to confront those who claim there can be no difference in value between these poets without the establishment of some ultimate value in relation to which both are placed. But the question of value can't be avoided, either, because it operates widely. On the level of oranges chosen from an open bin at the store, the side of the street one chooses to walk on, the music one cares for, the persons one spends time with.

The nervous system wants choice, and is built to make choices happen. Value, whatever it may be, retains a religious tint, ultimately resides in human nerves, and represents at least a worthwhile stopping place, a designated scenic viewpoint on a long highway. To discard value because of its religious stains is to become in some sense insane or blind. The body itself will place value, and in the absence of quality will invent value for itself in extreme lack of quality, or any debased versions of quality that succeed in catching the attention. One then becomes a connoisseur of hairstyles, sports activities, or other dissonances.

It's terrible to recognize the necessity of belief in value and at the same time accept the impossibility of verifying it. We are like birds who cannot write proper notation for our songs, and who are not certain that the songs are sufficiently instinctual not to be lost to the world when we ourselves lose our voice. If poetry is going to be a lost language, like that of the Cro-Magnons, then there can have been no ultimate value in it—or at the other extreme, society will have ceased to require any meaning for itself.

Marie E. LaConte

Suspended
(Journal from Saudi Arabia, 1986–1989)

The purpose of this particular journal, written during my residence in Saudi Arabia, was to contrast some of the many differences between East and West in a personal manner, and to record some of my thoughts and feelings about religion. I was particularly concerned with the place of religion in one's personal life, which is usually taken for granted by most people until something happens to cause them to examine it. In my case, an engagement to a Muslim man, along with my residence in a Muslim country, caused me to examine my relationship with God in a way I never wanted or expected.

I came to the Kingdom in 1986 as a medical professional. I had never traveled outside the United States before.

As a friend said of me one day, "You have the emotions of an Arab and the thinking of a Westerner. You are not living completely on either side."

&

2 SEP 86

During the early evening the hospital's main corridor is very crowded. Saudi men and women stream through the doors by the dozens, some with small children and their Indonesian maids, some carrying large brass coffee pots or bouquets of fresh flowers, and all wearing native dress. The men in long, white *thobes*, and the women in black, silk *abayas* illustrate the code of the culture—separation of the sexes. All heads are covered, and

251

the women's faces, too. By 7 or 8 P.M. most of the Western medical personnel have gone home, and the Saudis come to visit their relatives who lie sick in the hospital.

Several nights per week I am either entering or leaving the hospital at this time. My skin still crawls when I have to walk through a crowd of Saudis; I don't know if I'll ever feel comfortable. I walk down the hall in my white lab coat, wearing my badge, and I am an official member of this hospital's staff, yet I must brace myself against each wave of Saudis walking toward me from the other direction. The stares of the men are a challenge. I can imagine them thinking, "We will take your skills and we will tolerate your presence temporarily, but this is our country and you will never belong."

This evening on the way out, I fell in line behind Dr. S. and his wife. I was grateful that I wouldn't have to bear the brunt of the stares by walking out alone. The doctor's wife carried a baby, and wore a very short and casual dress—a yellow sack which had sleeves ending above the elbow and a hemline that showed her knees. The Saudi men nearly tripped over their own hems gazing at her legs. One of them, an elder, maybe a *mutawa* (religious policeman), couldn't conceal his shock: his eyes widened and his mouth dropped and he actually turned in the hall as he passed in order to prolong the sight. A younger man, perhaps a student, was overcome with lust at the sight of the foreign woman's calves, while yet another man was repulsed, wrinkling his face and pointing to her legs with one arm while elbowing his buddies with the other. The buddies, too, showed disgust, and wrinkled their noses. All of them turned as they passed, to get a look from the changing perspective.

The Saudi women, somewhat blinded by their veils, glided along as though hypnotized.

I, walking behind this ordinary Western woman, was fully clothed, and provided no interest by comparison, so I enjoyed myself watching them for a change. Mrs. S. and her doctor-husband trudged obliviously down the hall until they met up with another doctor, and the three of them turned a corner.

31 JAN 87

Christmas is a social and cultural event much more than a religious holiday, and this fact has never been more obvious to me than here in this Muslim country. Saudi Arabia does, however, focus upon that small kernel of religiosity inherent in the holiday. Saudi Arabia, the heartland of Islam, the birthplace of Islam, and ostensibly the champion of Islam, does not practice the religious toleration urged by the Holy Qur'an. Saudi Arabia calls Christmas "a pagan holiday" and increases security around the city in hopes of catching a few pagans in the act of celebration.

The Westerners carry on as if nothing has changed. They barge headlong into Christmas as if they were still in their own countries. They hang lights on their windows and wreaths on their doors. They plan their parties and brew an extra batch of wine. They buy Christmas presents for some friends and they ignore others. They whine and pine over their loneliness and they try to be first in line at the PBX to get their phone calls booked. This is Christmas! One must speak to one's family.

Christmas is the time one finds out who has a special friendship with whom, and who is most popular and who is most disliked. It is the time of year ordinary manners may be shed with impunity, and each has full rein to make his or her preferences known. Instead of saying "Good morning" to everyone, one can, on Christmas Eve or Christmas Day, say "Merry Christmas!" and hug and kiss one's friends while ignoring everyone else. One can extend dinner invitations to some, and not others, and not feel guilty. One can give presents to some and not others, with the full approval of everyone.

No wonder these people get so excited about Christmas: it's a social free-for-all, a temporary abandonment of respect for fellow workers through polite behavior. It is, indeed, a pagan holiday!

12 FEB 87

Tamimi grocery store is open in the afternoons, and I like to shop there because it isn't crowded then. Most stores are closed for four hours after the noon prayer, but Tamimi remains open, so I shop there on my days off.

Yesterday I had just finished at the check-out counter when the bus arrived. I started to carry my groceries to the empty bus. A dark and handsome man drove up next to the bus and got out of his car and said "Good afternoon" to me as he entered the store. "Good afternoon!" I replied. No other person was near enough to hear our exchange, and I felt light in spirit for having given a simple greeting to a stranger. In this country, men and women generally do not speak to one another unless they have business or mischief together.

He entered the store and I got on the bus to await the driver. Several minutes passed, and he came out of the store with a small bag. We glanced at each other. He reminded me of my brother Tom—abundant, coarse hair, generous in build and facial features, classically handsome. He sat in his car listening to the radio, and I sat in the bus awaiting the driver. I glanced at him again, trying to guess his nationality. He looked Italian but I guessed he was some sort of Arab. He glanced at me and I looked away.

Suddenly he got out of his car and approached the bus. "Mademoiselle?" he said, stretching his arm towards me. So he was French, or perhaps Algerian. He put four Hershey's kisses in my hand and retreated to the car. I said, "Thank you," and ate one. He started his car, and my driver came with two other passengers.

The man could have given me his phone number. He could have asked for mine. We had plenty of time to schedule a future meeting, but no, he did not attempt to establish a relationship. Four chocolate kisses were his only gift to me and he made me very, very happy.

14 FEB 87

This morning I caught the 9 A.M. shopping bus to Safeway 1. It goes every Saturday morning, but I am rarely off duty or energetic enough to go. This morning I forced myself to stay awake. I worked twelve hours last night, my feet hurt, and my head spun with the dizziness of extreme fatigue. I like this feeling. One's consciousness gets altered with lack of sleep. At thirty-six years of age, having outgrown my experimentations with alcohol, I still appreciate a slight deviation from ordinary consciousness.

I shopped quickly, picking up some salad fixings, cheese, bread, apples, Kleenex, and chocolates for my roommate. At the check-out counter the clerk began to punch the register, then said "Good morning" with a shy smile.

"Good morning," I said.

He was a short, brown man, and spoke with an accent I didn't yet recognize. He had the thin hair and smooth skin of an Asian. "Where are you from?" he asked me, with another smile, a more confident smile.

"The United States," I said.

"Yes, but where in the United States?"

"Wisconsin. It's in the middle west." I wondered whether or not he knew where Wisconsin was located.

"I love the United States!" he exclaimed, almost forgetting to continue with my groceries. "I love the United States. I wish to go there, but how?" He shrugged in resignation. His question was not a question but a statement.

"I don't know," I said politely, though I did know. The most common way to enter the U.S. is to get a student visa, but one must first arrange to go to some school, and one must show proof of ability to pay. One must also have some idea of where one will live, and how one will support oneself, and of course one must speak English far better than this man could.

"Where are you from?" I asked.

"Bangladesh," he said.

"Ah," I said stupidly. I know nothing of Bangladesh. I think it had some other name before it got to be called Bangladesh. Some vague prejudice then came into focus. I saw poor and hungry people, uneducated, unskilled, unwanted. How could someone like that get into the United States?

"I want to go to the U.S.!" he announced as he took my SR102 for the groceries.

"Can you get any kind of visa?"

"I don't know," he said pessimistically.

The other way, the easy way to enter the United States, is to marry an American citizen. I wonder how many men court American women, aiming for citizenship through marriage as their ultimate goal. My poor Bangladeshi store clerk had precious little chance of attracting an American wife.

Still, I can imagine him, day after day checking out the American women at the grocery store, packing their bags, saying, "I want to go the United States, but how?" Every girl is a new opportunity, perhaps his only opportunity. There are many American girls coming through the check-out lines. All he needs is one.

01 MAR 87

Even after having lived here several months, I was constantly aware of the "foreign" culture. I did not expect to fully adapt, and I knew from the beginning it was not possible. The most I could aim for would be a reasonable adaptation, a feeling of comfort, of ease in living without really forgetting that I was a foreigner. Clearly, I have come to this point. Indeed, I have actually forgotten, for brief moments, that I am the foreigner.

One of these moments occurred last night. My friend and I were walking through the narrow alleys of the women's *suq*. We stopped to examine a rack of cotton nightgowns, and I felt some wetness on my arm. I wondered where it came from, and I felt a few drops on my other arm. I quickly stepped aside then, realizing that I must have stood under some leaky pipe, and Lord knows what that liquid was that now struck my arms in large, single drops. I moved to the next rack, and again felt the drops. Finally I looked up, and saw the tops of the buildings and the navy sky above. The drops originated from the sky. These were raindrops! I had "forgotten" about rain!

12 MAR 87

When I first arrived, I did not make an effort to discover any Christian study group. True, I knew where to find active Christians, and I had promised both my mother and myself that I would not neglect my Christianity, yet I did not make an effort to seek out Christian fellowship. Even when asked whether I'd like to attend a Friday morning "coffee hour", I accepted half-heartedly and then made an excuse not to go.

During my last two years in the States I attended church nearly every Sunday. Sunday mornings were indeed the spiritual high points of the week, and I felt truly cleansed and refreshed on Sunday afternoons. That was because God was in St. Andrew's.

God was in St. Andrew's because the people wanted Him there, sincerely. The fact that St. Andrew's was Christian, Episcopal, was quite irrelevant. The people loved God, and worshipped Him using the format of Episcopal Christianity, which had been established at that church at the corner of 33rd and Lloyd thirty-five years ago.

The people here in the Middle East worship God using the format of Islam, which was established here fourteen centuries ago. Islam and Christianity both worship the same God. What, really, is important after that?

Prayer call can be heard five times a day, not just once per week. You can hear it in your living room, on your patio, downtown and uptown. Why should I bother to seek out Christian fellowship when I am surrounded, and even bombarded, by Muslim fellowship? Am I a heathen to wonder if Islam has something for me? Am I sinful for offering my own private prayer when the calls of "Allahu Akbar!" summon the faithful?

Not for that am I sinful. No, not for that.

When I came here I promised to say a short, silent prayer every time I heard the call. Of course I failed in this intention, and eventually forgot that I made it, until tonight.

Tonight, I became aware that I was actually getting into the habit of watching the prayers on TV as they were being offered in Mecca. At first, I watched out of curiosity and the lack of anything else to watch. Very shortly, I knew I felt differently after watching these prayers, and listening to these haunting, whining cries of Arabian holy men.

God is there, too, in Mecca.

21 MAR 87

My mother would be offended if she heard me say that I grew up in a household of mixed religions. My father would smile, knowing I was correct.

Sunday mornings in the household of my childhood often began about 7:30 in the morning, with my mother and father raising their voices in the repetition of an argument that ended only after all the children grew beyond adolescence. We would listen to the rumblings of it even before leaving our beds. As the argument gained momentum, we would cheer our father, who would insult all the rituals and illogical practices of a church that we could neither understand nor appreciate. But this was the only argument my mother ever won in all their married life. She would let my father rant until his bellowing woke the neighbors, and then she would bring it to a quick and dramatic climax with this statement: "If you don't want us to go to St. Andrew's, then get up off your behind and get dressed and *take* us to the church of *your* choice."

At this point, we knew it was over, and we dutifully rose and dressed for church. My father would never rise to this only challenge from my mother. We sensed how dearly she needed this triumph, and none of us rebelled seriously, though we all resented having to get up early on the one day of the week we felt we shouldn't have to get up. All of us vowed to forget about church when we grew up, and we all did. We all decided that we'd go to church with Pop as soon as we could. For many years after that, we joked about it.

"What church do you go to?"

"I go to the same church my father goes to."

Finally, even my mother wore herself down, and took a few years' breather.

But during those adolescent years nothing could keep her from dragging us to church every Sunday morning. Even in the coldest, rainiest, snowiest weather, when many Christians knew they'd be forgiven for not risking an auto accident, she stuffed us in the car and left the house fifteen minutes earlier than usual.

Like many single parent families, our life in Christianity developed as if we had no father at all. My mother's marital status remained a mystery to the adult members of the congregation. She did mention his name during casual conversations, and referred to "my husband" quite distinctly at times, but no one could really understand how any family could come to church year after year without the father. Not even on Christmas or Easter would he show his face, not even to drive us to church and then go home again. (Perhaps he no longer lives in the home, they must have thought.)

I forgot about church and I forgot about God for many years. Not even on Christmas or Easter would I show my face. I was much more of a heathen than my father ever was. My father never forgot about God. He did have a personal religion, one of the utmost simplicity. He believed strongly in God, in the Ten Commandments, in reward for obedience and punishment for transgression. This was all, yet I forgot about even this core of spiritual reality. Only during a moment of intense fear and anger did I remember God—that I could call on Him and He would help me. So I did, and He did. After that, I actually wanted to go back to church, as a form of discipline, to remind myself not to forget about God again, to know that I could always call on Him, and to worship Him, and to thank Him regularly for my blessings.

I went back to the church of my mother, the church I so scorned during my adolescence when I was dragged there Sunday after Sunday. I found God in that church, and I partook afresh of all the rituals and illogical practices that I never understood and still do not. I enjoyed the chanting, the incense, the magnificent organ music, the elaborate and richly colored vestments of the priests. I perceived an artistry in this form of worship, and enjoyed it without ever really believing in it as I should have. My father's simple religion had a good grip on me by then. Life was complicated, and his simple religion was a way to fit everything into a master-cast of order, a surety of direction. I still couldn't accept rituals and incomprehensible explanations. God never meant to make our lives more complicated by our worship of Him.

Occasionally, then, on a Sunday morning, I took coffee and bread before going to church. The Eucharist was not the first food of my day. In fact, Holy Communion was not the focus of my Sunday worship! It is true that the purpose of mass is, indeed, Holy Communion, but this was one of those incomprehensible matters that I could never fully accept. The wafer and the wine were supposedly transformed into the actual body and blood of Christ. We all acted as though we really believed this, especially the priests, and men, too, and I always wondered how many of us were putting on an act. The wafer and the wine were symbolic, of course, and no one could convince me that they actually became the body and blood of Christ.

Then there was the Creed, in which one professed belief in the Father, Son, and Holy Ghost—along with all the saints and the angels. Why couldn't I just believe in God? God alone was more than enough for anyone.

Good Friday mass was the worst, with its emphasis on pain and suffering and death. We were supposed to stay in church three full hours, but I don't remember ever being able to do it. At the end of the mass, the priest held a giant cross on which a good sized statue of Christ was mounted. One by one, we had to file past and kneel in front of this statue and kiss the feet. This practice was the most unpleasant of all. Every year I dreaded this barbaric act, and every year my mother forced me to humiliate myself by kissing the feet of this statue (and picking up the germs of everyone who'd kissed it before me).

Where is God in all of this?

As the years passed, and my mother became confident in her victory over my father, she did start to examine some of these church practices, and she finally recognized the foolishness of it all. Now she goes to a Protestant church, an evangelical church, one that is stripped of all ritual and ceremony. Her current religion is quite close to my father's. In fact, he actually attended a special performance of the Easter story several years ago. My mother sang in the chorus. I don't think he's ever gone with her to worship on a Sunday morning, but who knows? I'm sure she'd be delighted. She would have wanted me to come with her, and she did hint at it several times, but knowing that I am basically of my father's religion, she never pushed the matter. I would have gone with her to this new church except for one thing—she was becoming fanatical. She was going to Bible study groups mid-week, and reading religious books every day. My mother was becoming a Jesus freak. If this was the result of going to that new church, I would protect myself. I said, "No, thank you."

Does God want us all to become fanatics? Is He not pleased with ordinary human beings, honest, humble creatures who believe in Him and His commandments, and find difficulty enough within those ten rules? Everything points back to the religion of my father—simple, direct, moderate, and accessible. So many times I was made to feel sinful because I doubted the church. To embrace a religious dogma is to cast oneself to sin, because too few of those rules are easy to follow in ordinary life. Formal Christianity has made me feel inadequate.

16 APR 87

A few days ago I went to the grocery store. A new display was set up in Aisle 1, just before the fruits and vegetables. This new display offered dates, dried fruits, seeds, beans and nuts in large, white buckets. I scooped some shelled walnuts into a bag, noticing that the price was SR30 per kilo—reasonable, compared to the packed nuts imported from the United States.

At the check-out, the store clerk did not know the price. He was a third world type, maybe Bangladeshi, I don't know. He wasn't Arab, Filipino, or African. His English was as good as any third world expatriot in Saudi Arabia, adequate for his job, but he couldn't have gone to the United States with it.

He asked another clerk for the price of walnuts without shell. The two of them read and re-read the price list posted to the right of the cash register. Neither could find the price of walnuts without shell. I leaned over the counter to read the list myself. Three quarters down was "shelled walnuts—SR30/kilo." I leaned over the counter and said, " 'shelled walnuts' means 'walnuts without shell'," but their backs were to me and they didn't hear.

They asked a third clerk. All three read the list again and became very frustrated. Each uttered righteously, "Where is the price? They forgot to write the price for walnuts without shell!" One of them ran back to the display to read the price from the bucket. All of them failed to notice that the only walnuts offered were shelled walnuts.

"Cross this out," one said to another, pointing to the words "shelled walnuts." They all agreed readily.

"Put 'walnuts without shell'," the other one ordered, and again they all agreed. Their boss, who had written the list, obviously didn't know "good English", though I'm sure he was a Westerner. The three third world clerks, whose salary combined probably didn't equal mine, whose education combined surely didn't equal mine, were proud of themselves for discovering a "mistake" in a list of English language words. I kept my mouth shut.

08 JUN 87

Today I found a cassette of Peter, Paul and Mary's best songs and listened to some of these songs for the first time in eighteen years. I cried. These songs taught me something. They taught me, then, and they teach me now.

I knew these songs, all of them, thoroughly, by words and by notes. Some of them I played on the guitar. Some of them I sang with my cousin. By the time I was twenty, these songs were part of me. Their messages had gotten into me indelibly, though I didn't really know it at the time. Indeed, how was I to know that during the next twenty years I would experience all the loneliness, the separations, the sorrows and the injustices sung about in these songs?

My father hated these songs. He hated to hear about the idealism of a peaceful society where war was not allowed and racial prejudice no longer existed. Because he loathed these songs, I could not play them in his presence. When he heard them, he'd break into diatribes. He was afraid of these songs. I understand that, too—now. He knew what I did not, that these songs foretold my future.

These songs were about justice and peace and harmony and childhood and safety and clean living and honesty. These songs put me on a train bound for glory, and I'm still riding.

05 AUG 87

Egypt is rotting. The whole country is like a giant, succulent plum, thin-skinned and throbbing under the sun with putrid juice and overripe flesh. The cities ooze out decay from the cracks in the pavement, from the punched out windows, from the canals in Giza. I saw the body of a freshly dead horse in one of these canals.

A. and I spent two days in Cairo. After meeting me at the airport, he took me to the N. Hotel. I was expecting the Nile Hilton, but instead I got an old, tacky place not unlike the kind of place I would have stayed in fifteen years ago during my hippie days.

The hotel was big, and probably attractive at one time, many years ago. Now, though, everything in it had outlived its serviceability. The doors didn't shut securely, the toilets were crusted over with brown growth (non-organic, I assume). Though the air conditioners did work in both rooms, one leaked water from the ceiling and the other leaked water into the rug. The rug gave off a rotting odor that filled the room.

I fully expected to find cockroaches, and I looked for them. On the morning of the second day, as we were preparing to check out, we ordered orange juice, and we were brought some dry, stale biscuits. I found a baby roach lounging between some crumbs on the tray.

I wondered why A. brought me to such a decrepit place. It was cheap. Yes, that's the reason. It was cheap.

I'm not a hippie any more, nor am I so poor, and I don't have to settle for such a low standard. A. and I wrestled with this for the rest of the week. He wanted to be my host. He didn't want me to spend my own money. We really did learn about each other during that week, and I think we were both a little startled to discover such a great width in the gap between our respective economic positions. He had always emphasized that he was a poor man, but my understanding of "poor" was not sufficiently comprehensive.

We took the train to Alexandria. I'd expected Alexandria to be less oppressive. The pictures I'd seen of it showed such a bright, inviting city—his city. I was anxious to see these places, and prepared to like them, but I was not at all prepared for the reality of Alexandria in July—the overcrowding, the noise, the dirt, the stench, and the decay everywhere. The photographs did not lie. The beaches and the apartment buildings did look bright and inviting from a distance, with the sun pouring over everything, but at close range one can see the rot and smell the raw sewage.

Nobody seems to mind. The children run and laugh on the beach and splash into the polluted waters of the Mediterranean. Young couples walk along the corniche at night and gaze over the debris washed up onto the beach as if it wasn't there. Groups of men and women walk through the streets, stepping in donkey shit and half rotted fruit. Puddles of water, urine, and putrefaction run along the crevices of the sidewalks, and the men making falafel and roasting corn are standing in it. No one pays any attention.

24 SEP 87

Dr. M. advises us to call God. If we want to know whether or not He exists, we can simply call Him and see if He answers. S. advises me to pray for guidance. "Did you ask God to help you?" she asks.

Yes, I did. And He answered the prayer, as He always does, but I didn't hear Him. I was listening carefully. "God always answers prayer," they said. I believe it, but why does He sometimes send an answer we don't recognize? Worse yet, why do we sometimes interpret purely coincidental events as answers to prayer? One can make some serious mistakes this way. One can pray and pray for signs and guidance, but how can one dispute the claim of the murderer that God told him to do it?

10 DEC 87

Sometimes I am very sorry I ever began studying Islam, because now I am between religions. I am too far away from Christianity to return, yet I can't quite reach Islam. I can't fully reject Christ as Savior, but maybe my doubts are enough to cast me into Hell. Will Allah scoop me up? Perhaps He would if my faith in Islam were stronger, but it's not. As of now I have no religion, and I feel far away from God. If I died tomorrow I'd probably be sent straight to Hell for all this fooling around with religion.

This is a bad position I'm in. Christianity says I'll go to Hell if I reject the divinity of Christ. Islam says I'll go to Hell if I acknowledge Jesus as God. Either way, I am headed for the lower regions.

A. doesn't see my dilemma, of course, but he has no choice. He's never doubted Islam, so he knows beyond doubt how to point himself upwards. My mother, too, has never doubted that Jesus is Lord and Savior, so she knows she is headed in the right direction.

Now I understand how too much knowledge can harm one. One can put a curse on oneself with all one's doubts and seekings.

28 NOV 88

It's easy to fall into an agnostic state, with or without encouragement from home or society. Who wants to put faith in a God who permits suffering? What comfort can be had by uttering, "It's God's will," after a tortured death? How can any afterlife give more pleasure than the love and comfort of healthy human life on earth? A truly honest human being must answer these questions in the negative, thereby casting doubt upon the existence, or at least the goodness, of God. One can remain in an essentially agnostic state for years, regardless of whether or not one observes religious rituals. It is not uncomfortable. An agnostic is free to defy societal mores with impunity, at least regarding himself, and if he's not afraid of other people's opinions. An agnostic can experiment with new thought patterns; he can change and alter his thinking at any time. His attitudes are not dependent upon the master teachings of any one prophet. He can choose his heroes, and appoint new prophets if he wishes. He can also just plod along, insulating himself from the opportunities presented by the mental freedom of agnosticism. Either way, he is not yet a full participant in his own life.

If he does not die while still in this state, something will happen sooner or later to cause him to accept Allah. Maybe the event will be of minor importance. Maybe the event will be a process rather than an isolated action. The process of normal maturity, for instance, can be quite uneventful, but one day that agnostic will look at his face in the mirror and see his wrinkles for the first time. He'll remember his same face in youth, and he'll realize that the youthful face is already dead, non-existent. The brown hair that has faded into gray will never fade back into brown. For an instant, he'll feel a tremendous shock. He will know, then, that he's really going to die. How can any sane person keep on living once he knows he's really going to die?

Two options present themselves. First: forget you're going to die. Stuff it back down into the subconscious where it can't jump up and scare the shit out of you every waking second of every day. Let your subconscious keep custody of this knowledge; let your nightmares be the only testimony.

Second: accept Allah.

I think most people use both of these devices.

10 OCT 89

I know now that I cannot give up traveling, and I know the reason. The hours in an airplane—those cramped, dark and noisy hours—are the most peaceful and exciting hours of my life. In an airplane, high above any country, between time zones, between cultures, habits, and harnesses of life, one can experience a psychological and spiritual freedom unavailable on the ground. One's life is suspended, as it were; upon looking out the window, one is unsure of what lies below. The only surety is in what has been left behind, which no longer really exists except in memory. The destination also does not yet exist, except in expectation. Within this space, one's spirit is as free as it will ever be in earthly life.

The last few days before a trip may have been spent in an anxious agitation, packing the proper clothes, including the appropriate accessories, arranging for the care of plants or the pets, scurrying about performing little essential tasks that should have been performed long ago. Responsibilities are passed along to the next responsible person. Then, you are sitting on the airplane, and it's too late to make any changes. By the time you've reached cruising altitude, you no longer care, and can hardly remember what all the fuss was about. Whatever strings you failed to sever on the ground were automatically cut when the pilot pulled the landing gear into the belly of the plane. In the air, you have no appointments.

The daily routine you had followed the weeks prior to take-off will no longer be followed. The little habits will no longer be indulged; even your thoughts cannot possibly escape reorganization. Within this space in time and place, I never fail to experience a profound rest, coupled with a release of the imagination, a lightening of the soul. In an airplane, between your own lives, you are immersed in possibility. You can't possibly know what you'll walk into when the plane touches ground. All the most carefully made plans are still only plans, and only God knows whether those plans will be entirely fulfilled, or only partially realized. There is nothing to be done in an airplane. Nothing can be done to alter the life you've left behind, nor can anything be done to assure you of the life awaiting you in the next country. Here, so high above the earth that you can't even know exactly where you are, you are in a most helpless and dependent state, as the child in the womb—waiting, waiting, resting and waiting.

Kate Gale

"I Will Die in California on a Windy Day"
(From a Los Angeles Journal: September, 1990)

We wrote Kate Gale, "Your journal writing is not quite what we had in mind for our anthology, and yet we want to say we enjoyed reading it—as a rollicking humor piece. If we wanted to read a good parody of a common notion of what journal writing is, we could not have done better than reading your submission. It's uncanny because it is so easy for us to envision someone writing this piece in all sincerity.... Regardless of your intentions in writing what you submitted, we remain haunted by the possibility of taking it at face value...."

Ms. Gale responded, "I am reminded of the French who say, 'N'avez vous quelque chose un peu plus sobre?' (Don't you have anything a little more serious?) when they are choosing a book or film. As for what I meant by this piece, I can't tell you that, can I? Aren't readers supposed to take what they get? It is part of one of my journals, and we writers express ourselves on different levels, on the one hand we mean everything exactly the way it sounds and on the other hand we are playing with clouds. ...if you study theatre, you know there must be moments of comic relief, and now ladies and gentlemen for something completely different...."

—The Editors

ൟ

Kathy gets up early, begins immediately planning her day. She writes in a little black Daytimer which she consults regularly to see if she is getting everything done that should be done. Amy plays in the backyard while Kathy writes. Kathy can see Amy eating the dogfood and overturning the dog's water dish. She keeps tapping on the computer.

No matter how early she gets to the computer, it should have been earlier. She wants to write twenty hours a week, but finds it hard to get in even ten hours. Teaching five to seven classes a semester bites into her writing time, but she blames herself for lack of discipline. She thinks there are other writers who spring out of bed every morning at four, write non-stop until seven, work out until eight, and get to work by ten. She feels herself falling short of these ghostly writers. She looks out at her daughter between paragraphs and notices that the dog is humping her. She spanks the dog and goes back to the computer while Amy climbs in the wading pool and splashes the cats.

Kathy writes down how much she writes in the computer and in her journal every day. She devises new rules every week: ten hours a week on the novel, five hours a week of poetry, three hours a week on the screenplay. She ignores the rules and makes up new ones. She thinks that at some point she will slip into a disciplined form of life, jumping out of bed and rushing to the computer, but it never happens.

Her writing schedule mirrors her dieting. She will tell herself, no bread, no sweets, no starches. This lasts two days. Then she decides no sweets. This lasts one day. Her lack of concentration disappoints her. She would like to lose seven more lbs., but Honey continues to tell her that she is thin enough.

One day, it's September 7, 1990, she takes a new tack, or what she hopes will be a new tack. She's had lunch, and it's been one of her binge lunches: the rest of a bag of potato chips (about a third of a bag) with French dip and three cookies, and she's feeling disgusted with herself. It isn't so much how much she's eaten, but what. She decides that she will stop trying to be a writer, stop trying to diet every day, and just do it, like the Nike commercial. She doesn't want to tell Honey or anyone else for fear they'll laugh. She decides to keep track every day of how well she does. She starts to keep a journal on the computer.

September 7, 1990. What makes you think you can succeed this time, when you have always failed to be a disciplined writer and dieter? I don't know. No, really, I'm not making this decision again unless there's a way that I can make it. I don't want any more disappointments. What do you want? I want to be a disciplined writer and eat only foods that are good for me. OK, first, let's get all the foods that are bad out of the house, and let's not let them in the house any more.

How do you make yourself eat only foods that are good for you? You know what those foods are: fruit, vegetables, salad, raisins, yogurt, cheese, tuna. Just do it, one day at a time. Don't think about what you are going to do the rest of your life. Today. Today I will write and eat only food that is good for me. Today I am a writer. Today I am disciplined. Getting started is the hardest part. When you have done that, you can do anything.

September 8, 1990. A very bad day, especially considering my high hopes for it. It's 7:30 p.m., and I have just gotten to the computer. The problem is that I think I can.... I don't know what to do now, what goals to make. What have I done today? You ask. You know, first it was making his breakfast, then phone calls, then the mother-in-law comes by, then I do homework to prep for my classes.

Okay, I got it, this is the goal for Kathy's life. I don't seem to be so good at disciplining myself, so here's what. Every day, seven days a week, you get out of bed and go immediately to the computer, take your coffee and go. Write 1–3 hours. Three hours is the maximum, one is the minimum. Then go about the rest of your day, and don't worry about writing again. I think, if you can do that one thing, you will feel good about yourself, and you'll stop eating so much. You'll also have plenty of time later in the day for loafing, making phone calls, and running to bookstores. Tomorrow is a new day. I will recreate myself.

September 9, 1990. The day is starting off well, I can feel it. What I am doing now and will continue to do is I get up in the morning, get my coffee and go right to the computer. I don't even get dressed first. OK, I admit, I gave Hubby a toasted English muffin, and fed the dog. Now I'm writing, got here at 9:00. See my new thing is that I come out here right away and write as long as I have time to. When I need to go to work or go to whatever other commitment I may have, I go. I put in at least one hour at the computer. My day starts off right.

I wonder if I should incorporate these journal entries into my novel. They're so autobiographical. I suppose everything in a novel is a piece of the author, his or her fingers flew across the keyboard to make those words come from brain to paper. The lines connecting us to paper are so very fine, you know.

September 9, 1990 (evening). Still feeling a certain amount of dissatisfaction that I'm not accomplishing more but, at the same time, I'm happy that I am at least doing something. Today was a good day. Started off writing for an hour at the computer, made breakfast for my honey, he ate it, watched the game, not much conversation. I did dishes while I ate mine. Then left at 11:00 to go for a walk on the beach with Miya. We walked for an hour and a half, and I was carrying Amy, so I got an extra good workout. Then, let's see, I went to Sisterhood Bookstore where Amy demanded to be nursed. I sat in the restroom and looked at old art prints while she nursed, and then bought four books while she threw several books and records off the shelf. I got home, had my salad, and made my dance tape for the class I'm going to teach. Just making that tape took two hours, recording songs, but while I was recording, I ran in and out and weeded and watered all the flowerbeds and did the laundry. Now if Honey can just keep the place neat tomorrow when he's here with Amy. Tomorrow my full teaching schedule starts. I have my chicken soup packed for lunch, and my outfit—black tank top and shorts—all laid out, so I'll look spiffy but not too sexy to the darling little students.

September 10, 1990. Getting up at 6:00, nursing Amy, being at the computer by 6:30, writing my heart out, it seems so natural to me now. I wonder why I didn't start it sooner. Amy and the puppy play with Amy's toys and the puppy licks himself because he can. I sit here writing in my white cotton Victoria Secret night shirt. I've finished my first cup of coffee and will soon run in for another. Actually I'll wait until I've written for at least a half hour. Then I'll deserve a second cup of fresh ground coffee. Honey's sleeping. He worked until late. Amy's so fascinated with the outside now. She can sit for hours playing on the grass, stretching her arms into the fish barrel, trying to catch the goldfish, picking grass for the rabbits. She eats the grass too. If I can write every day, I can do anything.

September 11, 1990. Well, yesterday wasn't a bad day. I did write two hours in the morning, studied French for an hour, taught dance for an hour in the evening, and taught at two different colleges in the day, did the grocery shopping and got the car washed last night, made love.... I'm still not completely happy because, well, I didn't stay on my diet, which brings me to a point, should I really try to lose more weight? Of course, Honey thinks I shouldn't. But I think I would look better less maybe five more lbs. OK, here's what I'm going to do. I'm going to stick unfailingly to my diet for two weeks. 900 calories/day, and that is fruit, vegetables, low cal bread, fish and chicken, no sweets, no alcohol. I can lose these five lbs. I know I can. I just need to apply some stick-to-itiveness. Today I am only exercising 1/2 hour, and writing 1/2 hour, but that's okay. I will go teach from 10 to 10, so that's a long day. Tomorrow I'll exercise more and write more. I am happy that this writing every day is working out. I really must continue to spend my weekends with Amy. We need quality time together. I adore her, with her little smiles, her way of snuggling up to my shoulder and laughing in my face.

September 12, 1990. God, I woke up so tired, give me coffee. I'm late getting to my writing. I'm only going to do a half hour of writing this morning and a half hour of exercise. I hate that. I was dragging my butt this morning like a can of lead. Amy loves playing outside while I write. I keep looking out at her, and there she is, playing in the ferns. One of my students wrote yesterday, "The teacher looks young, so very young, and she wears no makeup. She's fresh looking." He was embarrassed for me to read this. I'm glad he thinks I wear no makeup. Some other guy wrote that for him orgasm is the pinnacle experience. He wrote that he always makes sure the lady has an orgasm too. How did he expect me to react? I smiled, and said his writing was very descriptive. I'm doing better, I have to admit that. I have been more organized and disciplined about my writing this week than ever before, out here every morning, in my nightgown, pounding away. I'll get better. I want to write at least an hour a day, and I can, I just need to work up to it. I wonder how Emiko liked Lifespring. I wonder if I should try it. From now on, I'll write at least an hour a day, and I'll eat less too.

September 13, 1990. Thursday, and I really am not writing much this week, but at least I am writing every day. I'll get better next week. This weekend I expect to finish my poetry manuscript. It's amazing how much time all this teaching is taking. I thought I would get more done. I wonder what I'll do with this journal. Today I'm only going to be able to write about five minutes at the computer, I'll write more in my journal later. Last night that writing workshop was so crowded, but I liked Jim. He said to call him Jim. I'd like to talk with him more after he's read some of my work and maybe liked it. That workshop is so cheap. I wonder if they'll like my novel. I suppose I'll try bringing it to them. I need to get the damned printer working. Well, off to another day of teaching. At least I have written something. I love myself, today and every day. I will write. I am a writer. I am beautiful, and I am eating only what is good for me. That walk this morning was wonderful.

September 15, 1990. Saturday. A very bad day so far, although I suppose that I shouldn't label it as such, that only makes it worse. But what am I going to do with the rest of it? And what do I do about Honey. I went for a walk this morning carrying Amy for 45 minutes, got some good exercise, then off to a birthday party where Amy glowed, running around in her little bare feet, running up to people she doesn't know, to touch them.

He has been angry all day, blackness hangs around him like the veil on an Islamic woman, shielding his face, his eyes, only his mouth shows and from his mouth leap spiders on angry mean hairy legs. I am not doing anything well. I suppose teaching is going well, although I don't have a full-time job yet. OK, let's write about one thing at a time here, it gets confusing.

One, diet, I haven't stayed on my diet at all, and I still weigh 135, and I would look better 6 lbs. thinner. I will stay on my diet every day, and lose 1 lb./week for the next six weeks. I'm going to be hungry, that's what dieting is all about, but I will lose the weight, and I will feel better as a result.

I will eat a 270 cal/breakfast, a large salad and veggies for lunch with tuna or cheese (280/cal), and the same for dinner (350 cal). I will do it, I can do it, and I will.

Exercise, I've been pretty good about exercising at least 45 minutes a day. I'll get that up to one hour a day.

Friends: I'll always see Miya every week, and Lisa I'll see every two weeks at least. Everybody else I'll try to see once a month. At least I can write notes to people.

Sometimes I feel like I'm losing control of everything. Tomorrow is going to be a fine day. It is the beginning of a new week, and it is the middle of September, a simply wonderful month, the air is cool in New Hampshire now, the leaves are turning crispy. I want to go back East so badly I can taste it. I need to spend less and save more. I don't spend as much on clothing as I did as an idiot college student.

We're going to the Hollywood Bowl tonight to see my favorite, Handel's *Fireworks*. God I love that music. I want to be that music, all orange inside floating over airwaves crawling into people's ears, making them feel things.

Maybe tonight when I hear that music, all the flame-colored chords will heal me. I'm slowly being ripped apart by not being able to write enough.

What am I going to do about that? OK, Saturday, the first thing I do from now on is to come out and write for at least three hours, same thing Sunday, the rest of the day I can do other stuff, like homework and exercise. I'll keep Amy with me while I write. Then Monday I'll write at least three hours. Tuesday-Thursday I'll write one hour a day. That means getting up at 6:15, and rolling right out here in my nightgown, but that's OK, I'm going to do it. Now the other thing is, this poetry book has to be finished tomorrow, then from now on, the 12 hours that I write, I want 10 of them to be on the novel. I have to write ten hours a week on the novel. I want to finish it this year. It is time for this novel. It is time to discover my own energy. It is time to stop fighting and start living. All that energy inside me. I will not die alone, afraid, cold. I will die in California on a windy day. The sun will not be setting, it will be rising. The clouds above the ocean will tell of much needed rain, they are tinged with pink, they float, waiting for me, the sun reflects on all that water where my ashes float along the crest, dip into a trench, and rise again and again.

September 16, 1990. I'm happy today. I have gotten off to a good new start. It is already 10:30, and I am just getting to my writing. But that's OK, as long as I write for three hours today, which I am certainly going to do. I am going to write from now until 1:30, and I am not going to pick my butt up once from the chair if I can help it. The only thing that will make me move from this chair is if I have to for Amy. She's sleeping now, but Honey may bring her out to play later. It's wonderful to have this little back room for writing. I can't hear Honey watching the game. I'm glad he likes football. It gives him a lot of pleasure, and he never minds that I don't want to watch it with him.

So, I'm off and running on my diet. It's 100 calories of fruit, 250–300 calories of yogurt and prunes, and 500 calories of salad, vegetables, chicken and tuna and eggs with an occasional slice of low calorie bread. I'm staying away from other foods until I can drop seven lbs. I want to drop this weight at the rate of 1 lb./week for the next seven weeks. I'm going to look fine at Thanksgiving. Once I get to 129, I'm going to just stay there by eating the same healthy diet: fruits and vegetables.

Today I'll finish writing by 1:30, make my honey his lunch, have some yogurt and prunes myself. Then I'll exercise, take my shower, and do homework. I would like to end off the day by spending time with my poetry journal. If I can do all this today, what a perfect day.

I'm becoming aware of my cycles. I wake up feeling like I have the day in my hand, fresh and blue like a new robin's egg, and I'm holding it, turning it over, admiring it. I drink my coffee and it's still fine, I'm looking down at my hips jutting out from under a white cotton shirt, and I'm ready for anything. If I don't get to my writing pretty soon, stuff starts to crowd in, like wine pressers running into a vat, and soon nobody can tell what a grape is, it is all purple confusion, the air smells so strongly of fresh juice you can't tell where the air starts and the grapes stop, and after that, I start to eat, slowly at first, then more boldly stuffing whole chunks of food that I'm not hungry for into my cavernous mouth, and then I am bloated, washed out to sea, the day is speckled and then rotten; it will never hatch, I close in on myself and wait for the next day.

Starting the cycle right means getting out to write as soon as possible, and continuing to write for one to three hours without a break. Don't try to write any more than that for now. I don't need any more pressure. After I've done that writing, I am overwhelmed for the rest of the day with a sense of positive accomplishment, the bird has hatched, is off, is flying.

11:30, well, I did take a break, I ran inside to go to the bathroom, and Honey says its half-time so let's make love, which we do, turning down the television so the cheerleaders will not distract us. The Rams are resting and drinking Gatorade. We are doing it on the carpet, laughing at ourselves, then washing off and going back to writing and football, feeling all happy and zingy on our insides.

Bianco Luno

Triple Lenses
(From Philosophical Notebooks: 1980–1990)

These, what have become notes to the soul, originated many years before as posted sour grapes journal-letters to someone who—perhaps understandably—grew weary of them…

The process of keeping a courageous journal is reputed sometimes to result in greater self-understanding. But what might it do for someone already transparent to himself? Here is proof that the process can act in reverse.

Welcome to the small, precious world of Mr. Luno, who has made a mental career of recording his descent into stupidity and cowardice.

> Of Consciousness, her awful Mate
> The Soul cannot be rid—
> As easy the secreting her
> Behind the Eyes of God.
>
> The deepest hid is sighted first
> And scant to Him the Crowd—
> What triple Lenses burn upon
> The Escapade from God—
>
> —*Emily Dickinson*

৪১

Fall 1980

Waiting for the bus I saw a woman dressed in red, black and white. Her long hair wasn't quite black but it was dark enough to suggest it. Her shoes were, though—they were matte black; plain and high-heeled, they settled the issue of her legs, which were exceedingly pale and made paler by ivory stockings sharp against and just below the fresh blood-red of her dress drawn in tightly at the waist. To her cheeks she must have first applied something to make them as white as her legs, and then gently bruised them to suffer the color of her dress and lips. (But there was the polite dissonance of her eyes, which were sparkling blue, and about these she'd smeared a hint of the sky.) It occurred to me these were classic Spanish colors: passion, and darkness in which perhaps evil lurked, plus the special purity that one expects of all women to some degree. She'd fitted them perfectly together this rainy day. In her hand she held a crimson bumbershoot, but as she turned to look away from me I saw something frightening: she hadn't noticed it, I'm sure, but a rib in the bumbershoot had pierced the ruddy membrane, and the shiny stick, in its metallic cruelty (invisible to her), spoke to some horrible vanity.

•••

What keeps me alive is the wonderful courage I see all around me. To think that all these perfectly unheroic and ordinary people are as unhappy as I am (and yet smile and keep busy and live life so fully) puts me to shame.

•••

Once when I was nine or ten my father finally tired of me saying I didn't believe in the devil. He stood up from the table and ordered me to go out into the night in our backyard, beyond the huge old white oak, and wait fifteen minutes in the darkness, pray to the devil and see if he didn't show up looking like a big black dog with fiery eyes. I hesitated. He said, *go on, what are you afraid of?*

It was dark; my eyes, used to the bright kitchen lights, were useless to me at first. The summer canopy of the great tree blocked out even the starlight. I stood around and waited. I might have imagined things moving in the blackness, or eyes (probably the neighbors' cats) watching me. I was pretty scared, no kidding, like I said, at first being blind and all. I kept expecting something to touch me from behind or suddenly hit me in the face. But nothing happened for the longest while. Then all of a sudden a terrific hatred welled up in me and I lunged forward into the darkness, hoping to grab the devil by the neck: I would beat the shit out of him, throttle him till I could feel his burning blood on my hands, thrash him about and drag back his battered pelt to throw at my father's feet and say, "There's your goddamn devil!" I lunged forward but only tripped and fell on the grass. I just lay there for another long time.

The grass was already growing moist and it was so cool, and by now my eyes had adjusted so I could see the stars in spite of the great oak. I could see into every corner of the backyard behind the garage and the big white oak. I started to feel pretty good. There was no devil around here! I decided I'd stay out until they started to get worried about me.

After about two hours I went in. My dad was watching TV—"Gunsmoke", I think it was, he always liked westerns. I could hear the music as I stepped up to the back door. He asked me what the devil had said to me. I told him he didn't say a thing to *me* since *I* was the devil, but that I did remember seeing a scared little boy out there and telling him to go to Hell. He turned into a big black dog with fiery eyes and went.

Spring 1981

Compulsively alienated from the ones I love.
You ask why I'm smiling.
It's the smile the devil wears when he's sad.
His sorrow amuses him.

Fall 1981

All philosophers have this one thing in common: they're all fascinated by fire. Some will sit content to watch the lovely flames dance for eternity. And some continually busy themselves looking for things that will burn, and try to understand the chemical reactions taking place. Finally there are those who, having perhaps engaged for a time in these activities, decide to leap in.

Winter 1981–1982

We are all under some spell or other. That we're not all under the same one makes for tragedy, comedy, etc.

•••

When my mother sifted for stones in dried pinto beans, or rolled out tortillas from little balls of dough, she held her tongue out between her teeth so that it almost touched her nose. It made her look inane, my father would say. It meant she was preoccupied—but more than that, it was a sign of deep contentment. She would be busy being what she was and that's all there was to it!

•••

Is it morally reprehensible for one to know the truth and not act accordingly? It can't be.
For if it were, morality would require us to search out the truth so that we could act upon it.
Meanwhile, until finding it, everything we could do would be wrong.
And suppose we never found it?
All would be lost.
The careful would take care not to act at all.
But it's plain to see we speak and do much without caring whether it's true or not. I shouldn't say we *don't care*; rather, we put out as much effort as the next person in search of truth, and then we're satisfied our intentions are good. Our main concern is to be loved, the truth be damned.
Admit this and even the *search* for truth is a dubious enterprise.

Spring 1982

Impure love is noisy.
The purest expression would be no expression at all.
Silence.
One of the curious things about the dead is how quiet they are.
This is the silence of perfection attained.

So perfection frightens us, creatures of a day.
Still, we call it 'perfection' not for no reason at all and think we will some-
day find it.
We can say we always have something to do.
I beat my drum, grind my ax, elicit reactions.
This is my conceit:
to find, to brush with the tips of my fingers, perfection.
And it would not be so hard if I didn't also insist on wanting to live.

•••

I am at a loss to explain my behavior.
Walking aimlessly about town at two in the morning.
'A stranger and a pilgrim', always.
Funny a stranger doesn't become familiar, at least to himself, after so many
years...

•••

"I, of whom I know nothing, I know my eyes are open, because of the tears
that pour from them unceasingly." (Beckett, *The Unnamable*)

•••

Sitting at the guard desk at the retirement home where I've worked now three
years, I watch widows and widowers pair off for no deeper reason than com-
pany. Courtship in the shadow of senility proceeds with such patience you
think they would live forever.
A little walk today, quickly tire, a little farther tomorrow.
Using each other as canes.
A dignified gentle civility so far from anything erotic.
An hour passes in silence, between words, on the divan.
An addled old maid is offered a gentlemanly arm.
I've noticed the women too far gone to powder their faces get the most atten-
tion from men.
From love, pity, companionship—I don't know.

I know of at least one case of a man letting it be supposed of himself he's more daft than he is only to occupy a certain woman's otherwise idle instincts. Probably she knows. Who could be so old and still fooled?
"It's not a question of being fooled," she would say to me, "I can see no joke from here."
Using each other as canes.
The word, rid of every trace of wit or disrespect, seen as a description of value rather than choice—a track and not a steering wheel…

•••

I would give an arm or leg to lose my eyes. (A gloss on the line from Beckett…)

Fall 1982

Sometimes I feel embarrassed and I want to apologize for the way things are, for life. For all the people who *could* be friends to me, who walk the streets looking in shop windows, who go home to cook dinner, sign report cards, who laugh and cry, show concern and kill—do all those things I won't let myself do with such abandon. I'm getting more polite with age and it must be a vice.

•••

Though the supply of lies may seem inexhaustible, we, for some reason, are restricted to a certain quota each. When you have exhausted your share you learn to keep your trap shut or risk speaking the truth in spite of yourself.

•••

Now every day I tear into K. Call her a bitch, a pig, an idiot. I expect her soon to move out, though I keep being surprised at the thickness of her skin. She abuses me, too. It's a regular pastime. We seldom spend time together. She comes home late from the clubs to sleep on the other twin mattress in the room. I tell her to shut up if she spontaneously begins to rant over the idiocy of the men she meets at the clubs. About how they pester her, the parade of petty drunken jealousies, the resentment from other women, the regulars…

"I'm the best-looking one around." My kitchen is spotted with the glitter, face paints and hair dyes, and rags she wears. She doesn't wash her dishes right. Lives on macaroni. She spilled shoe polish on my bed sheets. Eats and drinks on my bed. Methodically catching on every excuse, I tear into her. And she says, "You forget I have an IQ of 140." I say she's a piece of shit. For two months now, the time she's spent as my guest—at first because she had no money, then because she spent the unemployment she finally got—I've been tearing into her: It's paying off at last; she said today she's looking for a place of her own nearby, has even tried to get work.

She may be out of my precious space soon.

"So you can shout at your fuckin' books!"

Winter 1982–1983

I must define my terms as though I didn't speak the language; I remain foreign to my words, and I'm trying to show that I know how to speak them.

The hours pass like minutes and I keep moving farther and farther away.

My perception of things is still functional but increasingly false, my sentiments are colors on cheap postcards, my memories and plans are a collection of these.

The people who know me are incredulous.

And these are the people who *know* me.

I can't speak a word to them.

My true friends are perfect strangers.

They will always be far, far away, or long dead, or unborn.

•••

K. knows I have no friends and so she can get away, to a point, with what she wants from me. But every day I make it increasingly clear why I have no friends. This, in spite of her faults.

Spring 1983

Suppose I were to write without mockery, like Turgenev or [Sherwood] Anderson. But how can I be sure they were not mocking? Innocent writers don't write innocent books. No more than a child is nostalgic… Strange to say, I remember very clearly being nostalgic then.

•••

A child is taught manners (such as honesty) by friends and family. Sincerity, it picks up by spending time alone. Why it is dangerous for children to spend too much time alone.

•••

"The real morality of actions, their merit or guilt, even that of our own conduct, thus remains entirely hidden from us." (Kant, *Critique of Pure Reason*) Isn't it curious that we should have any notion of a 'real morality' over and above the apparent one? If I knowingly perpetrate an act of kindness, why isn't that enough for me to say "I did good"? Can't we see how so many people insist that it *is* enough?
I fancy that if Romeo had carried through some grave, courageous act—an undeniable testament of love—Juliet, on her balcony, would still ask twice and be justified in doing so. God, Himself, could not tell her what he would have to say or do to preclude the possibility of further doubt.

•••

Silence is the only eloquence adequate to the truth. Irony, even compassionate irony (humor), runs a poor second. Yorick's were Shakespeare's most lovely lines.

Summer 1983

A boy: I made great noises, though everyone spoke of me as quiet and well-behaved. In my head there were great scenes enacted, and the thunder of thousands laughing, as I swept the thick dust from the concrete floor of my father's shop. The epileptic dancing in my head sometimes convulsed my frame, and they would ask if I was alright. I was so happy when my parents went away and left me alone in the house; it wasn't often enough for me. I could have my fits in sweet privacy. The noise and dancing went on till I swooned against a wall, a wall stained with my hand marks. My mother was angry at me for racing from one end of the room to the other, bounding off walls like a caged monkey. Something very strong and terrible was inside me and clamored to be set free. With an iron will, remarkable in a child, I made it heel in the presence of others. I was so strong then. It will win in the end.

•••

The sun shines mornings on curbstones in towns near and far I've never been to. And yet it shines on this one where I'm sitting.

Fall 1983

There are murders so secret, not even the victims know; victims, so many, the murderers shouldn't be blamed.

Winter 1983–1984

Nine months now I've been living in a seedy rooming house, Bukowski-style, with ex-cons, derelicts, alcoholics, morons, drug-dealers, black homosexuals, over-educated middle-aged anarchists, fans of Céline, wavish punks, misogynists. (None of it has really rubbed off on me, available as I've been.) My only real complaint is that certain ones don't flush the toilet; the ex-con, in particular, has an irrational fear of flushing toilets and he also, I think, is in the habit of emptying stale food and other kitchen garbage into the bowl as well (the tiny kitchenette is in the hall right outside the bathroom door). There are no (resident) women in the house. K., visiting me, claims being attacked in the hallway by the bathroom by the ex-con (no more than a kid, whose usual crimes are stealing malted milk balls from Safeway and robbing parking meters). At present he's being detained at a correction center. Otherwise, I'm quite content with my room. I have a private kitchen and a bedroom, $120/month, all utilities included. It's quieter than you'd think, although a guy upstairs will periodically shout obscenities in the night, audible down the block, typically after a scandalous news event. (Just after the Russian downing of the Korean airliner, Reagan, the Russians, the Koreans, God,—all got their due of choice words. Similarly, after Grenada.) It's more than just words, the man seems to suffer real pain. Sometimes you just hear a wail—moving, but for the inopportune timing. His cat comes into my open window, a very friendly fixed tomcat. I'm thinking of getting a young cat myself soon to keep me company this winter. Company I don't have to fight with, like with K. I'm stocking up on used books in case of nuclear war. I think I have a fine collection.

The paltriness of the life I lead now would have frightened me a few years ago, fresh out of Princeton. Melancholy seems to mellow in time. Seems I feel free,—not knowing if it's real. Contentment is too strong a word. A greatly appreciated respite with a trace of guilt around the edges, set into a lovely mountain scene. Suspended in a curiously conscious coma, caged in a body paralyzed from the hair down...

•••

How long can I expect this charmed life I lead to last? Something nice happens to save me a thousand times a day. It can be as little as recognizing somebody I know on the other side of the street and the train of thoughts this starts up. It can be the smile I get from the 'billions and billions' served under the McDonald's sign. Forty-five billion, last count. Soon they'll be using scientific notation.

•••

A lie is an answer to a question.

•••

...Gradually, I sense I'm becoming more and more like other people as what is most peculiar to me cowers back into the infinitesimal core of my ego. If it doesn't kill me, I swear, one day I'll be the egotist *par excellance*, indistinguishable in the throng but for a slight sweet odor of decay.

Early Spring 1984

It is fortunate I am able to pass time so contentedly doing laundry, cooking dinner or walking to the Safeway, etc. If these distractions should lose their fascination for me…what would take their place in my life?

K. calls it making love, I call it sex (if I bother to call it anything). It's terrible, on reflection, what words can do…. I treat her with just enough tenderness to relieve my conscience. Either women are liars and they can rest content with just a likeness of love (and it's only men who are foolish enough to demand more than that), or she's awfully desperate, not caring to notice.

•••

It is very cold outside in the city I live in, and I'm very snug and warm here in bed.
I thank you, Lord.
Forgive that my gratitude is laced with malice.
If you can forgive my unwillingness to ever forgive *you*, you are indeed a great God,—still, not *my* god. You are not only dead—as an alert German said—you are buried now.
We have now to deal with your ghost.

Summer 1984

A point comes when an honest philosopher stops looking for truth, having found it—or better—*remembered* it. He starts looking for persuasion—and sees it everywhere—but never quite enough. The fact he doesn't die forthwith shows he's still open for suggestions, could still benefit from a tad more persuasion, still has a sock on.

•••

I went to a movie and spent the whole two hours wandering the aisles and ramps looking for the best seat.

•••

Women are liars just like men…
But women are *better* liars: they convince *themselves*. And when you've got someone who's convinced of something, why bother with honesty?
Men are not as good at this, which is why you have to watch them more closely. Instinctively, at least, every woman knows this.

•••

You may have noticed: I don't expect my uses of the terms 'men' and 'women' to reflect or represent particular men or women, still less, the essence of man- or womankind. The women or men I talk about don't exist anywhere.
If you think you recognize truths in my wisecracks, you're after consolation, not truth—and you're looking in the right place.
I wouldn't know what to say to you, if you asked for the truth.
I'm not in a position to know it. I still wander the aisles. I'm not a 'convinced' sort of person.

•••

Women lie beautifully. This is their saving grace.
Men face the ground when they lie.
Lying enhances a woman's beauty a million fold.
A woman can lie by herself, but a man has to lie with someone.
Women lie at rest, with men it is a chore.
When a woman lies she's a part of the world.
Men are always a little more there than here.
The thing about a woman is that she has a real chance for truth even if it's only half a chance.

•••

I dreamed I was at a philosopher's symposium. All about the room were tidy piles or pools of vomit. Over each a philosopher crouched. As they picked apart and sorted through their own and other's, I heard one to say, "I can't believe I swallowed that!" Another said, "How did you ever manage something so big down your trap?" "Ah, but I feel much better now!"

•••

On a table, there were bottles of sherry and one bottle of hemlock. The bottles of sherry were empty.

•••

Sad, year after year, after all this time. Near the window at a place that sells mostly hot-dogs, sitting, drinking tea or lemonade. It's summer and the hanging flower baskets and the lightly dressed women—it's odd.
It is not sad to be sad, but it *is* odd.
You're sad too, I'm sure, but I never see you.
I can't 'see' this sadness.
It smiles, makes faces, for all the world like it wasn't sad.
But early enough in the morning there is a heavy dew and the pansies, snapdragons, lobelias—not even the morning-glories, tucked patly away like umbrellas, escape.

•••

My conscience is never so tortured that *we* don't find it amusing.

•••

A lot of effort goes into the comedy—the striving to appear as what others are as a matter of course.
No wisdom is proffered.
I acknowledge the need for recommendations but that is not what I am doing.
Sometimes, I know, we settle on a course of behavior because our conscience is so calmed.
Mine has never been stilled for long: I don't say because I'm all that sinful or because it's all that deep. Only that it has never been a motivation.
I try my best to respect the values of the people that surround me.
And with as much success as most of them.
I say because my conscience is not especially concerned with my behavior.
Its concern seems to be with being hurt.
So I go on fashioning of my life an almost exact likeness of yours, mindful of being neither better nor worse.

If I'm different at all from you it must be in my practice of peeking, with the *steadiest* heart, at my conscience sealed away in a dungeon of its own making, privately, it imagines, in its throes:
The heart of friends, who surround me and who, while wincing at the thought of a small furry mammal being mangled alive, would dash a spider with a shoe.

•••

A rumor has it, in my family, that some of my ancestors were Aztec.
Legend has it that these folk were consummate heart surgeons.
Deftly wielding the obsidian, they could excise the thumper out of their sacrificial victims with all the speed and accuracy necessary to permit the victim the experience of holding in his hand his very own, spasming, before passing out. Managing our existence somewhat differently nowadays, our gods are neither so graphic nor so exigent. Our institutions (say, 'Freedom', Democracy' or 'Human Dignity', etc.) only trash the souls of their victims and leave their hands holding nothing in particular.

Spring 1985

The moral function of irony in literature is that of a speed bump in a parking lot.

•••

The seat of authority lies between the eyes and just above the bridge of the nose.
The child must be positioned at exactly the distance conducive to keeping this point in focus: too far and the claim to authority is ludicrous and vain, too near and only simple fear is inspired.
The wrinkles there represent all that is holy and firm in the universe.
Failing to compensate for my nearsightedness, my father did not position me correctly. This is what's wrong with me, I'm pretty sure.
By the time I get it in focus, authority subverts itself.

Summer 1985

To think and to live are two wholly separate things. This is a worthless observation except for those who suffer the presumption that in addition to being
alive they are 'thinking' people.
These can never hear it enough.

Summer 1986

And what can a woman teach?
She *shows*. What does she show?
Everything, simply. All that is showable
to one by another in the dark.

•••

La Rochefoucauld.
Like staring at the sun, the truth. Too long and you stumble for life. There is
only one truth, actually, and there are no words to describe it, see it with. The
words flee you like the colors from your eyes.

Summer 1988

Making love to a man who is going to die shortly is the secret dream of
every woman.
Men know this, to watch them behave...
So they live violently, kill and are killed. Because innocent women and children
(and when are they not innocent?) get caught in the fray not infrequently—they
say by accident, I, by design—a certain balance commonly prevails.

•••

The most horrible crimes ever committed are committed by children. Schools
and pre-schools are centers of detention, helping to curb their rampant crimi-
nality. At home they are tortured either physically or mentally or both. Still,

they do not desist. They outlive, they bury their victims. All the while innocent until the moment they engender.

All who are punished are deserving, simply in virtue of being punished and
not because of anything coming before. When they come to think they are
being punished *for* something, their innocence returns and they become trag-
ic. And yet their innocence never leaves them: They start out bloated with it
and end up that way, too.

Perhaps at the precise midpoint of their lives they understand best their guilt
for their innocence, the veneer then the thinnest.

•••

I went back to the house where neither of us live any more.
Not being able to remember the dividing line,
the mark, the boundary.
Having to pick out hers and mine from what was ours.
Not being able to forget everything else.

•••

We were so fair about it, whenever we bought anything we each paid exactly
half. Even to the point of brushing off the question of exact change.
We rounded off to the nearest dollar.
First we would settle exactly, *then* we would round off.
How is it supposed to be done?
From this you can see there was never any question as to being in love.
Every penny matters to a lover—or nothing at all matters.
Nothing at all matters.
All matters or nothing.
To the extent nothing matters, everything matters that much.
Everything matters not one bit more than nothing, etc.
Exactly.

•••

Your pain must be greater than mine.
You smile.

•••

I laughed and said I didn't have anymore to say. With amazing speed—it seemed so even to her—she found someone else and moved out. I don't want to laugh at things that are funny, I want to laugh at pain in great paroxysms, to see your expression change.
Until you get up to walk away.
Alone, then I'll stop and look at my hand shaking, my nerves still laughing.
You *were* funny but it was your pain I wanted to laugh at.

•••

More facetious and more accurate, one because of the other. At the store, I need soap and toilet paper:
my grip on "reality" depends on these.

•••

I only begin to cry when the pain stops.

•••

In a wheelchair at a bus stop, a minikin with cerebral palsy and the legs of a dancer. Eyes and hair exactly the same color. I find this woman extraordinarily seductive. Her puppet smile and her angular movements convey the *illusion* of pain. I feel in love.

•••

I write for women.
You don't expect to be understood, do you?
If I wrote for men I might get a pat on the back.
Isn't that better?
That would mean I was misunderstood. Understood, they would not come near me. A woman will react, get angry, feel sorry. No, she will not understand. But the silence of being understood is a horror. The sound a woman makes reacting is extremely pleasant to my ears.
So your weakness for music overrides any duty to impart information?
A woman can touch me and *of necessity* leave me alone at the same time. A man would just leave me alone.

Don't you feel a need to do anything for anyone but yourself?
Answer their questions.
Anything besides?
Suggest intelligent questions for them to ask.

•••

The space of an hour.
All the happiness in a lifetime sifted out might fill it.
For about that long I have worried my doubt.
With the same amount of control both breathe and hope.
Less than a second each week—
what it comes to.

•••

A woman can think things a man can't without losing integrity.

•••

We suffer.
At first by default, then by design.

•••

In these words I am as far as possible from the moment. Impersonal to be impertinent. Not your person but your *self* I wish to violate. Our "selves" are as contrived as anything I might say.

•••

When they are, which is never often, a man is quiet because he knows his words are false, a woman because there are no words.

•••

The vice of the sincere is intolerance.

Fall 1988

A vision.
Walking home from school as a child, making inventory of the contents of ditches, I come upon the badly decomposed body of God. He appears to have (had) the form of a dog.

•••

There are more melancholy women than men. I write for them: at their shopping carts and desks. I have so much in common with them. If I could write in a language they could read, they would understand, "thrown" as we are. But the men who are in power and the women articulate enough to notice and take exception have even more in common.

•••

Is it that we are so good with words or that words are so mercenary, so game that it doesn't speak much for our gift? I would worry if I believed them as you do. The finality and tragedy of words is evident in proportion to how well you know how to use them.

•••

Light can reach me, only if...
I don't know. In your search for
this man/woman connection...
It is always dark here.
My memory invests me with being.
You have no memory.
It is always light *now* for you.
For all its vast wealth...
and in your poverty
I can long to be you.
You never long to be me.
My pride, memory, all my wealth.
So dark.

•••

Truth is the loveliest jewel and most expensive lay in the whorehouse of language.

Winter 1989

All of my life has been lived in reaction to a woman. I cannot remember things being different. Yet they tell me (and how can I say they are wrong?) I have never been in love with them. All my life, knowing better than they what love is, unable to realize it, and made special through what I know, still, and not even being. You will know, I trust, what is wrong with *me*.

•••

My attempt to hold your hand was an attempt to bridge an unbridgeable gap. A slap each time would have been a sincerer gesture, more expressive of real feeling. But the gap is no less real.

•••

Whelmed by the burden and emptiness of words, and my need for the word-less touch of "a woman", and the thousand lies it takes to light up the darkness of the truest truths.

•••

Self-deception has no opposite.

•••

Like basking in the winter sun,
not for the light it sheds
but for its warmth:
What happens when I tell you
what you want to hear.

•••

Depth and purity of feeling are two separate things.

•••

It doesn't make any difference to this pain.
Whether I'm lying, sitting, stooping, standing, kneeling—could be dead even.
(There is pain after death.)
Whatever good reasons for suicide there may be, avoidance of pain isn't one of them.
Only this changes: the pain takes on sense.

•••

Stupid questions are unique in this respect: they can be answered.
You can feel honored to find me quiet before you.

•••

I dreamed, fully awake, as I was stepping into the shower, that a huge air-plane crashed into the street and the side of the building where I live. So vividly that, staring at the showerhead, only the water's finally turning hot brought me back.
In my visions everything is explained and, above all, with order and clarity.
My ex-wife writes to tell me that I was wrong in most of the things I said about her. Even though she is right in nearly everything, I cannot agree with her.
All is clear.
What is clear?—
Everything that ever happened between us I expected to fail.
Why? I don't know, I can provide no end of lies. It was unfair to her, this is clear.
This is my pride speaking now and not what you think.

•••

What does it mean for a condition to be temporary if it lasts as long as we do?
What does it mean for something to be untrue if we can never know the truth?
From what height can things befall us? Everything answered so far as we can strain to imagine.
"I do not believe this excuses lies being called truths."

The ancient scarred meanings of these words are at cross-purposes to the freshly riven values preserving this tension.
You can make the wound not bleed but it will always hurt.

•••

Forgiveness, the sweetest conceit.
As if any one of us could be so
wronged and any other so tortful.
And as for forgetting…
we may not remember, but we never forget.

•••

Human sympathy, in one of its talked about forms, would have it that, in another's place, I will feel pain, their pain as mine. Here, so plainly, you see how imagination, not a morality, can own the capacity for empathy. Does it make sense to ask: when is your pain ever like mine? I will find myself comparing histrionics, not pains. A person, once (and still) very dear to me, writes to tell me with solemn enthusiasm of her latest project, some new vision for restructuring her life. I imagine, in spite of myself, a deep sadness behind such hope. I imagine she suffers more pain than me, is a heroine for taking on life with such courage. I *do* imagine it as courage.

I live in a democracy, and at this time and place in history, democracy is considered the state of the art in the management of crowds. It is expected of me that if I don't vote, at a minimum, I should feel guilty about it. An opinion is expected of me. We are free to have one, aren't we? Likewise, with approaches to life.

Spring 1989

When I was ten, sitting on the front porch one fall afternoon, a woman I had never seen before came up to me and asked me how I was doing. She called me by a name that faintly recalled something, but it was not mine. She called me "Manuel". She seemed about fifty and had blue eyes. A quarter of a century later, my mother tells me my real father's name was Manuel Perez and that this woman was probably a social worker. From the woman's visitation and a few other odd hints I had growing up, I had gathered already what my mother revealed to me.

I remember the woman crossing the driveway, coming up the curved concrete walk my stepfather and I had poured and inlaid with small round stones. There were leaves all over the driveway I was supposed to sweep and rake up. I don't know what I was doing—whether I was reading something or just staring time in the face, looking at the front lawn and the street, the leaves, and the sad color of the autumn light. The woman approached with a pleasant expression I could see from a long way off. I don't remember much else about her. She stayed a few minutes, asked some questions about how I was treated, smiled and left. I didn't tell my parents about her then—but I scarcely told them anything about anything. My stepfather believed in work not discussion, which suited me somewhat because I didn't believe in talk either, though work was no special interest of mine. And my mother was shy about the past.

After the woman left, I kept at whatever I had been doing, probably nothing. In kinder, more romantic, nostalgic moments years later I would describe my childhood as a time of infinite wonder—when I would stare at the pattern of leaves, thinking I needed their specific names (pecan, white oak, sycamore), thinking that by these names I could better conjure them up whole and exact when all that had really fascinated me was their nameless existence. As idiotic leaves, they were more real to me than by their names. But nothing, then, was very much real. The *real* was still a romance to come.

I ask*ed* questions of books or the things themselves, but never of people. Predictably, I questioned authority only to question the authority to question authority. About God, I started out a militant atheist, then a devout junior member of the Holy Name Society; finally, my increasing stupidity precluded opinion.... As an adult my mental retardation reached the level of profundity that completely occludes an opening for curiosity.... This first-hand experience proved invaluable when eventually I took up working with the retarded. I became mute, lost the power of conversation, fell easily into a lethargic silence. And only when roused...but then the certainty and righteousness of my tone was mistaken—when not for arrogance—for wisdom. I came to understand how important words were to people, and how silence was an ambiguous, anxious thing to them. The lesson was painful: that words should *flow* like feelings…. What did this woman want from me? She could have just walked by and from the street seen that I wasn't being abused. And if I *had* been, she wouldn't have found it out from the questions she was asking me. Another part of my brain shut down.

My father would be home in a few minutes and the leaves were still covering the driveway. Abused, yes, alright these leaves abused me, the color of this woman's eyes…from where I trace all my wretchedness and pride. Pity me, if you dare! Afraid, ashamed, I hid from others (at home, in school, at work) my developmental disability: that I had no recognizable feelings and no words to fake them. So the pattern was set from then on: women were to stop and question me, see that I wasn't being abused, and then leave. From my position on the porch, through her questions, I sought and found the only genuine intimacy I was ever to find. If she was a social worker, her work must have been easy. Before then, I had never seen her and have never since. Maybe she's seen me? Perhaps she hailed from heaven or rose from hell. A fall breeze drew up the leaves and curled them into a little devil's screw behind her. Here, there was at last some sense in the pattern of the leaves. Usually a quiet child, I outdid myself being still at this thought. I went onto the lawn and felt the need to lie down and rest. I lay in the grass, face to the sky. A leaf wafts down to fall beside me. Weary already, how was it going to be for the rest of my life?

My autistic tendencies grew and grew. Finally, you were engulfed and my responsibility accrued for having gutted the presence of your body and soul of any independent significance, hollowed you out for my purposes, which even for me were inscrutable. Busy, fidgeting with my body parts and my ideas, you, as a separate self, your integrity, receded to the horizon of the afternoon, the pattern of leaves, and to an obligation for me. And you picked up on this notion of duty and made of it a cause for your indignation. In it you found excuse to place me in a class of stricken unregenerates. I did my violence, you do yours.

But from my vantage point on the porch, or from here looking up (not at the sky, but at the heavens), you were still real and, hence, a romance. From here there is no view. I can't see clouds or the color of the sky; I don't see God or any of his angels. The half of the world, it has been decided for me, I can't perceive; the other half, I have decided not to. My mother tells me (finally) about my real father. She was only waiting for me to ask (she said). He was a drunk—a nice man, but a drunk, whom she left. From Veracruz, no less.

•••

So long as we must have unattainable ideals, let them be the highest—further, let them go on to rise hysterically ever higher every time we turn to look at them.

•••

Modern: to have no illusions.
Post-modern: to have had no illusions, to have forgotten what the illusions were.

•••

More mine than my pain nothing is.
You would take this away from me.
I say this even as I beg you to.

•••

Is it that I am strong?—
That I can talk this way about pain, hope, God, women?
What is so much gall in the service of?
Can I be heard to weep when my gut is twisted enough?
Am I really balled up in a corner of my bed, afraid of death, as you read this?
What would you do for me if you could?
The face of death is what frightens me. It resembles mine.
But, you see, I'll be okay tomorrow or the next day, and I'll go about looking and breathing for all the world like you.
I will pose again.
Be for you a cynical poseur.
I will cast from nothing a hope (for the nihilist is the most adept of hopers) and keep it to myself.
I shall look brave and strong until I keel over:
I do this for you.
Out of love for you.
I will.

Summer 1989

When I quarrel with an intimate it is usually over my impassivity, or how little my "true self" resembles my available self. Or how hypocritical I am in the face of what ails me. I have the verbal facility to make the barest truth sound like a lie. I sound like a genius telling you how stupid I am. My wit is that of the mentally deficient I work with. It flatters *you* to think otherwise. To think I have a "true self", an ailment to be hypocritical about, a truth to pass off, I have...
do I have *anything*?
An immense, immense conceit.
It's a kindness to you that I don't always hide it.

•••

Mired at a generic level, my problem may be that I haven't yet learned to single out the various pains. Grief from convulsion, sadness and heartbreak from death throes and the suffocating presence of others and the fine nerves of a cat snapped by the wheel of a car...and so I talk, I whine some adolescent sententiousness—as though I knew and could tell what was coming later and so was authorized to subsume under one figure the whole of the richness of your world. What I know of it and what you do compass it; but *my figure*, chiseled with a moralist's sledge hammer, an ironist's pick and maybe sometimes even a boy's explosives—my figure is beautiful, baneful, ugly and sublime. I can see what comes later because I know there are only so many possibilities, and I cut my figure to include them all: actually, *they* cut my figure.
I miss the point, don't I?—
"the" point I make a point of missing; yours and mine, however, never stray from my sight:
I saw a young cat, its spine snapped, emerge from beneath a moving car, bounce and twist above the pavement, spewing blood from its silent mouth...my arm went to my face, I cried (I cry even now) and I thought of you.
It's only a cat, yes, and you are not yet that.
Your consciousness leaves me cold.

•••

"Human life is precious."

I will not be forgiven for asking, "To whom?"
The pity we feel for animals and small children does not have to climb over a wall.

•••

But this is real compassion: a kind of tone-deafness to the music of pain. Hitler must have suffered 11 million times more for our sins than Christ ever did. Or,—he was blameless and history's outrage, a plaint about the weather.

Fall 1989

Maybe I am not serious. We could agree that I am being ironic. This is possible, but I will not offer proof because maybe I am in earnest. It all depends on you. When I cry out in pain I am only joking,—or my pain is not a joke but *you* are. You make me laugh so hard you deserve more respect than my laughter can convey. You should be glorified, someone should kill you to put *me* out of my misery.

•••

I can speak as I do about women because I am not a man; by *our* own admission, I am a boy and so share in his dispensation.

•••

So sensitive, I lie to myself continually, just to get by.

•••

My biggest failing:
I want to go on living.
In the face of it, smile, maybe laugh.
At least until tomorrow.
Like this from day to day.
Tomorrow, I'll decide about the next day.

Winter 1990

But there is something in you I cannot touch, so far away…. My eyes well up.
My heart sinks, my poetic nihilism is a hair's breadth away from mysticism.
From across these "infinite spaces" can you hear me weep? We "share illusions", why isn't this enough? (I mumble when I say anything; where do you
get the words?)

Spring 1990

A voice overheard: "The truth makes you lonely."
I overhear others talk even—especially when—they are talking to me.

Summer 1990

At their most extreme, the notions I contend with are interchangeable. This is
a key to understanding both what I say and don't. Pride/Humility, Truth/Lie,
Women/Men, God/Nature, Hatred/Love, etc. Pay close attention: I won't
often deign to be so explicit. Where you see "you" plug in "I"…
Now, having leaked a secret, I proceed to call it disinformation. You really are
free to read me as you please. I grant you only privileges you already possess.
I am only as alien and hostile a spirit as you reflected in a mirror. Only that
tangible. True to form, the nihilist may amount to nothing.

•••

I am no threat except to those who dream.

•••

A philosophy that feels no pain.
A sound like slapping a ghost in the face.

Fall 1990

Pain and beauty.
The beginning and end of the *Goldberg Variations*, Gould's humming.
He doesn't hum so much on the theme and its reprise, the end pieces. Dumb from pain, a whole philosophy is splayed like a fan. From the first stirrings of doubt through despair to resignation. (Truth having never made an appearance.) The history of philosophy in 33 aphorisms, 33 machinations of the spirit.

•••

To voice the truth is to hum.

Essays on Journal Writing

Kimble James Greenwood

Meditations on 25 Years of Journal Writing

I
The Personal Journal: history, genre and defense

I started writing journals in 1967, age 13, at the conjunction of two events: I was given a blank notebook for Christmas by my mother (who wrote journals, primarily for therapeutic reasons), and I read the "half-sexy diary" of my brother, then in the army and on his way to Vietnam. His diary was an awakening for me. Therein I found wit, exuberance, adventure, loneliness, sex and Art. I began in imitation, wanting to cultivate in myself what I saw in him.

&

Age 13 was also the age that I recognized that my long-standing love of science, and desire to become a scientist, was compromised if not precluded by my disinterest in math. A painful reorienting took place. I began to admit interests and proclivities that my concentration on science had all but adumbrated. From that time on I began calling myself a "poet, writer and philosopher" and set the course of my life accordingly. These are roles, goals and loves I've held to since—though, at any given time, favoring one or the other.

My journals, then, became the working notebooks toward these goals—a place to experiment, to write-up my life, to describe the world around me, to honor beauty, to consolidate, play with and augment vocabulary, to work on poems, to think things out or through, to recopy quotes from books I liked and found inspirational, to remember. As I grew older and the process continued, the journals themselves split off and diversified, specialized—so that my main journal, the "personal journal", was now accompanied by adjuncts: poetry journals, dream journals, fiction journals, quote journals, journals to list memories in, to list books read, movies seen, vocabulary lists, curious gleanings from newspapers and magazines, etc.

&

One more component is necessary to understand how and why I structured and took to journals as I did. From the age of nine onward I have been afflicted with the speech impediment of stuttering and stammering. It comes and goes, severe to negligible, determined by its own rhythms, expressive of its own will. In my youth it was the central psychological pole around which my personality, my sense of self, was constructed. My social self atrophied; to speak was to humiliate myself, to lose power, to misrepresent myself, to invite criticism, mockery or pity from my peers.

As compensation, the journal became my place to speak, to speak with what I felt to be my true voice. It was the place for me to hear my true voice. In my outward life I was inarticulate, introverted, stunted, halted, stymied, frustrated. In my inner life, my journal, I was extroverted, expressive, fluent, prolific, articulate, full to overflowing. My outer life felt characterized by weakness. In my journal I showed my strength. In my outer life I had no voice. In my journal I came to know and trust my own voice, my own voices. In my outer life I stumbled, was often seen as overserious, shy, awkward. In my journal I could dance and show wit, playfulness, gusto and irony. In my outer life I was often a coward; in my inner life—journal and imagination— my courage went unfettered, I dared everything.

In this way the journal became friend. I talked to it as if it were other—the ubiquitous and promised "You" as balance and countermeasure to the "I". It was open and receptive to me, comfort and harbor to me. I felt it to be the place I kept my best self, my identity, my wholeness, love and soul.

&

I talk in past tense, I state beginnings. Time has modified, changed, even refuted some of these initial causes and intents. Age works its integrations.

308

Fate determines the course, impervious to the ego and its will. The journal has become its own entity now; it has led to nothing else—neither poetry, fiction nor philosophy, per se. It is my major work, perhaps my only work. I think of it, still, as context, as my context. I can take position *e* now, because I have taken positions *a*, *b*, *c*, and *d* earlier. I reread the journal constantly, discovering anew themes, patterns, directions, crossroads, intent. It is much more of a psychological testament to me now: the text of the self, of the creation of the self. In this way it holds, shows, renews, and constitutes my sense of wholeness; it gives me consistency.

Rereading it as much as I do has proven to be an exercise in and revelation of time and memory. How I have learned to distrust human memory—my own no less than others'! The journal is where I keep my memory; to reread it is to refresh and renew *memoria*. It is not memory of myself alone that I find there. Not at all. My journals are full of the voices of others, full of the people in my life. Through my endless rereading of them, the people of my life are still very much a part of me now. I reflect on them, feel them, learn from them; they remain relevant, viable, alive to present concerns. I do not, I can not—as they always warned me not to—forget them.

Anais Nin remains my favorite journal writer. She has taught me much—as have reactions to her by others taught me. When I mentioned memory above, I recognized that I was paraphrasing her. Let me quote directly from *Volume V* of her published diaries: "The diary gave me a frightening mistrust of memory. Memory is a great betrayer. Whenever I read it, I find it differs from the way I remembered the scenes and the talk. I find scenes I had forgotten, thoughts I had forgotten, and precisions noted at the time have become foggy or vanish altogether."

Writing in a diary developed several habits: a habit of honesty (because no one imagines the diary will ever be read); a habit of writing about what most closely concerns me; a habit of improvisation on any theme one wishes; habits of spontaneity, enthusiasm, naturalness. The emotional reality of the present. A respect for the present mood.

—Anais Nin, *Volume III*, June 1946

Though I am delighted to concur with the bulk of what Nin has said here, I take exception to one statement. Quite the contrary, I would say that everyone imagines that the diary will be read. The traditional lock on the diary, the obsessive gestures of hiding it, guarding it, disguising it, writing in code—are all manifestations of the anxiety, the fantasy, that the diary will be read. To commit anything to writing is to create physical evidence—an extension of the self that, once committed, exceeds the control, guardianship or restrictions of the self. I have had people tell me (especially adolescents) that they dare not write a diary for fear that someone will find it, particularly the someones who would serve as subject matter, who inspire the negative energies that seek or need expression or melioration in a diary in the first place.

Sixteen pages into my first journal, I allowed myself the freedom to write out a sexual fantasy a page-and-a-half long, seeking to claim the honesty, privacy and freedom I felt a journal promised. Was there not also the pressure, an expectation, to be forthright, honest, and whole? Within a month of writing it, however, I could no longer stand the tension, the anxiety or fear that my mother, siblings or schoolmates would discover it and so know—or assume they knew—who I *really* was. I went back and crossed the whole thing out, taking my sexual self back into privacy, where no one but myself had access to it.

But anger, sexuality, and bad thoughts aren't the only secrets we keep in journals. The dark shadow isn't the only kind of shadow; mention is made of the white shadow as well. I think particularly of our enthusiasms—our infatuations for a loved one, a book, a film, music—enthusiasms that build so ethereal a structure, such overstatement, that time cannot help but ground them. Aren't we no less embarrassed for the inflated enthusiasms of an earlier age? For rhetoric that proves untrue? For being caught with the mass, found out in our immaturity, shamed by our tastes?

In my second journal, in celebration of July 4th, I did a messy full-page spread, drawing an American flag and a portrait of Uncle Sam:
"HAPPY BIRTHDAY AMERICA—
192nd BIRTHDAY. CONGRATULATIONS!"
The fact that this is the way our recent presidents still talk does not inhibit my own tendency to roll my eyes.

৵

When man begins to permit himself full expression, when he can express himself without fear of ridicule, ostracism or persecution, the first thing he will do will be to pour out his love.

—Henry Miller, *Sexus*

I have returned to this quote over and over again. It is another way to regard the enthusiasms which have animated my life. The journal has always been the safe place to record the enthusiasms, to pour out my love.

৵

Very early on I recognized that I was trying to preserve *life* in the journals; I was trying to hold on to what proved endlessly ephemeral. It was not just life that was ephemeral; I was ephemeral—an unknown, uncalled for, undifferentiated cipher on the earth. Writing of my life gave me substance, a solidity that I could return to and build from. Writing does not only give others access to what would remain unexpressed in the self, it gives access to *oneself-as-other*. Time and mood will always make one *other* to oneself. We are legion—endlessly forgetting we are legion, or forgetting the *extent* to which we are. How many lives we have lived! How endlessly flows the water under the solid bridge of our hardened memories. Are we the bridge, or the water? The journal gives me access to my selves, access to the range of lives I have lived, cherished, and loved. The written documentary proves no less evocative than the photographic documentary.

৵

Several years ago I heard the late French poet and writer Edmond Jabés speak at a seminar at U.S.C. in Los Angeles. A beautifully warm and wrinkled face, a mellifluous voice. My notes have him saying the following:

"Perhaps there is in every writer a mythic book, the book of books, that he attempts to write with every work he composes.

"The writer becomes the text; as long as he is writing he is still recreating himself, the book of books.

"Every creation of a new book is a case of a writer protesting the text he has created, arguing with the text he is becoming."

I find these thoughts beautiful—and as succinct a description of what my journals mean to me, and have meant to be, as anything.

Journals are how we appropriate *the story* of our lives, reclaiming narrative and drama from the social institutions that otherwise, by default, document our passage from birth to death in the stolid prose and bare facts of bureaucracy. Within the pages of a journal we fight back against case history and business time, filling in the colorless outlines, the machine convenience of standardized forms, with the pavonian quirkiness of our peculiar colors.

The life journal, in fact, documents and constitutes the *creation* of a self, gives words to the timeless initiations that come to qualify the life as mythology—the old and vital stories, heroic journeys, that undergird human existence, weighting our surface efforts with the depths of archetypal profundity. In the pages of a journal we are invoking the old magic whereby humans approach godhood: *we are creating ourselves with words!*

My biases are wholly existential. I believe our first, major, real, vital and genuine creation is ourselves. We are, in theory, ontological, protean, unlimited, heir to all that is or has been human. We are, in practice, ontic; limited to physiology, body, gender, heredity, the family, the culture, the society, the times—the accidents, details, and limits that so shape and give us individual form and distinction.

The journal becomes the logbook of the creative journey, the workbook of the character, the text of the individual, the confluence of self and other, and its turbulence.

క్

I wrote in my journal in 1984, "Within this space, this room, the selves expand and separate. A field of exaggerations. Numerous caricatures. Drama takes place. I watch the drama. This is the stage where I watch it: a journal."

క్

The journal is the place to *be* self-conscious. But the literary impulse I began with allowed and encouraged me to play with self-consciousness, to play with the necessary solipsism of the personal journal. I became self-conscious in the way any actor must become self-conscious. In the very feeling of anger, for example, one preserves the consciousness, the detachment, to note the mechanisms of it, the expressive units (whether words or body signals). To become supra conscious and familiar with something becomes the license, the inclination, to play with it—fascinated with the energy, eager to shape it in interesting ways, urge it down curious byways, follow it to the shadowlands, the boundaries.

The journal was the place I could *play* with my various selves—introduce them, give them voice, let them speak to each other, overhear each other, fight with each other. First person gives way to second person, to third person—ad infinitum.

Deliteralize with the literal creation of words.

Construct and de-construct.

Modify by addenda, not by destruction.

Write, reread, remember.

క్

One can not talk of journals without bringing up a major polemic: what of the narcissism, the solipsism, the egoism, the claustrophobia, the arrogance of the sovereign Self? The "I, I, I" of the journal. All the attention, care, focus, voice, view, time, pampering and puling rooted in the self?

We have been taught to distrust and recoil from such self-preoccupation. We might allow someone the right or reason to write their self-aggrandizing diaries, but to publish them? to inflict them on others? to presume our interest?

࿓

As for 'Every man his own poet', the more every man knows about poetry the better. I believe in every one writing poetry who wants to; most do. I believe in every man knowing enough of music to play 'God bless our home' on the harmonium, but I do not believe in every man giving concerts and printing his sin.

—Ezra Pound, "A Retrospect", 1918

Details in themselves did not interest her—she disliked Chekhov for having made much of them—but when a person was 'dear' to her, as she once wrote to Pasternak, his *whole* life' was dear, 'the most beggarly detail precious.'

—Muchnic reviewing a work on Marina Tsvetayeva, NYTBR, 10/12/80

To these I add two personal anecdotes. A friend of a friend, paid to type up the journal-novel I wrote in the early eighties, once asked me ingenuously, "Who would be interested in the journal of a nobody?"

Again in the early eighties, full of enthusiasm for my life and meditations at the time, I sent a photocopy of a journal to my brother and sister-in-law. My brother wrote back after awhile and honestly told me they found the stuff "tedious, exhausting and embarrassing."

࿓

I cannot ignore these charges; I engage them. Let them remain alive, and teach us by the very vitality of their polemic. But here are some obverse perspectives.

The theme of the diary is always personal, but it does not mean only a personal story: it means a personal relation to all things and people. The personal, if it is deep enough, becomes universal, mythical, symbolic.

314

—Anais Nin, 1946

❧

What manner or presentation of details obscures the universal, and what enhances it? This is a fundamental question of Art, for its successful determination marks the line between high and low Art. The great Artists convey a human relevance, a fundamental aesthetic, within or beneath a surface of individual detail and specificity. At the same time, universality is no guarantee of Art—the non-artistic universal yields the stereotype, the artistic universal yields the archetype. The mechanics of this are subtle.

As in all Art, a mysterious and harmonic balance is sought: a surface with depth, depth with surface. Too much surface, like too much ego, can prove deadening, tedious and untranscendent. But too much depth can sink us into undifferentiated darkness—which is, at base, always and ultimately death itself, death of the individual. The personal, if it is too deep, becomes impersonal.

❧

The succession of generations insures that we all begin as nobodies. The heroic challenge is to rise out of that entropic given, and—as is said—make a name for ourselves, proving, as we hoped all along, that we were somebody. My friend's friend was simply recognizing and passing on what we all know—that journals, like autobiography, have traditionally been a retrospective art. One qualifies one's fame or worth in some other genre, some other activity, and only then does the "beggarly detail" of our lives, our incidental writing, gain value by association, so to speak.

If one's primary genre *is* the journal, however, and one's art is both the life that goes into it and the consciousness and care with which it is told, then the journal claims no less than any other literary text—seeking its measure and interest according to the standards of any and all Art. The journal-as-art claims no reflected glory but must stand alone, demonstrating therein a vision, voice and style that grabs and holds us, intrigues and entertains, giving us the rush we recognize as Art—that combination of form and content so apt that, once apprehended, the world becomes incomplete or less interesting without it.

❧

Or is it that the journal writer takes our interest for granted—is this what so irritates us? For is this not the presumption of any ego: my life (in all its beggarly detail) is fascinating, worth writing about, worth insisting that you read and value no less? And all the techniques of social intercourse and Christian manners, where we set aside the self in endless apology to consider the interests of the other, to eschew the ego-speak of "I, I, I"—is it the nakedness of the self without such garments that so disconcerts or repulses us in the personal journal?

What of the selves that don't abandon the garments of social intercourse in their private writing, but remain apologetic, deferring, self-conscious: I know I'm talking too much of myself here... This is only my opinion... You must think I'm... Gentle reader, perhaps you remember from your own life... And how are *you* today?

Do we not lose something here—betray the very essence of a journal, where we go to find the self naked, the id in full bloom and bellowing?

ॐ

Or full bloom and bawling.

Ideally the personal journal is the compensatory private place that serves as balance to the personae and pressure of our public roles. It is not only ego and its aggrandizement that is not allowed in the public sphere. What of all the so-called negative emotions? Not only anger and hatred, but loneliness, sadness, depression, fear, bewilderment, foolishness, triviality, boredom, self-pity. For most of my teens and twenties these comprised the tone scale of my journals. I called it "whining"—my journals were full of whining.

But the whining was real, true, human. It constituted my vulnerability in the world, my honest worries and anxieties over my perennial sense of failure and insufficiency. I knew such tones and perspectives were not a social asset. I knew, at the time, I was not a social asset. All the more to have a place where I could indulge the imperative to question and lament—that essential doubting of my position and meaning in the world. To deny it or cover it over seemed false, dishonest, and counterproductive to me. But to indulge it in public felt unseemly, *also* counterproductive.

Out of this sense of self, and what I came to learn of the extents of self allowed and disallowed in public, my sense of humanity was developed.

Indeed, my concept of humanity is that *we are all* internally wounded, uncertain, lonely…but that we learn to create the public selves that foster the public illusions: the self as strong, confident, clever, successful, in control, etc. If I am drawn to journals, and to literature, it is because I am drawn to the soul and its wounds—as nakedly, wholly and honestly presented as I can find.

ॐ

As a journal reader, it is not the ego I seek in journals—it is the soul, the psyche. Preponderance of ego remains distasteful to me wherever it is found. Too much Apollonian light can blind and bore, freeze the obdurate surface into facile form. It is the Dionysian darkness that intrigues me, the depths that shimmer and lap at Apollo's carefully crafted columns, threatening to de-construct them with a laugh, a leer, or a wail. I enjoy the psyche in all its mess—its emotions, moods, ages, faces, freakishness, eroticism, and theatre.

ॐ

If the Freudian unconscious is the place where all the repressions reside—driven there by social training, civilization's need for order, temperance and morality—and dreams the stage upon which these repressed contents play out in code their pressured needs for expression, what then can be said of the personal journal whose *raison d'être* is the same? The journal is *also* meant to be the stage where repressed contents can play, where pressures of social personae are relieved, where the subconscious can rise to the surface like magma. Hence the journal's famed therapeutic value, and the shame and nervousness we feel at the eyes of others apprehending it.

The real shame to me is when the ego and its self-consciousness—its need for control, its need to appear pleasing to others, its absolute terror of mockery—closes off the doorway to the psyche and its profligate shadows, and so hides its most genuine and interesting depths, perpetuating the mass illusions that sustain mass inhumanity.

ॐ

[Anais Nin's] relentless self-scrutiny is at first fascinating, then exhausting and, finally, tedious.

—Barbara Fisher Williamson, in a capsule review of Nin's *Early Diary, Vol. III*, in *NYTBR*, 1/29/84

Most did not like Nin's work, felt the diaries were self-aggrandizing, written for publication, dull, solipsistic.... Miriam Sagan says, 'I began with Anais Nin but her self-engrossment seemed too massive....'

—Lyn Lifshin, in her introduction to *Ariadne's Thread*, 1982

Self-engrossment results in a gross self, a massive self. Or is it a massive self that results in self-engrossment? The focused attention of the journal writer upon the self results, inevitably, in specialized knowledge; one becomes a specialist in oneself. But no, not the self alone, in *selves*—provided, as Nin indicates, that one goes deep enough, far enough.

I doubt Henry Miller, Otto Rank or Antonin Artaud found Nin too massive a self, her diaries self-aggrandizing. Their own self-engrossment was equal to if not excessive to hers—which is, one could say, the typical imbalance of the sexes. In this regard, it occurs to me that all the criticism I've heard of Nin's ego and self-aggrandizement has come from females. Aren't women traditionally forbidden by most cultures to have selves, trained instead to set it aside, keep it in embryo, imprisoned? The imprisoned aren't known for celebrating the presumptions, the exploratory verve, of those, especially of their kind, who are free. The imprisoned aren't known for taking the complaints and woes of the free seriously.

For fellow specialists, for those on the same or similar path, the journal writings of the serious thinker or Artist are endlessly fascinating and relevant. The language spoken there is a language recognized, a language charged with familiar ironies. There is no threat. Quite the contrary, there is, often enough, sly play, much humor.

And lest we forget, in contrast to the women Lyn Lifshin mentions, there has been no lack of women who have said to Anais Nin, "You have published *my* diary; you are telling *my* story." I have passed out the first volume of Nin's diary to as many women as I could over the years. No other book-as-gift has elicited such positive regard, such liberating energy. But perhaps it should be remembered that these are women who are coming to the book fresh, approaching Nin as if she were another unknown, like themselves. Reputation and canonization continue to destroy the honest individuals who were often pariahs in their time.

&

"Endlessly fascinating"? An overstatement, an exaggeration. I actually understand and concur, in part, with Williamson's progression: fascinating, exhausting, tedious. I have felt that progression in rereading my own journals. I consider it a phenomenon of the journal genre itself—the journal-as-life genre—and so attempt to come to terms with it phenomenologically.

What causes tedium? A preponderance of detail? Unnecessary detail? Unnecessary to what? To narrative? But detail is what distinguishes the individual. Detail determines the lived life. And narrative—flow and story, beginnings leading expeditiously to ends—is no less the journal writer's need, desire and aim than the journal reader's. But how often is the life characterized by its being stuck, blind, without transcendence, movement or oversight? The journal writer thrashes about, spitting out the vapid details of her or his cage—trusting and hoping that therein clues will be found, the way out, the overlooked will reveal itself.

The bog of detail, the tedium of life, is ideal counterbalance to its transcendence, the grace of flow and plot; the "dry stodge of time" eventually yields learning and enlightenment. "Tedium" is a charge leveled at certain artistic works as well—e.g., Melville's *Moby Dick*, Joyce's *Finnegan's Wake* (or even *Ulysses*), Pound's *Cantos*, Lewis' *Babbit*. But the tedium, in these cases, is part of the point, the conceit of the art. It is the very dissonance which creates a tension that all the more dulcifies the eventual release into melodic flow. Tedium and boredom are the necessary stuff of life. Artists employ them in their simulacrum of life—but at their own risk.

The real clue to tedium, I feel, is the "exhaustion" which preceded it in Williamson's progression. For, in fact, details unordered, or details resolutely held to someone else's order, especially self-consciously so, can be chaos if one doesn't have the energy to hold, correlate or translate them to one's own order. Nor is the problem only detail, per se. It is also a matter of attention. The seriously introspective self in the journal bestows a concentration of attention on both self and world. But the attention and concentration are *cen-*

319

tered within the idiographic self—which cannot help but be at variance with all others, by definition. *The extent of that variance determines the extent of energy expenditure needed to encounter or engage the journal writer.* Or it may not be "extent" so much as *kind* of variance. Sometimes the most subtle or hidden variance can prove more annoying, exhausting or benumbing than major and obvious discrepancies.

Then again, it may have something to do with the balance struck between introspection and extrospection. The self commenting on the self, interrogating the self with full attention and bias, can create an airtight chamber—the chamber others are wont to see as solipsism. Others find little air there; they suffocate and recoil. Whereas if the commentary is turned outward, and especially if dialogue—or the voices of others—is allowed or brought into the journal, the effect is to strike windows and doors into the hermetic chamber; energies of light and air ensue.

These are all known mechanisms. Speak long enough in your own voice, in one voice, and you will put others to sleep. You can even put yourself to sleep in that way. But others will awake, regain energy, once they begin speaking—or once you incorporate their voice or their concerns into your monologue. These mechanisms prove especially troublesome to journal writers who would have others read their journals, since one of the main points of the journal is to speak in one's own voice. It may be, however, that if one goes far enough into the self, or allows the imposed societal impositions of consistent images to fall away (and so becomes more honest with oneself), then one will fracture into one's natural diversity, becoming two, three, four…and so come to speak in many voices.

One last hypothesis is this: I bring to the journal each day's highest energy. Or several days' worth of energy. Or weeks'. Like a capacitor, I store energy, I keep it in, until the tension, volume or intensity compels me to discharge. The journal is where I discharge. It is false that high-energy writing necessarily provokes high energy in the reader. The opposite can occur as well. If not met with equivalent energy in the reader, the effect of such concentrated attention will prove exhausting. I know this, as I've said, from rereading my own journals, and have learned that I can reread them only for a limited amount of time.

And here lies a clue and technique. It has always bothered me that journals aren't read as they are written—with requisite, correlative time and space between each entry. When journal reader meets journal writer two entirely different time systems are meeting and clashing. The journal was written in attenuating time, time attenuated with space and silence. But the journal is read in foreshortened time, compressed time, as if it were a story, a novel, a narrative.

Therein lies the mistake. It is my suggestion that journals-of-the-life be read differently. Rereading my own journals I observe the rule: *No more than thirty pages at any one sitting.* The trick is to stop whenever one feels one's attention flagging, interest dropping, irritation growing. It surprises me again and again how bringing fresh energy to the reading invests *it* with fresh energy. The trouble encountered by Barbara Fisher Williamson, I think, was that she was reading several years of Nin's journal life as quickly as possible, under deadline for the review—and so learned how quickly enough fascination can turn into exhaustion.

In the breakdown of repression, the artists do their part by first dreaming the forbidden thoughts, assuming the forbidden stances, and struggling to make sense. They cannot do otherwise, for they bring the social conflicts in their souls to public expression.

—Paul Goodman

Those who charge the journal with solipsism inflate the word. How is such purity possible? The journal records the *dynamic* between self and others. I think of those wonderful lines in the Talmud, "If I am not for myself, who should be for me? If I am only for myself, what am I?" The journal is the place where one is *for* oneself, but not *only* for oneself.

We are told that Jung was fond of saying that one could not individuate atop Mt. Everest—the point being that one comes to understand oneself by interactions with others. I do not carry into my chamber, where I must write in solitude, a singular self. I carry the whole history of all my interactions with others, the extent of the history of my times: media-fed, school-fed, thousands of books read, movies seen, magazines and newspapers read, discussions engaged in and overheard with thousands of people. Where is the isolate self, the pure self, amidst such feeding?

For this reason, I'm attracted to the post-structuralist claim that there is no self, per se. The self is a construct, a locus of social intersections, social codes, the way things constellate at any given time. A lecturer I once heard presenting this idea used as example, of all things, writing in a diary. "There I was in 1967, scribbling away in my diary what I thought were my own private concerns and ideas, my own problems. Several years later when I read other women's diaries, or went back and read mine, I saw how we were all writing the same things. We were trapped in the concerns of the society, the clichés of the times, and couldn't see it until later."

Solipsism, or ego, seems more clearly demonstrated, to me, by those who have the audacity or the naiveté to assume that they're the "only one". You know the phrase: "I thought I was the only one...."

II
The Journal-as-Art

William Saroyan once suggested that good writing was writing done by "a good man". It could be said, no less facetiously, that the journal-as-art is a journal written by an artist. Or—to take it to a level a little less facetious—the journal-as-art is the recording of a life *lived* as art.

&

But what is Art: harmony of form and content? Loving attention to detail, to *le mot juste*? Charm? Magic? Beauty? Mystery? Articulate emotion? Consciousness? Consciousness masking itself (irony)? Intelligence? Sophistication? Play? Passion? Truth? Lies?

There is no need to be ingenuous; Art is all of these things—and more, and less—in proportion.

&

Art implies standards, quality. Written art implies something well said, well thought out—felicitous insight, aesthetic substance. Art also implies integrity: the personal voice, intelligent voice; implicit morality.

I use morality here as John Gardner used it in his work *On Moral Fiction*, where he argued that literature is life-affirming, representing an integrity that does not cheat, sneer, trivialize or otherwise cheapen the work and aspirations of the *condition humaine* and its endless fights against entropy, death, and—to be circular—demoralization.

ॐ

We well know how humans develop and compose themselves for their public roles, duties and responsibilities. Socialization, if not professionalism, is a matter of preparing a face for the faces that one meets.

The personal journal has long been seen as the place where one can be real—let loose with what one "really thinks": what's personal, sincere, honest, the truth behind the mask, the unconscious and immediate feeling behind the self-conscious composition of thought.

With this, I think, we finally get to the basic problematic of the journal-as-art: journals are meant to be—valued as being—spontaneous, real, human and true. Whereas literature is known—if not valued—as being conscious, contrived, controlled, created, chosen, care-full, manipulative, etc. Art is meant to be Sunday best; journals are everyday clothes. Art is the golden egg; journals the internal workings that produce the egg.

ॐ

The problem is that we have been trained to love the golden egg more than the visceral workings. The golden egg remains powerful and mysterious to us. We love to be taken, tricked, overwhelmed or surprised by the magic of Art. But sophistication brings the magic within reach, turns the golden egg into a magician's trick.

As much as we may thrill with the trick, we simultaneously long for the secret behind it—the technique that humanizes the trick and makes us equal to it, bringing it within range of our own imaginative appropriation.

We go to the journal for the secrets behind the trick.

ॐ

We're accustomed to regarding the journal as *found art*, if we think of it as art at all: a secret cache uncovered, lost voices revealed. Since journals, by definition, claim to get as close as possible to the personal voice, the voice of one's unguarded thinking, this becomes the particular virtue we, as readers, seek and expect from them: the moral treasures of sincerity and honesty, the immoral treasures of gossip and secrets.

The outside discovery of what ostensibly was meant to be an inside secret, of what could only *develop* as an inside secret, is thought to insure the integrity and genuineness of the voice. Had the journal writer been preparing a journal manuscript for public consumption, had the journal writer intended her or his art, we would feel that the journal's secret, mystery and integrity had been somehow tainted or compromised.

Private writing made public is a paradox that cannot and must not be explained away. The literary approach to journal writing is to consider this an essential irony. Essential ironies are not meant to be dissolved; they are to be engaged, they are played with.

John Fowles once described his method of writing novels as a simplified two-step process. The first step entails keeping the internal critic asleep while one writes as volubly, freely and passionately as possible. The second step is to waken the critic and slash, delete, clean up and edit.

Though this idealizes a much more ambiguous and mixed process—as I'm sure Fowles knew—it also epitomizes, I think, the differences that concern us here: the first step constitutes the process and purpose of the journal, the second step exemplifies the process of *making* art.

Having caricatured and so illustrated the difference, the division, let us now remember the natural ambiguity, the mix.

First of all, who can ever put the critic to sleep? The development of an Artist is also the development of the Artist's inner critic. Knowledge and experience necessitates comparison and contrast, a greater apprehension of the standards and models whereby one aims and measures oneself. It seems self-evident that the first draft of a master, an Artist, can command greater worth as Art than the first draft of a novice. Mature Artists have so incorporated the basics of Art, of critical standards, into their style, being or craft that even their incidental writing, their throw-away pieces, have comparative value. In this way we can bring together Fowles' first and second steps into one line, one process, and recognize that editing is coterminous with creation. We edit ourselves before even a word has been put to page. Our spontaneity arises out of and through our critical standards—whether consciously or unconsciously. Absolute eschewal of the internal critic is disingenuous.

Secondly, we must remember that Art alone does not constitute value. There is such a thing as bad art, poor art, or inferior art. The art, in these cases, is mere show and little substance; form without content, content without form. Though we can and do use Art as a measure of value, we must keep in mind that art has its more pedestrian affiliation to craft, skill, process, manufacture, technique. The utilization of the techniques of art may qualify one's product as art, by definition, but says nothing of the value of the art.

Thus, it is instructive to remember that Art, like any value or definition, transcribes a continuum; in this case, a continuum from Low Art——to—— High Art. The journal-as-art genre may be defined as any private writing that has been edited to facilitate its aesthetics. But the degree to which it has achieved its aim, the degree to which aesthetics serve content, is the degree to which it moves toward High Art. High Art remains the value.

The journal's art is *not* for someone who considers unfettered invention more valuable or interesting, as text, than creative adherence to the lived life. The journal's art is *not* for someone who finds that self-consciousness disrupts narrative and interferes with pleasure. Nor is the journal's art for someone who feels that truth is only accessed through objectivity or impersonality.

The journal's art is one which retains the texture of the lived life. It's very *purpose* is to traffic in and subtilize self-consciousness. Its allegiance to truth is to the truth of subjectivity and personality.

The longing for the personal voice, the hunger for unadorned psychological reality, the need to get beyond or inside of all personae, basic curiosity (love of secrets and gossip), and even weariness with the monotheistic gloss of the topical fashions of professionalism and the consequent love of amateurishness (its mix, vulnerability, enthusiasms, even its *un*consciousness)—these are all motivations, expectations and hopes we legitimately bring to the reading of journals.

ॐ

But the journal *artist* cannot (and must not) claim unconsciousness. The journal artist can no longer be the amateur; a differentiation is taking place.

The writer *designs* the text. Though the inceptive outflow comes out of mystery, though the outcome means to be magic, the process between is one of design and intention.

Still, too much design and intention can kill the art. Artists become *arty* if they overreach themselves, or rely too readily on formula, or if their consciousness or self-consciousness becomes too evident, too claustrophobic.

ॐ

Art—as in artifice—exists whenever consciousness has entered. Art and artifice share the same root. This simple but central fact wreaks havoc with the notion of the journal-as-art because two of the distinctive values claimed by the journal, peculiar to its art, are the values of honesty and sincerity. Like the disturbing paradox of private writing designed for public consumption, so, too, we are faced with the problematic: honesty and sincerity pull one way, Art pulls the other; an existential dilemma.

Irony and the ironic arts are the way one *dances* with the unsettling paradoxes of public/private, sincerity/artifice, I and Thou. What is irony? The immensity of the unsaid that pressures the said; the tension of two disparate surfaces meeting—often ignorance and knowledge, or complexity masking itself as simplicity, or the many taking on the guise of one—a tension felt as

326

a kind of humor; a distancing and reserve that allows the author to be simultaneously involved and "innocent" while remaining detached and commenting. Done poorly, irony can become coy, cute, posturing, clever; done well, it becomes essential to the sophistication of the journal's art.

෧

To me, people are art. The human life, *each* human life, is and becomes an inevitable creation—and creation itself constitutes art, but art as process, not as value per se. The value comes as people mature and so come to appropriate themselves, honoring the choices that define them, body and soul. The value comes when people shuck off the pale imitations, stereotypes, worn roles and clichés of their upbringing and times, and come to know and value what makes them distinct and individual. Out of mature individuality comes *voice.*

The personal journal is the given place where we learn, practice and prove the method to our madness, the art of our lives, the mature integrity of our voice.

෧

For many years I imagined myself writing journals in the way Keith Jarrett improvised his piano concertos. Each journal was meant to be a jazz novel, so to speak—a spontaneous, impromptu, immediate work of art.

This involved giving each journal a title meant to be reflective and expressive of its contents. It meant beginning and ending the journal with requisite energy and attention; setting mood and theme in the beginning, and resolving or restating theme in the end. It meant finding and following the themes or peculiarities that determined the course and temper of any given phase of my life. It meant pacing myself, attentive to when too much of any given tack or tone had accumulated, and so moving the register to fresh or alternative tacks or tones. One sees the process whereby I was creating my life *as* I was creating my journal; the two informed each other, played off of and depended upon each other.

෧

Lest we become caught up in our own paradigms and so fail to see the wider picture, I must remind us that we have been approaching the journal-as-art as if the art involved were relevant only to the literary enterprise, as if the journal's art were only or strictly literary. This is too narrow a view.

Psychology, philosophy, and sociology could each claim the journal as a primary text, if they were so disposed, in the way history has long recognized and valued the personal journal as an invaluable source of the historical record. The art, in these cases, would remain a measure of the quality of the prose, attention to form; but each discipline, with its distinctive content, would also necessitate its own emphases, and so come to demand and construct an art peculiar to itself.

If we're to imagine the journal as psychological art, for example, I *don't* mean something of the nature: Diary of a Breakdown, or Diary of a Pathological Mind—though this kind of writing has been and can be expressive of psychological art. Rather, I have in mind the seriously introspective voice applied to the interrogation of one's particular feelings, memories, moods, fears, fantasies, dreams, etc. I have in mind journal writing as the inevitable therapeutic process that accompanies individuation—a written travelogue of the long and painful differentiating between self and other, the lifelong appropriation of the Self. Examples of this genre might be Kafka's diaries or Sylvia Plath's journals.

As for the journal as philosophical art, I'm drawing on the vital but neglected notion that philosophy comes from and must be applied to *the lived life.* Academic philosophy, by contrast, has become the perpetual motion whereby ever greater abstraction is generated. To find and use philosophy—the art of thinking—to understand, explore, choose and cherish a life in accordance with one's values or principles is a worthy activity, an artistic enterprise, and a process aptly serviced by the personal journal. I think, as examples, of Thoreau's Walden journals, and Sartre's *War Diaries.*

Sociological art has a relation to historical art, for it recognizes that the individual is also a subset of any number of social structures—gender, age, race, family, religion, state, etc.—and so illuminates or exemplifies social categories in microcosm. Each individual is or can be (the degree determines the art) an expressive epitome of the locale, the times.

In summary, the journal-as-art describes a mix; it is not for purists. It is informed by a dynamic of tension: the bringing together of public and private, truth and fiction, professional and amateur, conscious and unconscious, sophistication and innocence. These tensions, handled poorly, create only tenseness and irritation; handled well, they can energize and excite. This remains the challenge we place before the journal writer who would be artist.

Victor Muñoz

The Journal as Art: "Impossible Text"

I

Every journal begins as a self-communication and, to remain purely that, must pass from existence before or with its author. Related to the unposted letter, its privacy is warranted by the same conditions, and, when successful, a difficult subject to discuss since, by definition, no one ever sees anyone else's, like snot among the polite.

A journal becomes, for present purposes, *literature* when it makes its way through intention or inadvertence to other eyes, when it becomes an intersubjective communication—the published version, of course, being the most extreme.

When a literary journal is, in addition, rich in intersubjective meaning and interpretation, we may call it to some degree an instance of the journal as art. This is a discussion of what I think is peculiar and significant about this kind of self-communication.

II

> To while away the idle hours, seated the livelong day before the inkslab, by jotting down without order or purpose whatever trifling thoughts pass through my mind, verily this is a queer and crazy thing to do!
> —Yoshida Kenko (1283–1352)

All they say about the literary journal is true. That it's too easy a form, too much an outlet, a drain for the run-off, the excess, the scrap of expression attending the main business of living or writing. That it can become, through congeniality, a trap for creative energy, an impediment to artistic development. That perhaps its best literary role is the one of a dedicated workbook, the place out of which a recognizably finished form will emerge but not in itself subject to the same scrutiny art begs. Nearly always its penchant for narcissism narrows concern to the moment, or to the past—but only as a collection of personal moments. It is melancholy (as Baudrillard reminds us), except, perhaps, when it is taken up with some program of self-improvement and becomes sticky with hope. Usually, it has scant structure. It is directionless, neither forward- or out-ward-looking, nor polemic. Not "architectural and premeditated," according to Barthes, it is an "Album...of leaflets..., *infinitely suppressible*: rereading my journal, I can cross out one entry after the next, to the complete annihilation of the Album, with the excuse that 'I don't like this one': this is the method of Groucho and Chico Marx...." Finally, with all this, it appears to sponge criticism so effectively it repels critics.

But as strictures disqualifying the journal from competition for a place in our aesthetic affections, these commonplaces are themselves too facile. Defects of motivation, social responsibility, utility, etiquette, etc., perhaps they are, but not of art. A proper defect in an aesthetic form would have to imply a failure to realize the integration of its essence, of the elements which compel its existence. To help raise the level of the argument and show respect due the subject, I will try for a measure of clarity concerning the mission of the journal, pressed to its limits. Its reputation, nurtured by the distracting commonplaces, has obscured what draws certain genius to a writing crazed by time.

III

> EGOTIST, n. A person of low taste, more interested in himself than in me.
>
> —Ambrose Bierce (1842–1914?)

Probably none of the truisms is more patent than the diary's or the journal's egoism. The feral tangle of the self, a formidable obstacle to effecting sympathetic motion in another's sensibility, is a convenient snare for boredom. But exactly why the idea of self-absorption is so distrusted is somewhat obscure. Either it is the *subject* we cannot bear, or some peccancy in the manner or depth of presentation. The latter is the more defensible objection, we have to suppose.

> *April 29.* Marian let me see her diary. This is what she writes every day: "I got up at 7:30; I got dressed, I had breakfast at 8:30 and went to school. Sister was very cross today and I had to stay fifteen minutes after school to repeat my lessons.... I went for a walk with Anaïs and had a nice time. I came home at 6. I did my homework and had dinner at 8. I wrote in my diary. It is already 9. I am going to bed now. Marian."

> ...That gives me an idea of what a real diary is like and I think I'll do mine like that....

(But the young Anaïs reverted to her already old ways and went on to pursue her form to its now famous length and self-direction.) Marian's is an example of a superficially self-absorbed journal, classically boring and susceptible to the withering effects of the truism's accusation. We may excuse it as a child's diary; but a child's diary is the archetype that informs almost any beginner's journal, so many of which never survive long enough to break from the elementary template. The circuit of attention at this basic level of egoism is too small for a depth of consciousness to develop and validate the effort. The journal project is then left undefended from all the moral and social forces that seek to break the circuit altogether and pull us away from ourselves. At this point the charge of egoism begins to sting. Commonly, just before it dies—is abandoned—the journal degrades to an annoying mirror, or worse, an object of self-loathing. To its credit, the pruning effect of the truism does help to keep the numbers down, a seldom noted aesthetic benefit of the moral criticism of art.

So, provided the self-absorbed circuit is ample, tries our intelligence or imagination, what still irks us? Isn't *acknowledged* self-absorption a possible step toward self-transcendence and, as such, an advance over the all too common naive or semi-conscious varieties?

On the first page of his *Diary*, Gombrowicz bows to the obvious: "Monday: Me, Tuesday: Me, Wednesday: Me...," and proceeds anti-methodically to ply his spleen and genius to his exquisitely and deceptively narrow subject. Every aspersion of moral irresponsibility only makes more intrepid the true journal keeper—the one who has learned to speak in *its* voice and heard there something vaster than whatever we oppose to the ego. And while the narcissism of art should be confronted, the critic who can't see past it, nowhere more glaring than in the diary, is too well-meaning to understand the need for it—art, not the narcissism. The charge is welcome when it serves to curtail the spread of mediocrity, but inappropriate at a level that matters—the level of beauty—and when it serves to distract from the greater problems of the form. At the level that matters, in any case, few have or develop enough 'self' to seed the notorious process. First class egotists are really quite rare.

But there is an even more basic reason why we must go further than merely tolerating a self-attention. If we expect inter-subjective communication ever to penetrate beyond extended biological exigencies, beyond the animal grunts facilitating joint enterprises a vast proportion of the *practice* of language functions as, beyond a supporting role in the cohesion necessary for survival—it is important that we develop *individual* selves worthy of the discourse our putative collective self-image ordains. Our own depth is exercised through others, certainly, but from where will these deep selves arise if not, on their part, through self-attention?

Self-love is an antecedent of any other kind of love, speaking of truisms.

IV

> I am unable, yonder beggar cries,
> To stand, or move; if he say true, he *lies*.
>
> —John Donne (1572–1631)

Why we should value sincerity, particularly in art, is not always clear. In its absence, where is the insult? Call a piece 'sincere' and the artist may rightfully pause since it is not a predicate with an unambiguous emotional train. So minimal an expectation is bound to seem almost off-color, if not irrelevant. Except at times in the history of art and literature when a cult of sincerity has raged—and even then what the artist sees in the concept is not what the moralist sees—the comment has usually smacked of understated compliment or overstated slight. Yet sincerity is often the star claim made on behalf of private writing, its moral *raison d'être*.

The moral expectation may be that the narrowness of the concept of sincerity—so complained of—acts profitably to crowd out the plump graces of social approval or the invitations to personal cowardice an audience seduces with. A leaner picture may emerge, it is hoped, of the truth or what self-gossip in the coziest quarters purports to worship as such.

In my little notebook I am obliged to practice an ostentatious sincerity, attempt the work Poe proposed entitling "My Heart Laid Bare," the one "no man *could* write…, even if he dared. [For the] paper would shrivel and blaze at every touch of the fiery pen." But a compromise occurs early in the diarist's act, perhaps in the very *will* to keep this account. Even supposing I do not intend or anticipate another reader, it is myself I can wish to persuade. And when is it we are *not* persuading? Surely not in the absence of others, though this might be when we have the best chance of success. The more private the lie, the more likely the hearer will be duped. One of the most 'sincere' philosophers, Wittgenstein (whose almost entire literary output was cast in the form of highly tentative, fragmented, private writing), prefaced a collection of his 'remarks' by saying he could not expect it to be freer of vanity than he himself was. The aspiration and, perforce, the pretension to sincerity is dubious when I have so schemed the event to exclude any judge but myself. Alone (in my garret, by candlelight…) can I appreciate my own sincerity? If I say yes, who am I sucking up to? Who cares? If I say no, *who* is making that judgment? The very idea of sincerity as ever an *accomplished* act is problematic, at a minimum, and, likely, a conceit. So it is no wonder pretensions to it get a side-long glance. (Even when no one is looking!) It only begins to look good when I consider the alternative.

We might (somewhat insincerely) salvage an aspect of the concept by straining to see it as a process, a dance of lies veering toward an extreme but truthful exhaustion. A willingness not to lie could begin with an admission that one might be. As Gombrowicz said of his *Diary*, "'This is how I would like to be for you', and not 'This is how I am'." In this mannered step back, the form may have a moral superiority not only to its own more naive manifestations but to verse, plot or polemic. It is just conceivable it might gather into itself all the qualifications necessary for the truth, make itself ready, *lie* and wait for it—at least, if no more: The lucklessness of the enterprise explains, I suspect, a portion of the melancholy.

V

> An unshaped kind of something first appeared.
>
> —Abraham Cowley (1618–67)

The most distinguishing formal characteristic of private writing is its fragmentation. Times, dates, incidents, occasions—but beyond these and, more
fundamentally, what determines the shape of the writing is an openness to
revealing the *seams* of perception and deliberation. Where they appear, actual
dates have only an historical (if that) importance for anyone but the writer,
though they may function as the native punctuation of the form. The fractur-
ing needn't be so obvious as that following upon a calendar. When the date or
hour, as an index, is so stressed that the diary's function becomes mnemonic,
then it also turns scientific, instrumental and, as such, imminently disposable
but for the facts it reports—and not our topic here. The muse, concerned with
accuracy of a different order, suffers little compunction in making of a date,
time, etc., a stylistic device (as in Gombrowicz, Frisch, Baudrillard and many
Japanese diarists). Though it may expand the genre to unforgivable propor-
tions to include a mass of philosophical literature, doing so would help to
dissolve some of the puzzles of style and classification connected with the
writings of some of the Pre-Socratics, Montaigne, Pascal, Kierkegaard,
Nietzsche, Antonio Machado, Karl Kraus, Ludwig Wittgenstein, E.M.
Cioran, Vilhelm Ekelund, Fernando Pessoa, Elias Canetti, Andrei Sinyavski,
Laura (Riding) Jackson, et al. To the extent deeply experienced time is creative
and in constant strife with the eternal, it has become increasingly conscious
of its passing significance, its necessary tentativeness and incompleteness.
The existential stutter reaches such a pitch that even crowning a thought with
a date is judged so much frippery. Obviously all writing bears at least a casual relation to time, but only in the journal and related forms does the calendar
insist on leaving tracks. The journal's relation to time is essential without
needing to be specific. The question, here, most pertinent to the keeper of
these forms, is what has its explicit indication to do with substance?… There
is, in effect, *always* a reference to time, however muted. Mortality insures that
even a seamless journal (reflecting the lyrical aspirations of its keeper) is broken
at its heart: It must be ready to leave off any moment. Novels, treatises, sym-
phonies might remain unfinished, but who has ever heard of the unfinished
diary? More cause for melancholy.

But do we abdicate an artistic responsibility to uphold the crafted, labored
image? Art shouldn't be so easy, aren't we being lazy? Assuming the question
is not meant in the same philistine spirit we might hear Munch or Klee
unfavorably compared to Vermeer or Botticelli, I take it to express the understandable fear that so democratic a form as the diary, allowed pride of place,

would somehow bring on a general devaluation. Too many responses one could make...but I retreat. *While insisting that I don't argue here for the existence of a single instance of the journal as art, I do assert the formal space should one come about.* I would rather cast my argument as a challenge: You, as a private keeper of what you would have us believe is a truth about your experienced or reflected life, are up against it more than you, as a weaver of fiction or builder of theory. Still, I imagine I have glimpsed a rarer beauty in even a lame truth.

VI

> But everything human is fragmented.
> Not even Plato himself was dressed for the music he spoke of.

—Vilhelm Ekelund (1880–1949)

So glibly we excuse the journal its untidiness...but why, granting and setting aside the plea for space, should it be abetted? The fractured, aleatory, episodic we accept; the room is theoretically there, but where is the urgency to fill it? Moreover, while nothing logical may prevent a self-communication from evincing a wealth of intersubjective meaning and interpretation, doesn't the integrity of the one preclude the artifice of the other? This seems to be what makes the very idea of the journal as art psychologically paradoxical.

In Max Frisch's *Sketchbooks* the search for authenticity—the state of being whose expression sincerity is—finds its vehicle in the diary. In discussing it, Evelyn Moore states:

> Everything must be alluded to, nothing should be fully delineated. Essentially, the outline conveys the meaning. To state anything explicitly destroys the ability of the words to express universal truths because that limits the reader's ability to expand upon these things, to fill the gaps with imagination. Completeness forces upon the reader a vision that, if it is too concrete and complete, he cannot accept as authentic.

This is also the aesthetic of the 14th Century Buddhist priest and diarist, Kenko, as Moore explains in her paper comparing him with Frisch.

The heritage of the *nikki bungaku* (poetic or literary diary) can be traced at least to the 8th Century. The highly elliptical, vibrantly allusive, temporally present traits of Japanese literature—familiar to us from the Japanese novel (our form, given back to us, transformed) and such poetic forms as haiku—were nurtured in the interstices of the *nikki*. There, time, made intimate with being, is entrusted to craft a form for it, in contrast to the willful, teleological inclination of Western figures, but now diminishingly evident, for instance, in certain forms of the avant-garde novel. Why persist calling it a 'novel'?—the heart of which, the plot, is a millenarian vestige and ought to be an embarrassment to our more edgy sensibility. The contours of much of our art still remain an homage to what we are not but vaguely imagine that we should be, still aiming at catharsis through edification, a *building* toward and away. Though awareness of the formal lag is hardly new in the European tradition (a few voices having always carried—witness the list above), certain trappings haven't fallen away and still seem able to dim perception of the change in our relation to time and what this requires of the forms we express in. The truths about our being, the ones we used to have to squint to see at the vanishing point of our efforts, have passed over the horizon and left us with an undeveloped sense of the present—a particularly critical state if those ideals, visions of the future in the distance, have collapsed. If we continue to see them, it is a stark act of faith.

Not to suggest anything so simple as a move toward Eastern principles of art or living—rather, that we shouldn't have to feel so adventurous or revolutionary in fashioning a timely vessel for the expressive contents of our being. While we may have been (and will go on) inventing remarkable shapes, the wheel has been around a good long spell. The East/West link here is instructive, principally, for bringing to focus the two essences of time-bound private writing, *authenticity* and *fragmentation*. The two notions come to define the journal (diary, notebook, etc.). Their coincidence is not arbitrary.

Keen to the journal's temptations and snares, Barthes conceded at least one diary keeper he could read "without irritation": Kafka. Why is revealing: the *non-artificial rhythm* of his diaries. Kafka contrives to find and maintain the voice to speak *more* truthfully in the face of an inevitable artifice than under a licentious honesty (and all honesty, on a conscious plane, is affected). Not surprisingly, "K." barely manages a discrete identity even in his fiction.

Blanchot saw in Joseph Joubert one who made of his "journal-as-trap" an expression specific enough to his literary debility to seem genuine but not without torturing a fit to the traditional genres; the language of a 'book', of a 'work', always eluded him, the pieces resisted those patterns, insinuating, rather, their own integrity—that of the journal. Joubert, like Wittgenstein, it could be argued, never got past his pile of observations and reflections, but the possibility that the quality of his reality came to feel *thus* correctly presented is too abiding to be dismissed.

A morally inescapable lucidity and the passionate structuring of an aesthetic faculty, in the interest of wholeness, may both insist on expression in the same medium at once. When this *"virtually* impossible text" (Barthes) succeeds, a slightly invisible coherence emerges. Blanchot tries to speak of it:

> Fragmentation, the mark of a coherence all the more substantial for being attained through the necessity of undoing itself—not by a dispersed system, nor through fragmentation as a system, but by staging in pieces (a shredding of) what has never existed (ideally or otherwise) as a whole and may not again in some future guise reconstitute itself. The spacing through a timing that can only be grasped—fallaciously—as the absence of time.

But the occasions for their false coming together, for travesty, in a form as generous are proportionately great.

VII

> ...maybe consciousness even preceded us in death, maybe it arrived before us to initiate us into the white light of nothingness that awaited us there...
>
> —Marie-Claire Blais (1939–)

The conventional journal, as a record, is too mindlessly empirical, too inhumanly serial; the fictional literary forms, too visionary or escapist—they step out of time. Human time *sits* on the journal, keeping at bay the "unbearable lightness" of the purely aesthetic. This is why we push the journal toward art and not, say, the novel toward some time-bound state to which it has historically been only too willing to submit but rather as a consequence of its lightness. (The number of published fictions in journal form is vast and ever growing.) We push against a natural current, a fact belied by the *apparent* ease of the project.

This most difficult of shapes for art to inhabit, yet, is exactly the literary challenge of the time. Watching committed writers with increasingly disfigured countenances haunting the old houses of literature may continue for some time to offer entertainment, but the range of elicitable, unmannered reactions is diminishing. We are invited to share in a sarcasm or an ankle-deep nostalgia. They keep wanting to replace the mirrors their faces break.

A set of ambitions, entailing the 'work' or finished piece, accompanies the act of writing. The value of the premeditated work is extracted at the price of a distortion of being—a call to undo which, one would think, would be forthcoming. The entire set bears down as a pridian commitment and seeks to extend itself, grow and develop apart even from the writer, and actually puts words in the writer's mouth or on the page, as it were, that—together with the writer's vanity or because it is that vanity—urges a grander, more *momentous* statement than a clock or a calendar has room for in its parceled spaces. *You will dissemble under this pressure in any event*, but not in a human way unless kept to a schedule. At a certain elusive pace the truth, or what of it we are to be treated to, will get accomplished. To find that pace, it is our *will* that we should subject to our will; it is, to itself, a stintless enough charge.

The will to consciousness has so failed to locate us, to find us any place, and so corrupted—made a ruse of—every craft, every reach for order or form, that time, its steady givenness, is (again) offering to become the arbiter of authenticity, that supreme object of conceit. The space it clears for the soul is both lavish and quartered. Allowed to sing in its cell—but it is allowed to sing! Under the auspices of the day, the moment...the journal, vademecum of the soul, the literary form of consciousness itself, through its rhythmic circumscription, reintroduces ritual to the abandonment of the lyric, plays moralist to the aesthete, secreting for awhile (until the next thing) the truancy of any higher illusion, any God or the big Self...

The set begins to bear down too hard on me.

Should it have occurred to anyone (but myself) that the journal tending toward art might require justification in terms of whether it is a good or a bad thing "to while away the idle hours" with, or in some salvation it might offer, the best I have prepared is a moral excuse and aesthetic permission. But it would be wrong to think that all literary genres have these equally, or that once acquired they cannot be lost.

Notes

I

The typology based on exposure is derived in part from Andrew Hassam's article, "Reading Other People's Diaries", *University of Toronto Quarterly*, 56:3 (1987). One based on motive can be found in Roland Barthes, "Deliberation", *Partisan Review*, 47:4 (1980), also printed in Susan Sontag's *A Barthes Reader*. There are others based on focus, public or intimate, and ones sorted by their relation to time, whether time is measured by events or experienced as flow. Earl Miner considers these last two in the introduction to *Japanese Poetic Diaries* (University of California Press, 1969).

Is my subject just introspective private writing? Where do I place outward looking journals (nature, travel, historical, etc.)? To the extent the keeper's perspective has no critical bearing on what is being described, I would call the writing an incipient micro-history or a chronicle in the making—not a diary proper. It would be a report to someone, even if that someone was only the keeper. The writing must come *from* an individual subjectivity for what I am going to say here to apply. So these ostensibly extroverted orientations are not automatically disqualified. Thoreau's vision of Nature, for example, was stamped with his individuality, his mental economy.

II

Kenko's words are from his diary, translated as *Essays in Idleness,* excerpted in Donald Keene's *Anthology of Japanese Literature* (Grove Press, 1955). Six centuries later Jean Baudrillard echoes, "The journal is a subtle matrix of idleness" (*Cool Memories*, Verso, 1990).

Baudrillard, Ibid.

Barthes, Ibid.

III

The Bierce definition is from *The Devil's Dictionary* (Hill and Wang, 1957).

Nin quotes her young friend, Marian, in *Linotte: The Early Diary of Anais Nin, 1914–1920* (Harcourt Brace Jovanovich, 1978). I owe this reference to Olivia Dresher.

Witold Gombrowicz, *Diary: Volume 1* (Northwestern University Press, 1988).

IV

"A Lame Beggar", one of the *Epigrams* in *The Complete Poetry and Selected Prose of John Donne* (The Modern Library, Random House, 1941).

On the subject of sincerity and journals, see Henri Peyre, *Literature and Sincerity* (Yale University Press, 1963), especially chapter 7.

Edgar Allan Poe, *Marginalia* in *The Centenary Poe* (The Bodley Head, 1949). Also quoted in Peyre.

Ludwig Wittgenstein expresses his modesty in the forward to *Philosophical Remarks* (University of Chicago Press, 1975). He published only one book, one short article, and one review during his lifetime, and much of what he said there he repudiated.

Witold Gombrowicz, *A Kind of Testament* (Calder & Boyars, 1973), Chapter 8.

V

The Cowley quote came to me from Poe, who gives it a wry gloss in his *Marginalia*. It is from a poem, "Creation".

VI

Vilhelm Ekelund, *The Second Light* (North Point Press, 1986). The fragment quoted is from the selection, *Elpidi, 1939*.

Evelyn Moore, "Aesthetic Records: A Comparison of Max Frisch's *Tagebuch 1946–49* and The Diary of Kenko, *Essays in Idleness*", *Comparative Literature Studies*, 25:2 (1988).

Barthes, Ibid.

Maurice Blanchot, "Joubert and Space: An Author Without a Book, a Writer Without a Manuscript", in *The Siren's Song, Selected Essays* (Indiana University Press, 1982).

Maurice Blanchot, *The Writing of the Disaster* (University of Nebraska Press, 1986), Ann Smock, translator. However, the translation used here is mine and differs slightly from Smock's.

VII

Marie-Claire Blais, *Deaf to the City* (The Overlook Press, 1987).

An extensive bibliography of diary fiction can be found in H. Porter Abbott's *Diary Fiction: Writing as Action* (Cornell University Press, 1984).

For the impetus behind some of the thinking in this paper I am in debt to many heated discussions with Olivia Dresher, whose knowledge of the subject and collection of journals is impressive. Any errors or infelicities, I'm sure, are the result of my stubbornly not listening to her.

Biographical Notes

Biographical Notes

C. F. Asmusson was born in Ann Arbor, Michigan in 1937, and grew up in the Midwest. Following preparation for a career in the visual arts, she lived in New York City in the 1960s, where she worked on the staff of two well-known art magazines, meanwhile acquiring her real education through the public library. While her work was first published in literary magazines at the University of Colorado in the 1950s, there were many years of silence during which she attempted to enforce on herself a "normal life". Her present work has its origins in journals or logbooks begun in New York in the early 1970s.

Sean Bentley is an editor of *Fine Madness* magazine. His poems have appeared in *Poetry Northwest, Cincinnati Review, ACM, Northwest Review, Miscellany, Seattle Review, Old Red Kimono, Slackwater Review, Poetry NOW, Writer's Forum*, and many others, as well as the anthologies *Intro 6* (Doubleday), *Iron Country* (Copper Canyon), *Pontoon* (1999), and *Island of Rivers* (National Parks Association). His most recent collection of poetry, *Grace and Desolation*, was published in 1997 by Cune Press. His first full-length collection, *Instances*, was published by Confluence Press in 1979, and his chapbook, *Into the Bright Oasis*, in 1976 by Jawbone Press (now Brooding Heron). He writes, "I am currently masquerading as a technical editor at Microsoft. I spent the Eighties writing, singing, and torturing a guitar in the underground band Walk Don't Walk." Currently, he is desultorily working on a novel.

Audrey Borenstein, a native of Chicago, lives in New Paltz, New York. She has been writing and publishing in a variety of literary genres since the 1960s. Her short fiction has appeared in more than thirty literary magazines and collections, among them the transition issue of *Kansas Quarterly/Arkansas Review, North Dakota Quarterly, Ascent, Nimrod, Webster Review, Northwest Review*, and in the anthology *Womanblood: Portraits of Women in Poetry and Prose*. She also has published essays, poetry and manuscripts of

Journal writings in literary magazines, four books of nonfiction, and is co-author of a chronicle of local history. In 1990 she completed a trilogy of three novels—fictional explorations of alternate lives in a community in the Mid-Hudson Valley that was founded by French Huguenots in 1677; excerpts from these novels were published in 1988 and 1989 in *Oxalis*, *The Albany Review*, *Resoundings*, and *The MacGuffin*, and in 1994 in the literary anthology *Paradise*. Borenstein self-published fifty copies of the third novel, *Simurgh*, and donated them to family and friends of her literary estate and to special libraries throughout the U.S. with collections of Jewish-American fiction. Her awards include an NEA Fellowship and a Rockefeller Fellowship. Formerly Adjunct Professor at Louisiana State University, Cornell College in Mount Vernon, Iowa, and SUNY, New Paltz, Borenstein resigned from academia in 1986 to devote full-time to writing. She has published manuscripts of her Journal writings in *Medicinal Purposes*, *Resoundings II*, and *Journal Shares*—a publication she co-founded with a member of the National Journal Network; and in the anthology *Women of the 14th Moon* (Freedom, California: The Crossing Press, 1991). She is currently at work on a series of volumes of her Journal writings from 1964 to 1999.

Kathleen Hunt Dolan was born and raised in Northern California and has lived in the Pacific Northwest for 30 years. She has a degree in Comparative Literature, and has published scholarly articles, poems, and a book on baroque poetry.

Olivia Dresher has been writing and collecting journals and diaries for over 30 years. Her poetry has appeared in various literary magazines, anthologies, and self-published collections. She has been employed as an editor, as well as a music teacher/performer. She is the founder and curator of the Library of Diaries, Journals, and Notebooks at the Richard Hugo House literary center in Seattle, Washington. She lives in an award-winning restored 1918 Craftsman Bungalow. Seattle has been her home and inspiration since 1981.

Kate Gale is a Ph.D. candidate in English literature at Claremont Graduate University. She teaches English at the University of Redlands and at California State University Northridge. She is the author of five books: three collections of poetry, *Where Crows and Men Collide*, *Blue Air*, and *Selling the Hammock*; one novel, *Water Moccasins*; and an edited anthology which has widely been adopted for classroom use, *Anyone is Possible*. Ms. Gale has had numerous poems and short stories published in literary magazines, including *Arshile, Portland Review,* and *Bakunin,* and has read at venues ranging from universities to coffee houses throughout the West Coast, including readings at California State University Northridge, Claremont Graduate University, Portland State University, and Cody's in Berkeley. She is contributing editor for Red Hen Press. She is the first place winner of the 1998 Allen Ginsberg Poetry Award.

Guy Gauthier was born in Winnipeg, Manitoba. He graduated from the University of Manitoba in 1963. His poems were published in Canadian magazines in the early Sixties, and his plays were performed in Winnipeg. In 1959 he went to New York on a Canada Council grant, and decided to stay. Many plays were performed Off-Off Broadway, and some were published by Breakthrough Press and anthologized in *The Scene*, Vols. 1 & 3. He started writing a journal in 1971. A book of his poems, *Zone*, was published by Midnight Sun Press, New York, 1976. He has written a non-fiction novel about his grandmother, *Léona*. In 1988 he moved to Louisville, and also started to write in French again. His French poems have been published in two anthologies, *Répertoire littéraire de l'ouest canadien* (1984) and *Anthologie de la poésie francomanitobaine* (1990). He has continued to write his journal in both French and English. He moved back to New York in 1991, and has published his poems on the World Wide Web, and reviewed the work of new Canadian poets.

Kimble James Greenwood lives on the Olympic Peninsula in Washington State.

S. Afzal Haider is 59 years old. He has studied electrical engineering, psychology, and social work, and has worked in the respective fields about ten years each. For the last five years he has been trying to become a full-time writer. Most of his stories come from his journal and life experiences, and a few have been published in the *Clothesline Review* and *Tomorrow* magazine, as well as in the anthologies *Sacred Ground* (Milkweed Editions) and *A Dragonfly in the Sun* (Oxford University Press). He is married, has two sons (ages 10 and 21), and lives in Evanston, Illinois.

Marie E. LaConte has written journals since she was 12 years old. She has published a short story and poetry. She writes in her journal, "The power of writing is like the power of education and superstition: one who partakes of these things is changed forever.... I've transcended all my previous reasons to write, and what is left to me is the writing of the artist, the writing that touches one's soul and causes one's senses to forever perceive some new aspect of an old truth.... The writing left for me to do is the writing of art, the writing that illuminates, for an instant or a lifetime, a new truth I thought I'd never learn. This kind of writing is the most powerful of all, and worthy of fear. One must stand before it temporarily paralyzed, in awe of its power...."

Bianco Luno worked with the developmentally disabled until 1992. Now that he has discovered his own disability, he doesn't have to anymore.

Ja Luoma writes, "A friend left this message for me: 'The dark flowers of the psychic garden are the loveliest and most fragrant.' I am a dangerous-looking dusk, purple in color, with twisted leaves coming to pointed tips, mottled green and white. My words are my fragrance, singular in that I cannot be untrue, no matter how volatile, how bitter the scent. Loveliness is measured in the depth to which my roots travel. My psyche is my garden. I do not leave it without a sense of dream. When I go I carry my work with me. I listen to the sounds of the animate and inanimate with equal care. A part of my soul is anchored in the mountains surrounding me, giving me weight and stature that isn't seen but felt. I am the dark flower. Sometimes I am recognized."

Victor Muñoz tutors logic and philosophy at the University of Washington and edits the Philosophical Notebooks of Bianco Luno, soon to be published on the web at "http://www.aporia.net". He lives with his friend, Fellini, a cat.

Noëlle Sickels is the author of two historical novels, *Walking West* (1995) and *The Shopkeeper's Wife* (1998), both from St. Martin's Press. She has also had short stories, poetry, essays, and articles in a number of magazines and small press anthologies, including *American Fiction*, and was editor of *Time Was*, an anthology of reminiscences by Los Angeles senior citizens.

Sandi Sonnenfeld is a graduate of Mount Holyoke College, and holds an MFA in Creative Writing from the University of Washington. Sandi's fiction and literary essays have appeared in a variety of journals, including *Sojourner*, *Emrys Journal*, *Voices West*, and the anthologies *Family: A Celebration* (Princeton, NJ: Peterson's Publishing) and *Sex and the City* (London: Serpent Tail's Press). In May 1998, Sandi won first prize for the David Dornstein Creative Writing Contest, a national competition sponsored by the Coalition for the Advancement of Jewish Education.